# New Directions in Bookbinding

Philip Smith

# New Directions in Bookbinding

Philip Smith

Studio Vista

To a man who knows nothing bookbindings are just
bookbindings. When he has studied and knows a
little, bookbindings are no longer just bookbindings.
But when he has thoroughly understood (and knows
All) bookbindings are once again bookbindings.

*(Adapted, with apologies to an unknown Zen Master.)*

*For F.C.R. and dedicated to the memory of J.R.R.T.*

Studio Vista
Cassell & Collier Macmillan Publishers Limited
35 Red Lion Square, London WC1R 4SG

Copyright © 1974 Philip Smith

First published in Great Britain 1974 by
Studio Vista

Library of Congress Catalog Card No 74–5943

Published in the USA in 1974 by
Van Nostrand Reinhold Company
A Division of Litton Educational
Publishing, Inc.
450 West 33rd Street, New York, NY 10001

ISBN 0 289 70324 7 (UK)
ISBN 0-442-27788-1 (USA)

Set in 9pt and 11 on 12pt Ehrhardt

Printed in Great Britain by the Shenval Press
London and Harlow

# Contents

## Acknowledgements and Notes

When I undertook this book I conceived the idea of asking practitioners from related areas of the craft to contribute something of their specialist activities (conservation, restoration or particular techniques). I received also statements from different countries on attitudes to the art there. I am most grateful for the effort these busy bookbinders have made both in writing and in supplying photographs; and to those collectors and others who have allowed photographs to be used. Some omissions are intentional, or caused by lack of availability or are due to circumstances beyond my control. I would be grateful to readers who draw my attention to any important developments in creative bookbinding which are missing.

The help and advice which many others have given is also gratefully acknowledged here. Thanks are due to Messrs John Harthan and Fuller, of the Victoria and Albert Museum; Mr John Latham for his other aspect of the book in art; Mrs Monique Lefevre and Mr Anton Scheck for help with translations; Mr Kenneth N. Lyne, Reader's Digest Association; Mr Bernard Middleton for allowing me to use his incomparable library of books on bookbinding; Miss Dorothy Miner, Walters Art Gallery, Baltimore; Mr Howard Nixon, of the British Museum; Miss Elizabeth Roth, New York Public Library; Mr G. L'E. Turner of the Oxford Museum of the History of Science; the late Professor J. R. R. Tolkien, for much inspiration; and many others.

I am especially indebted to Mr Edgar Mansfield for his continued encouragement and his kind remarks in the Introduction and for his helpful criticism and his checking of the manuscript; to Señor Emilio Brugalla for the unexpected and generous assessment of my work in his Foreword; and to my wife Dorothy for her help in correcting the typescript and for so tolerantly putting up with my almost complete absence from family activities.

C.P.S.

*Notes*
The diagrams in this book are not drawn in proportion or scale but in the form of profiles and cross-sections which convey simply a maximum of information. The hand written notes with the diagrams fill out the general information in the text. Initials by some of the diagrams acknowledge the immediate source of idea or information, where known. Bracketed italic numbers in the text indicate a bibliographical reference.

The following continuously supplemented reference is substitued for a nominal list of suppliers of equipment, materials and chemicals; it is international in scope: *Designer Bookbinders' Directory*; available from Mrs D. Lubett, 2 Oakwood Mansions, London W14 8LB, England.

The following are some of the Institutions and Societies which have encouraged the development of the hand-bound book:

Centro del Bel Libro, Ascona, Switzerland; Director is Herr Josef Stemmle.

Designer Bookbinders, London, England.

The Guild of Bookworkers, New York, USA.

Internationale Vereinigung Meister der Einbandkunst, Munich, Germany.

Nota Bene Club, Copenhagen, Denmark.

La Société de la Reliure Originale, Paris, France.

*Photographic credits*

All the colour plates are by Sidney Pizan, London, except for Plate 35 (by Tony Evans), Plate 100 (by the author), and Plate 101 (from Spain). All the author's black and white plates are by Godfrey New of R. B. Fleming and Co., London. The details were photographed by the author and inter-negatives made from his colour transparencies by R. B. Fleming and Co. Plate 1 is by courtesy of the Victoria and Albert Museum. Plate 104 is by courtesy of the Art Institute of Chicago. All other photographs were kindly supplied by the binders of the books shown. The sketch diagrams were drawn by the author.

*Notes on some contributors*

*Edgar Mansfield* is a sculptor and bookbinder. Past President of the Guild of Contemporary Bookbinders (now Designer Bookbinders) (MDE). He now lives in New Zealand. Born 1907.

*Emilio Brugalla* is bookbinder, restorer, historian. Member of the Royal Academy of Arts and Science, Barcelona. He is Spain's greatest living exponent of the tooled bookbinding. (Father of Santiago Brugalla) (MDE) Born 1901.

*Anthony Cains* is bookbinder/restorer/conservator. Until 1972 Technical Director of the Restoration Centre of the Biblioteca Nazionale Centrale, Florence (BNCF). Now Technical Director of the Conservation Laboratory at Trinity College, Dublin. Born 1936.

*Gotthilf Kurz* is bookbinder, graphic designer, teacher. President of the Internationale Vereinigung Meister der Einbandkunst (MDE). Born 1923.

*Roger Powell* is bookbinder/restorer/conservator, scholar. Honorary MA (Dublin). Binder of the Books of Kells, Durrow, Armagh, Dimma, etc. Born 1896

*Henri Mercher*; bookbinder/designer/finisher since the age of thirteen. Member of the Société de la Reliure Originale, Paris. Born 1912.

*Monique Mathieu*; bookbinder/designer. Member of the Société de la Reliure Originale, Paris. Born *c*. 1936.

*Ivor Robinson* is bookbinder, designer, teacher. Past President of Designer Bookbinders (MDE). Born 1924.

## Introduction by Edgar Mansfield

This is a very important book, at the right time, and one which transcends its subject. It is important because it reveals the philosophies and techniques underlying some of the most creative works in a discipline which has recently penetrated the field of art. It is at the right time because it follows, and thus extends, some of the finest books on standard and traditional techniques – including repair, restoration and conservation. It transcends its subject because the reader will, in retrospect, discover the nature of the creative act which makes a particular artist become a part of history rather than simply one more skilled performer.

Philip Smith brings to bookbinding one of the most original minds ever to add technical mastery to design competence: his parallel training and experience as a painter is of equal significance in bringing to bookbinding the mind of an artist. While this combination of talents may be adequate, maximum creative fulfilment demands two more: creative craft imagination, and the perceptive functional mind which can equate means with ends. He possesses both of these.

'Creative craft imagination' – the discovery of new technical possibilities during practice or in retrospect – is more rare than might be assumed. 'The perceptive functional mind' distinguishes between two aspects of technique: (a) its expressive use as an appropriate means of communication, dictated by the artist's intention (without which the most imaginative concept may become diluted or ineffectual) and (b) its decorative use, a kind of narcissism, not infrequently motivated by novelty. Philip Smith uses only the former and his mind is stored with numerous technical innovations which await relevant and significant application. In his work, creative craft imagination embraces the entire binding operation and not simply the decoration; the 'functional' mind is always in control.

Whether or not one agrees with all his experiments – and like most creative artists he also may occasionally disagree later – there is always an intuitive or calculated reason. Nothing appears on his bindings just for the (creative) 'hell of it', though such forms do sometimes emerge within the design and are exploited and gently integrated, or else rejected either before or during its execution. Certainly calculated reason for all *structural* experiments on a functional object is essential, but how far this dogma should be applied within the expressive image itself may be controversial and personal. In 'expressive design', however, anything not specifically relevant will interfere with the maximum creative intention.

On the cover and even sometimes within the structure, the vital feature of Smith's work is his personal involvement with the author's thematic material. Whether one accepts or disagrees with his creative interpretations – and some are remarkably penetrating – the imaginative creations which come to life under his magic hands are never adventures in irrelevant pattern, and even his magnificent colour schemes are totally expressive. Philip Smith's bindings are, without creative loss, the unique reflections of an intelligent mind on the author's content, even if these may sometimes be as original as the creations themselves (both his and the author's). While his covers may become the vehicle for a work of creative art, they are never the excuse for it – although to the creative artist the temptation can be great and is often followed by rationalization – plausible claims to relationship – in this age of reasons. Creative compulsion is disciplined and guided by a deeply rooted philosophy. There may appear to be something almost 'fanatical' in Philip Smith (i.e. complete dedication to an ideal), a factor not uncommon among unique creative artists. Indeed its absence, or tolerance, may be debilitating. Extreme 'tolerance' – a much overrated virtue – frequently leads to the abdication of values, and to inertia.

Almost from the moment he left the Royal College of Art, Philip Smith's creative vision in this craft caused a sensation among his fellow bookbinders: opinions were – and still are to a lesser extent – divided. This may be inevitable. 'Probe' minds tend to challenge and disturb (even similar minds), while the 'orbital' mind confirms and reassures. The best of both always survive, but only probe minds may contribute to and thus expand scope and vision.[1] The creative artist's indifference to

1 In practice, of course, most creative achievements retain many elements of conformity.

accepted boundaries should not be confused with anarchism. In common with other potentially successful mutations in this creative universe, each work of art evolves its own special form of discipline: in its design, structure, technique and other components, as it explores the unknown; or changes, penetrates, or illuminates the known. This is no digression from the subject. It concerns the crucial question – 'is it possible to evolve a creative work of art through a book cover while at the same time exploring and respecting another's creative act – the author's content?' The great works of art inspired by the Bible answer this question. In the case of bookbinding, however, indoctrinated barriers of prejudice and history tend to blind the judgement. The 'pecking order' of media and utility dictate that only 'painting' and 'sculpture' qualify – and the object or surface must serve no additional function. The whole book cast solid in bronze, or even a cover removed from the book and framed, would immediately qualify for consideration as 'art'. A visit to the Tate Gallery or to the Museum of Modern Art in New York will provide adequate precedent (Plates 108, 109). Even the probably valid 'decorative' distinction appears no longer to apply to 'art versus design' since the arrival of 'Op' Art – 'probably valid' because mere repetition impoverishes creative magic, without which 'art' becomes pedestrian. Picasso's brilliant dictum 'First you find, then you start looking', in fact illuminates the whole transcendent and reciprocal process which operates during the evolution of a creative work.

One point must be emphasized in connection with this book. It deals primarily with one convincing philosophy, the close relationship between binding and content. The reasons given are logical and irrefutable, but as Smith observes, the creative act may sometimes transcend or ignore reason. Until the end of the last century, the idea of a relationship between cover design and content rarely occurred to anyone. The function of decoration on all objects of utility was simply to enhance, and this attitude continues to produce works of great beauty, glorifying the book cover. Penetrating expressive design, and this philosophy of Philip Smith, is a very recent phenomenon, and may be regarded as an 'Everest' in a chain of peaks which include the imaginative extension of decoration, abstract art and numerous other directions revealed by the questing mind. Many of these creations will be partially relevant, neutral, or even totally irrelevant to the content of the book and more appropriate on a wall panel. They may even include the 'Easy Rider' product of uncertainty – restless change and its bed-fellow, 'Happening'. The problem however is not simple, despite the permanent function of the binding to which these designs may be applied.

Assuming the designer will not or cannot work in any other medium, it may be better to execute a product of the creative imagination on a book cover for 'bad' reasons, rather than leave it 'still born' for good ones. Furthermore there is often a feed-back from creation in other media which may achieve relevance. Without birth there can be no progeny. While the content of this book closes no past and future doors to other directions, and can even illuminate these, it crystallizes values by offering an ideal – a total unity of creative integration for the whole book.

Edgar Mansfield
Napier, New Zealand, 1973

## Foreword by Emilio Brugalla (*translated by Kenneth Lyons*)

European bookbinding in our day possesses unsuspected riches, with a vitality that is quite alien to traditional concepts. Decoration, which may give the book a symbolic aesthetic quality, obeys intrinsic demands that leave any sort of gratuitous ostentation out of the question. Such splendour as it possesses must come from its own significance as an original creation, which will express with witty subtlety, suggestive vagueness or sharp contrasts, the intrinsic essence contained in the pages of the book.

Those two champions of the art of bookbinding, Legrain and Bonet, with the help of the excellent craftsmen of Paris, revolutionized the bookbinding scene of their day. They created a new conception of decoration which altogether changed the face of the book. They both taught the professionals – the trade practitioners – new ways and means of working, and they both inspired followers. But their early endeavours, timid and tentative, were childishly clumsy compared to their later achievements. Pierre Legrain, without arrogance or rancour, pronounced the significant words: 'S'échapper à l'obsession du passé' (To escape the obsession with the past). This was his motto.

Paul Bonet, overburdened with the responsibility of his many commissions, uttered this *cri de cœur :* 'Pas de délais de temps, ne jamais connaître un prix d'avance, ne jamais voir la maquette.' (No time allowed, never to know a price in advance, never to see the mock-up).

After all the triumphs, both past and present, that have come to the art of bookbinding, triumphs recorded with erudite and painstaking detail in the catalogues to the exhibitions of the *Société de la Reliure Originale,* it seemed that the possibilities of decorative ideas, images and figures had finally been exhausted. But this was not the case. Today we can discern against the backdrop of history new hopes, new values, new fashions. The surprises are continuous. The most recent does not come from the deliberations of Legrain or the powerful imagination of Paul Bonet. Nor is it one of the many that the art of bookbinding has received from Pierre-Lucien Martin, Henri Mercher, Coster-Dumas, Cretté or Leroux, Lobstein, Monique Mathieu or Knoll, all active members of the *Société de la Reliure Originale* who exhibited their latest creations at the 'Helmhaus' of Zurich in 1969. No, this time the surprise comes to us from Great Britain, the homeland of such men as Samuel Mearne, Roger Payne, Cobden-Sanderson, Cockerell, Roger Powell and all those others who kept alive the flame of English bookbinding, a flame fanned to new life in our own time with the creation of *Designer Bookbinders,* a growing society of bookbinders and book lovers.

A special place in English bookbinding must be found for Edgar Mansfield, one of its most powerful influences in recent times: he it is, as draughtsman, painter and sculptor, who in his *Modern Design in Bookbinding* reveals his lively imagination as it exploits the covers of beautiful books, covers of 'Oasis' and native niger leathers, mostly with the wrinkled, shaded African tanning and with strange imperfections which this artist turns into expressive elements, combining them with a tangle of thin and thick lines in his original style.

The greatest surprise, however, was the one which caused such astonishment and perplexity in August of 1970, in the 'Casa del Crocefisso' in Ascona, the premises of the Galleria del Bel Libro. Our good friend J. Stemmle, its founder and director, provided us as usual with photographs, slides and brochures which reproduced some pieces from the extraordinary exhibition of fifty bindings by Mr Philip Smith, an English artist of very great talent whose star now shines high above the international horizon.

In speaking of his work in bookbinding let us forget the prejudiced outlook of the trade and all orthodox methodology. Let us half close our eyes in order to see more clearly! If we are to appreciate the scope and objectivity of Smith's work we must recognize the sincerity of the abstruse pictorial sense of our age, which is so unlike any other we can remember. We must accept with tolerance the hypnotizing effects of a developing technology, of *avant-garde* painting and sculpture, and the new manifestations in ceramics, plastics, metal, leather and any other means that art makes its own in the ceaseless search for truth which is heedless of local feelings or tradition.

Philip Smith is forty-four years old and is already an outstanding designer of the new school, trained in London's leading centre of bookbinding and the graphic arts. His imagination is filled with ambiguous figurations, symbols and diffuse lyricism. Speculative rhythms and cadences, hyperbolic in intention, take on lucid transparencies and iridescences of sparkling colour, the antithesis of the withered realism which leaves the shrill imperatives of the surrealists and their immediate ancestors far behind. He makes absolutely no use of compasses and rulers or other instruments proper to his art and trade. He does not deny the past but neither does he make common cause with it; nor is he attracted by what is called 'the beauty of speed', though this is an invention of our age. His achievements are meditated and systematic. He is ruled by a will that defeats all difficulties. He stands apart from all the vaunted rigidity of those who are faithful to rectangular precision. His penetration is not based on geometrical reasons or grammatical rules, but on a spontaneous and intrinsic discipline, from which he tries to extract a vital essence, much as a painter might, but using leather as a means.

His ingenuity consists in making the leather of the binding present hypotheses which will induce the aesthetically-minded reader to reflect before venturing into the maze of fiction and ideas, whether they be those unfathomable worlds of Tolkien or Yeats, of Leonardo da Vinci or Shakespeare, worlds which he daringly attempts to explore and explain through the silent medium of his subtle art.

The absolutely original liberty which he takes, for instance in his book-walls, may offend some opinions and give rise to controversies regarding the inalienable function of books. But it is the profundity of the subjects which inspires him, especially those based on philosophical or poetic theses to which he submits all the potential of his pictorial wonder-working.

In his eagerness to give a book all that can be imagined by his energetic creativity, this original bookbinding artist is not content simply to compose sketches and leave them to be carried out by expert craftsmen, as is usual in Paris. Smith prefers to carry out the work with his own hands and in his own medium, which gives rise to many of the improvisations which further his expressive effects and the credo of his inspiration. In the use of this material, leather, he is partially faithful to tradition, but now he seldom uses tooling except in some of his titles. His chromatic range is derived from a great variety of leather cuttings set side by side in amorphous pieces like jaspering.

His art seems enclosed in a hermetic individualism that delights in apocalyptic depths and digressions suggested by the books he binds (often selected by himself), which inevitably include the 'Shakespeare Canon'. It is without precedents or professional formulas permitting any approach or the formation of a school.

Books today, just like those of ancient times, are on the threshold of an enigmatic future, facing a period of rapid expansion and change which can already be felt. Will tomorrow's leaves be made of paper? Will the shade of Gutenberg finally vanish? Will leather still be the material of the art of bookbinding? These questions about books – both contents and containers – only future events in the life of mankind will answer.

Emilio Brugalla, Royal Academy of Arts and
Science, Barcelona, 1972

## Author's Preface

The hand-bookbinder now has little part to play in the service or social needs of the general reader. The mass demand for literature of every kind has left him in a social back-water. Bookbinding was never a folk-art and cannot be considered as such. Patronage has always been from the rich and the scholarly. Now more than ever it is less a functional (trade) than a therapeutic (amateur) activity, and most bookbinding done by hand is concerned with the repair and conservation of books which have been with us for a long time.

Private presses producing special editions of distinction grow fewer, with periods of growth or decline according to fluctuations in fashion and demand. Where new work is demanded of the handbinder he is thrown more and more into the realm of 'art'. His work can be seen widely only in exhibitions and so there is greater emphasis on hand-bookbinding as exhibition or collectors' pieces. The book remains a functional object but it is an open question as to how many of these elaborately constructed objects are actually used for reading. It is an expensive way of reading to pay anything from £500 to £1,500 or more for a copy of *King Lear,* when it can be read for less than £1 in paper-back editions. Like all significant but 'purposeless' objects the hand-bookbinding can be justified on the level of 'art'. But to be truly on a level with other traditionally art disciplines, like painting or sculpture, the same creative spirit must inform it. The text itself must also be of a quality of content and materials worthy of such fine treatment; but this part of the process is generally up to the client.

This book has several objectives and, I hope, many uses. One is to throw some light on the new approach to hand-bookbinding with a view to aiding the discrimination of bibliophiles and bookbinders. Another is to say something about bookbinding at a more creative level where it begins to move away from the realms of traditional decorative, or applied, art. The book is also an attempt to explain some of the newer techniques and inventions originating in response to an exploratory approach and to the special requirements of creative bookbinding. Because bookbinding as a means of artistic expression is entirely unfamiliar and perhaps indistinguishable at a cursory glance from the activity which has gone into it before, I have tried to communicate the fact that bookbinding can be different, not only in style and degree of decoration, but *in kind.* Most people interested in fine books have seen and treated bookbinding at best as a minor art, more usually as a decorative craft, and mostly as a dead handicraft which has been replaced in its useful function by the machine in the trade edition bindery. All these views contribute to the truth, and even bookbinders must accept them as a fact of life. But there is a different species of bookbinding validated by a different kind of activity; this is the kind of activity which distinguishes the pursuit of art from the work of the designer and the craftsman, each of whom can nevertheless use his own kind of 'artistry'.

This new species of bookbinding can only be written about from the inside, and I hope to show in some detail how it happens. It does not happen at the design stage, nor at the making stage, it happens in the heart as an act of love, not of function, nor of necessity (except to the artist). I do not want to confuse the issue with overmuch philosophy but the argument cannot be stated without some, which I will make as factual as values can be!

A stool requires three legs with which to achieve its greatest stability. The art side of the new book-binding is its vital third leg. During the period of its functional necessity up to the nineteenth century hand-bookbinding has managed to get on very well with two active ingredients, put there by the craftsman and by the designer, if they were not the same person. It is only when the content of the book, especially the thematic idea of the creative writer, is sought out as the vital and peculiar springboard of this medium that it can be justified as an 'art' medium, for it is this hidden essence which informs the whole point – if not the only reason – of using a book and not a canvas or panel on which to display visual images.

In the past no other concepts existed but the application of 'standard' or traditional decorative motifs to the functional object. This was often accomplished with great skill and taste; objects were beautified by a richness of surface for its own sake. Today with our heritage of new discoveries in every field – science, psychology, art – the crafts also are turning in new directions. In retrospect we now see, with regard to the possibilities inherent in bookbinding, that the task was begun at the second step. The book, in depth, was overlooked.[1]

I have implied that advanced bookbinding is not only concerned with more complex technical operations, but with the introduction of specific purposes and conceptual direction in the work. It includes a creative and original approach rather than an automatic and habitual one. In basic bookbinding one learns *how* to do; in advanced bookbinding one learns *what* to do with the acquired skills of experience. A quite different connection is made between the operator and his work. The new factors include increased awareness and sensibility to the demands and potential nature of the medium, and solutions come about through understanding and discrimination. No longer is he concerned with making pretty designs applied to a surface in the form of either fumbling or sophisticated arrangements of abstract elements. The elements and their compositional disposal are directed by creative purposes and insights from higher regions of the mind, generated by his special relationship with the book.

One of the greatest neglected potentials of bookbinding has been the area in which the aim is the integration of the binding imagery with the book content, in such a manner as to evoke in the viewer's mind an experience corresponding to that which the bookbinder – as reader – has found in the book, and further, to allow some new truth about it to reach him. The role of the image on the binding is analogous in part to the scenery and lighting of a play. It may provide a setting to the reading and throw light on its essential quality of meaning.

The book narrative consists of two parts, the outer part or 'letter' (the descriptive information or dialogue) and the 'spirit' of the content (the theme, idea or experience which the author intends to communicate). The author uses words, the binding artist uses visual images (colour and forms) and certain materials. The image does not correspond to the literal aspect of the writing but to its thematic quality filtered through the understanding of the binder. This may go beyond the author's intention and the binder will interpret what the writing actually conveys to him. For example: *The Lord of the Rings* is simply a tale without ulterior motive on the part of the author. One does not analyse or interpret this with the intellect; one absorbs its meaning emotionally as it applies to one's own picture of the world, without attributing the meaning one has discovered to Professor Tolkien. Such tales appeal directly to the emotions from which they stem, and it is in this way that they can influence one's attitude and behaviour.

With expressive bookbinding the artist hopes to tap and convey more than one of the possible meanings of the book, which cannot be fully grasped by casual reading but only by a depth of appreciation gained in getting to know the book thoroughly.

This calls for special requirements of the artist as bookbinder. He must be capable of detecting the spirit of the book to create a new experience from it. He must be capable of selecting from the repertoire of his imagination those symbols and relevant material equivalents which most closely correspond in character to the mood he wishes to evoke, and of organizing (designing) these without losing control of his theme. He must be a master of structural techniques and of graphic representation and have cultivated enough manual skill to achieve 'invisible' craftsmanship. At any stage the unity of his representation may be marred by lack of attention to any of the details which make up a fine binding. Professor Maslow (*37*, pp. 143–44) in speaking of creative work says:

> In the first place, the great work needs great talent . . . In the second place, the great work needs not only the flash, the inspiration, the peak-experience, it also needs hard work, long training, unrelenting criticism, perfectionist standards. In other words, succeeding upon intuition comes rigorous thought; succeeding upon daring comes caution; succeeding upon fantasy and imagination comes reality testing. Now come the comparisons, judgements, evaluations . . . selections and

[1] Since the nineteenth century it had of course been realized that *some* reference to the book to justify the expense of elaboration should be provided, and it was probably the illustrative imagery of early advertising in the cover which gave a lead in this direction after the beginnings of mass production.

rejections. The necessary passivity and receptivity of inspiration or of peak-experience must now give way to the activity, control and hard work. A peak-experience happens to a person, but the person *makes* the great product.

It is possible to draw a parallel between the painter or sculptor who derives his inspiration from observation or insight into nature, and the creative bookbinder whose springboard is another created thing (the writing of a poet or dramatist, for example). There are obvious differences, of course; not the least of them is that the bookbinder keeps 'the landscape' with his interpretation of it. The combination, properly integrated, makes for a most powerful communicative art. The term 'art' is used far too liberally today so that every object exhibited in an 'art' context (for example, Duchamp's Hatstand) is called 'art'. For the purposes of this essay I understand art to be a kind of communication generated from a certain creative source in man, not contrived wilfully by mental acrobatics but stemming from a point of anonymity which transcends individuality.

Designing is a combination of mental processes (such as discrimination and selection) which the operator uses to organize what he has received as insight, or by other means, such as a client given or self-initiated specification, into a form or prescription from which the finished artifact may be made up.

Craftsmanship – ingenuity with techniques married to manual skills – is what the operator uses to manufacture a physical transmittable replica of his insight.

The task of the craftsman or the designer is to become so conversant with his means of expression that it does not interfere with the re-generation of the insight or idea. Skill becomes an automatic tool controlled by the latter and guided by the design plan. The designer masters analytical procedures until they too become second nature in problem solving. His work subserves the insight as craftsmanship subserves design.

In advanced creative bookbinding, which aims at an integrated object, it is necessary to unify the working of these three departments. It is apparent that there is a difference in kind between the works of an individual bookbinder and between the work of different bookbinders. This difference seems to come from either a dominance of one or other department or in the insufficient development of one of them. It is evident from the appearance of their products and the way they naturally work that each bookbinder 'leans towards' one of the departments; that is, there seems to be a dominant function in his make-up (modified by external influences such as training, opportunity and experience) which causes his bias towards one or other aspect. One bookbinding will reflect more or less faithfully the thematic mood of the book(1);[1] another will display ingenuity in the design of its working structure(2);[1] another demonstrates the skilful composition of graphic elements(2);[1] yet another shows clearly the bookbinder's delight in manual skill(3);[1] This predominant characteristic or feature recurring in his work will naturally be strengthened by use, and others atrophy through lack of it. Each of these features can be detected in the bookbindings shown in the Plates. Sometimes a fair balance of all the characteristics can be seen in particular works.

> The great artist is able to bring together clashing colours, forms that fight each other, dissonances of all kinds, into a unity . . . To the extent that creativeness is constructive, synthesizing, unifying and integrative, to that extent does it depend in part on the inner integration of the person. (*37*, p. 140)

[1] Anyone sufficiently interested can learn the craft of bookbinding, but far fewer have learnt how to inform it. In this book we hope to indicate how the highest level may be developed. In a hierarchy of *completeness* (1) would represent art/design/craft bookbinding; (2) would represent design/craft bookbinding; and (3) would represent craft bookbinding. There are of course permutations of degree in each kind or level; for example, nothing can be *made* without some degree of organisation (design) or some kind of motivating impulse. Skill can rise from the crude to the highly polished; design from the vague and immature to the analytically sophisticated; and motivation from the banally imitative and self-protective to a highly emotional but disengaged originality. Chart 2 develops this idea – applicable in fact to any activity.

The aim of the artist-bookbinder is to direct and integrate all the various departments so that one function does not dominate to the weakening or exclusion of another. For those fortunate enough to find some purpose in life through their work, of which the goal is the production of the perfectly integrated bookbinding, their activity can be seen as an analogue of the search for personal fulfilment and integration. Both areas have a mutual feed-back. It is possible by studying the processes and factors which lead to the one to discover equivalent methods of accomplishing the other.

C.P.S.
Merstham, 1973

# 1 Historical notes

An avalanche of volumes has been written about the history of bookbinding in both its decorative and technical aspects and it is not the purpose of this book to repeat, with less scholarly knowledge, what has been done so ably by experts. I merely wish to draw attention here to the relatively few precedents of expressive rather than decorative bookbindings.

I have included a photograph of the famous *Stonyhurst Gospel* (Plate 1) made in the seventh century AD, because it has a quality of expression uncommon in the earlier days of bookbinding. Some of the techniques exemplified in this binding are still being explored and developed by modern designers. The binding is not purely expressive because the monks who made it added decorative motifs within the panel borders. Until the present century indeed there are few bindings on which the decoration is not enclosed by a border of lines or pattern. What is especially interesting in this binding is the design on the upper or front cover. Instead of the usual Christ in Majesty surrounded by the four Evangelical beasts, we have here the more subtle allusion of a tree with a heart-shaped bud and four 'apples'. The design is in leather modelled over cords, the panel lines are built up over cords which are laced into the wooden boards and the central 'Jesse-tree' probably over glued cords. The finer lines seem to have been marked in with a stylus and coloured with pigments. The lower cover is quite flat and appears unfinished with just a kind of Coptic chequer-board mark-up scribed on the surface (*48a*).

The relationship of binding decoration to text until quite recently has been a relatively superficial and accidental one, with the exception of liturgical bindings. The history of book decoration may be looked upon as a gradual movement towards a closer integration of inside and outside, with a few periods when completely arbitrary decoration was customary.

Most early Western European bindings protected religious books, and, at a time when the Church was the leading repository of knowledge, a sophisticated symbolism was developed and widely disseminated. Everyone used and understood this symbolism, and in a largely illiterate world pictorial imagery was an essential element of communication. The content of the liturgical book was easily recognized in the binding decoration, but for books on other subjects it was, with a few exceptions, a different matter (*35*, The Introduction by Howard Nixon. Also *65*, Plate XLVIII, No. 344).

With the development of printing and the demand for more books, secular artisans, rather than monks, were employed in binderies. The hand-bound book was the mass-produced book of its day and there was no time for the bookbinder to contemplate the contents, even if he had the ability to design or could read. It was the patron, the printer or the bookseller who would decide how the binding was to be decorated. Occasionally a more talented artisan would devise a pattern, and expensive tools, rolls and panel stamps would be cut for a special job. These motifs would be used on other books which came in for binding. On rare occasions a design would coincide with an appropriate text. Some books on architectural subjects happen to be decorated with architectural features, but this may have been fortuitous. Thomas Maioli's *De Architectura* by Vitruvius, produced at Venice in 1511, is one such binding executed by Claude de Picques.[1]

The Elizabethan passion for embroidered bindings, often made by ladies of the Court, has induced works demonstrating the integration of binding and text, but here again it is the religious books which receive this treatment. A charming example of this type of work may be seen on a Book of Psalms[2] at the British Museum (*35*, Fig. 2). This seventeenth-century bookbinding depicts Jacob's Ladder on the back cover and Jacob wrestling with the angel on the front. It is interesting to note that the design 'bleeds' off the edges of the covers but the two parts are separated by a panelled spine.

Development of the concept of integration of cover and contents had reached the stage of the illustration of one incident rather than the total impression of the spirit of the book. Apart from the examples referred to it is extremely rare to encounter evidence of content/binding harmony throughout the whole period from the sixteenth to the nineteenth century.

Since the early nineteenth century there has been a more deliberate concern by book designers to create some rapport between the two dimensions, but the ideal – often expressed but not achieved – has had to wait for visual developments in the 'pure' arts to prepare the ground and make our present achievement possible. The Industrial Revolution freed the bookbinder's mind from manual concepts and allowed more artistic and technical experiment. There was, however, no training in the use of visual elements comparable with that available to the designer today; consequently, design and decoration, to our taste, was very amateurish and lacking direction. Manual skill, as always seems to be the case, was never lacking. Nevertheless, the urge to break out of the closed circle of stagnant traditional[3] ornamentation is apparent, and some very interesting bookbinding objects resulted.

The mid-nineteenth century proliferates with novelties in the techniques and materials used in book production.[4] The appearance of printed cloth and paper for bindings gave rise to new directions in bookbinding and almost every conceivable material was brought into experiments to allow the more permanent binding to compete.[5] Covers moulded from a mixture of papier-mâché and plaster were patented by the London firm of Jackson & Son, but only a few titles, on medieval subjects, were bound. By happy chance these rather heavy bindings have a curiously medieval quality (*38*, p. 139). The firm of Remnant & Edmonds specialized in the use of unusual binding materials and apparently they were responsible for the first use of Parkesite (a celluloid Plastics). Tortoiseshell, porcelain and art silk inlaid with gold and flock were some of the novel materials used, as well as decorated vellum, paper inlaid on cloth and stamped in black and gold. I also discovered in an old patents specification by Samuel Leigh Sotheby one of the precedents of interchangeable cover decoration of 1861.

1 This belongs to l'Ecole Polytechnique, Paris, and is reproduced in *Maioli, Canevari and Others* by G. D. Hobson, Ernest Benn, London, 1926.

2 Vide: *English Embroidered Bookbindings* by Cyril Davenport, Kegan Paul, London 1899.

3 The term 'traditional' should not imply that everything stops (at the Victorian age). It has its growing tip, watered by the genuine *avant-garde*, which in its turn is absorbed into the main trunk of traditional knowledge.

4 The pre-occupation with novelty and sensational appearance, and with new methods of manufacture, led to the neglect of quality and soundness in materials and structures which only recently, following the Florence flood episode, are being given wide and serious scientific consideration.

5 Vide: *The Collector's Book of Books*, by Eric Quayle, Studio Vista, London, 1971, gives a good account of early commercial book-production.

The outside of the covers of the book or portfolio is made so as to have the appearance of a panel in frame and a long slit or opening . . . is left in the inside of the cover (or top or bottom thereof) and an ornamental design on paper or other substance is inserted through the opening and held secure between panel and frame.

These adventures with newer materials and techniques thrown up by machine production must have inspired the more creative hand-binders to experiment with the traditional leather binding and this was especially true in France, where efforts to break away from 'persian carpet' style and other prevailing forms of decoration were made by Marius Michel, Gruel, Ruban, Romain Raparlier, Petrus and Meunier, who encouraged initiative and imagination in their workshops (49, where several illustrations of their works may be seen).

A new approach to text/binding relationship began to predominate in France, being passed on to Pierre Legrain by Michel and thence to influence the modern binding designers there, but, says Miss Prideaux:

> This idea that the decorative outside of a book should be emblematic of what is within . . . proved a complete snare to the craftsman who was not an artist, but also apparently to the wildly imaginative, who considered that eccentricity of motive could cover any amount of technical inefficiency. (49)

In France and later in England this tendency led to pictorial bindings, but the pictures remained strictly within the tooled panel. Much of the work was modelled in a naturalistic way and hand coloured. Raparlier, a one-time student of the Ecole des Beaux Arts in Paris, produced imaginative designs which never repeated. He built up the forms immaculately by working leather inlays and onlays with small modelling tools while the leather was still wet and then hardening it, and imparting shaded tones with the modelling tools heated.

In 1894 W. Y. Fletcher remarked,[6] lamenting the lack of originality, and the copying of tradition in his day:

6 Vide: *Bookbinding in France*, Seeley and Co., London, 1894, p. 80.

> The invention of a new style of binding seems as little likely as one in architecture. Still, we venture to hope that some genius may arise who will be able to unite originality of design with the marvellous accuracy and finish which distinguishes the work of the present day and thus make bookbinding once more a living art.

During the present century too the prevailing attitude amongst bookbinding designers has been moving around the concept of content/binding unity, but it has been found easier to pay lip-service than to act upon it! Vestigial traces from earlier periods – carried on by the untutored amateur or the trade man (usually uneducated in design concepts) as well as in pastiche in the book-clubs – co-exist with the progressive work of today, the ethos of which is developed in this book.

The deaths of Bonet the designer and Mondange the skilled technician[7] in 1971 brought to an end an era where innovation in decoration and abstract design reached a high peak.[8] Before us lies a new era where not only the designer and technician but the artist also will find a legitimate place in this field.

7 Vide: *Paul Bonet*, by Paul Valéry and others. Librairie Auguste Blaizot, Paris, 1945.

8 In the *Société de la Reliure Originale* they have a large group of followers and imitators. (Their influence is also felt, but applied with far less skill, in other bookbinding societies.)

1 Stonyhurst
*Gospel of St John* (St Cuthbert)
Brown leather modelled over string on wooden boards. Indented and coloured lines
135 × 95mm (5⅜ × 3¾in)
*c.* AD 650 Stonyhurst Library

## 2 A framework for thinking

The framework on which integrative bookbinding is built can become a useful tool for bookbinders pursuing different goals from different standpoints. It may be used as a check-list on the completeness and validity of the approach. In advanced creative bookbinding at least four stages may be separated out for the purpose of examining the factors and processes involved. In practice some of the factors from different stages overlap or occur simultaneously and it is not possible to draw sharp dividing lines.

### Preparatory work (input stage)

Reading the book stocks the memory with all the data relating to subject and theme, and notes are made. This is followed by quiet contemplation of the book over a period to allow unconscious processes to form and crystallize ideas and images in the imagination. At this stage all one's past experience of working, one's training, understanding of symbols, colour, materials, etc. influence these unconscious processes (7, 9, 26, 29, 37, 63). Essential preparation would include a wide training in sound methods based on a thorough understanding of bookbinding principles and aims, so that the binder can match the binding to the content of the book.

### Inception of idea (insight)

If one can quieten the mind, all the preparatory and background work seem without warning or contrivance to be synthesized in the upper reaches of the mind and to present the imagination with a clear insight of what the solution is to be. Whatever it is that comes into contact with the mind at such moments, the trace it leaves there is usually interpreted in terms of the bookbinder's current visual idiom. It seems almost *miraculous*, and happily releases one from meritorious personal claims. If, as is most usual, there is no such insight, one has to muddle along intellectually working-up a design from one's notations, and hope to generate emotional interest leading to a breakthrough (to something less contrived). Other factors which adversely affect this stage might be: unsympathetic relationship between binder and the content of the book (he must be able to open his heart to it!); ideas insufficiently registered in the memory or in one's notes and sketches; loss of idea due to time lapse and cooling down (if the idea is registered with emotional impact it is rarely forgotten); and finally, undisciplined imaginative faculty leading to an incoherent image.

### Design organization (planning stage)

Unlike the second stage this one is quite straightforward. From the insight a design specification is formulated (all the notes and sketches are referred to in this) and the structure is worked out. Possible expressive elements are tested against the original concept (or the design specification, whichever is available). The designer will check the feasibility of manufacture of his idea; the availability of materials, processes and services; and the possible extent of his abilities. For success at this stage a methodical approach and ability to formulate visually are necessary. Sufficient data from one's background and experience should be available together with a grasp of bookbinding techniques. Second thoughts or associative thinking can superimpose on or swamp the insight or one may lose trust in intuitive decisions. Continual reference to a check-list specification, drawings and colour sketches is useful. Each factor in structure and surface design is given due consideration so that there can be a complete synthesis of data leading to integration of image and book. Clear insight is a rare occurrence and the predominant designing methods will be those summarized under D1 and D2 (Chart 1) originating as a self-initiated or client's specification, which substitute for it. This stage is the bridge between the 'idea' and the viewer. It is the prescription which is to be given tangible form at the next stage. The role of the reflective part of the mind is as an observer keeping attention tuned on what is relevant to the design.

Where there seems to be an influx of creative energy at the 'insight' stage, at the design stage there may occur an unconscious synthesis of various ideas in the mind known as 'invention' giving what later seems the *obvious* solution to a long-probed problem (e.g. the book-wall structure or carrier of the image rather than the creative image in it).

## *Making (output)*

At this stage it is necessary to have control of tools, materials and structural methods. The appropriate techniques and skill in handling are vital to a successful manifestation of the original idea. Dis-abilities include lack of skill (or insufficiently developed skill); too much emphasis on virtuosity of handling for its own sake; poor tools (or lack of maintenance); low quality or inappropriate materials; poor physical awareness. In working with onlays and maril (Section 10) there is an intuitive handling of the materials; spontaneous decisions seem to be made by some swift co-ordination of the practised eye and hand. There is the feeling that the right instinctive decisions are being made, like a blind man moving about so *certain* of obstacles that he has no need to put out his hand.

One can see that no amount of intuitive handling of materials will invent the book-wall, and no amount of inventive designing will bring about emotionally meaningful images. But the great bookbindings will include elements of the operational harmony of all three sides of the creative act. A practical example of this process is described in Section 18.

Industrial production lacks the humanizing touch of the hand-craftsman, and this is unavoidable on that scale, but even in the province of the hand-made object some designers prefer to hand over the work to technicians to make up. Where the particular material can be shaped without reference to idiosyncrasies in it, such as by the use of hard-edge onlay and paper-pattern tooling designs, i.e. fixed prescriptions, this delegation is possible; but it diminishes direct intuitive control, cuts out initiative and inhibits the spontaneous working of materials such as leather.

## Chart 1   A Framework for Thinking

*Notational analysis of operational factors in hand-bookbinding design*

This chart represents the determining factors of bookbinding work and their separate roles related to functional facilities in the bookbinder. This is necessarily an artificial division in order to check-list the various ingredients of the three main processes. The factors should be considered as possibly cross-fertilizing rather than conflicting. The categories can indicate the approach of the particular bookbinder who may work from one or a combination of different categories depending on his type, training, inclinations, special abilities, above all upon the kind and quality of his attention, and of course on the type of book (creative writing, technical etc.) he is dealing with. The chart, which is not comprehensive, should be studied in relation to Section 2 and the theme of this book. See Appendix I for factors determining physical make-up of book.

| Factor | Category A<br>Art aspect, includes expressive bookbinding | Category D1   Surface design<br>Category D2   Structural design<br>Designing aspects | Category C   Structural technique. Craft aspect |
|---|---|---|---|
| Working definition | Art is a communication generated from a creative source in man, it is not contrived by mental acrobatics. | Designing is a combination of intellectual processes used to organize the insight experience into a form from which the finished artifact is constructed. | Craftsmanship is ingenuity with techniques married to manual skills used in manufacture. |
| optimum operative condition | Emotional content of 'mind' is synthesized. Seems *miraculous.* | Intellectual content of 'mind' synthesized in 'invention'. Solution seems *obvious.* | Intuitive or instinctive co-ordination of eye and hand in spontaneous handling. The rightness of the operation seems *certain.* |
| Motivating impulse | Unexpected creative insight into the nature of the text. The experience generated by the text is all important. The medium of expression (including the operator) is a vehicle of the creative source. | D1. Play on an empty surface; work from 'nothing' by intuitive or contrived relationships made between graphic elements. D2. Works from self- or client-initiated design specification. The design is all important. The medium is a vehicle of the design. | Physical book and materials. The medium is all important and is the vehicle of func-tional use. |
| Physio-psychological tools; methods | Imagination<br><br>Reading and contemplation encourage spontaneous incep-tion of idea. Work from the 'given' intuitive synthesis of factors. | Analysis leading to planned synthesis<br><br>D1. Works with acquired compositional rules | Motor skills, physical awareness.<br><br>(Craftsman thinks of decoration as *applied* to materials). |
| Predominant function | Emotional (initiating)<br><br>Works by creative and ori-ginal thinking. | Intellectual (guiding)<br><br>Works by Lateral (inventive) (cf: *7, 10*) logical (consolidative) or associative (random) processes, i.e. different kinds of selection and ordering. | Manual (executive)<br><br>Works by traditional rule of thumb, imitative and habitual thinking (in the non-pejorative sense). |
| Dominant factor in work | The concept (open-ended, ambiguous but integrative meaning) | D1. Composition designed to express personal idea. D2. Ingenuity working on struc-tural needs. Aims at solving design problem. | Execution and finish. Aim is to produce an object with good technical finish. |
| Visual basis of work | Isolation of thematic mater-ial and use of symbolic analogy (with objective or universal meaning). Each creation is original and develops new forms | Play of graphic elements (perhaps signs given specific but arbitrary meaning) based on title, general subject, illustrations or past art styles. Generally developed by formula from previous works. | Arbitrary pattern or motif or naturalistic illustrations. Usually self-imitative or traditional. |
| Intention | Promulgation of artistic truth | D1. Elegance; pleasing decoration; design in the 'abstract.' D2. Well designed structure. | Slick finish. To make a useful object with fine presentation of materials. |
| Relationship of binding to contents | Integrative | Not considered of prime importance; the work is treated as a design problem. | Rarely considered. Separate. |
| Operator directed by | Inner necessity of insight | Requirements of the graphic or structural design | The needs of the materials. |

# 3 The fine binding – the principal parts and their functions

Satisfactory bookbinding depends on so many interacting factors that it is not possible to give a simple do-it-yourself formula. If it is known what is necessary for achieving a goal, decisions can be made within a framework of constraints. The variety of factors which regulate how a particular book shall be treated and bound are listed in Appendix I and in the 'framework for thinking' which precedes this section.

This book is not intended as an introduction to bookbinding for beginners, but some generalized information is necessary to provide a context for advanced bookbinding techniques and design. Figs. 1, 3 and the chart in this section show the main parts of the codex and some of their functions.

The main element of the book is the carrier of the image (the surface bearing the illustrations and/or text). The problem has always been how to arrange the text and pictures in such a way as to make them readily intelligible to the reader. The image carrier has evolved in its portable forms from clay tablets and rolls (where accessibility was poor) to the present codex form, and has been made from such organic materials as ivory, wood, wax, bark and leaf strips (i.e. papyrus), parchment, vellum and finally paper; developing from permanent materials (slate, clay) through relatively fragile and impermanent materials (papyrus and paper) to sheet material made from the organic polymers (plastics and plastics impregnated materials) of the present day. Multiples of these image carriers have been attached together by rings, cords and thread.

The codex form of grouping the image carriers or leaves is a pile or polyptych of sheets held together at one edge. The outer leaf at each end is usually stiffer than the others and is known as the cover or board, and is designed so as to protect the rest of the leaves. Binding methods consist in a variety of solutions to the problem of holding a number of leaves together so that they remain together and accessible to use and resistant to wear for a prolonged period. Binding creates the mechanism whereby this becomes possible. Generally a book will last as long as its weakest material and structure; as books are still made from relatively fragile and vulnerable materials these should be of the soundest, tested quality and durability. Binding is the last process in book making, a chain of events beginning with an idea in an author's mind and including such processes as paper-making, designing of type and format, printing ink technology, printing and all the print finishing processes such as gathering, folding and collating. The hand binder, with whom we are concerned in general, and the creative designer-bookbinder in particular, will take it up at these latter stages.

Since the codex form of book appeared around the end of the first century AD no sudden mutations have appeared in its evolution. Materials and structures have in principle remained constant and unchanged. Differences lie not so much in new principles but in variations and refinements of the original ones: so 'advanced' bookbinding is concerned with these variations and refinements and special methods used in special cases. No simple formula can be given on what to do in binding a book, because each book is so different and the variables (weight of paper, number of sections, etc) are often so critical that the wrong sewing thread or wrong sewing method, for example, will seriously and adversely affect the operation and life of the book. Bookbinding methods can best be taught or demonstrated by reference to particular books. In this book, methods will be described and illustrated by some actual examples and the problems which occur. By reference here to the charts and check lists and his experience as a bookbinder the operator will be able to determine what treatment is best for other particular books. The main concern of this book is with the design and the artistic use to which a binder may put his knowledge of techniques.

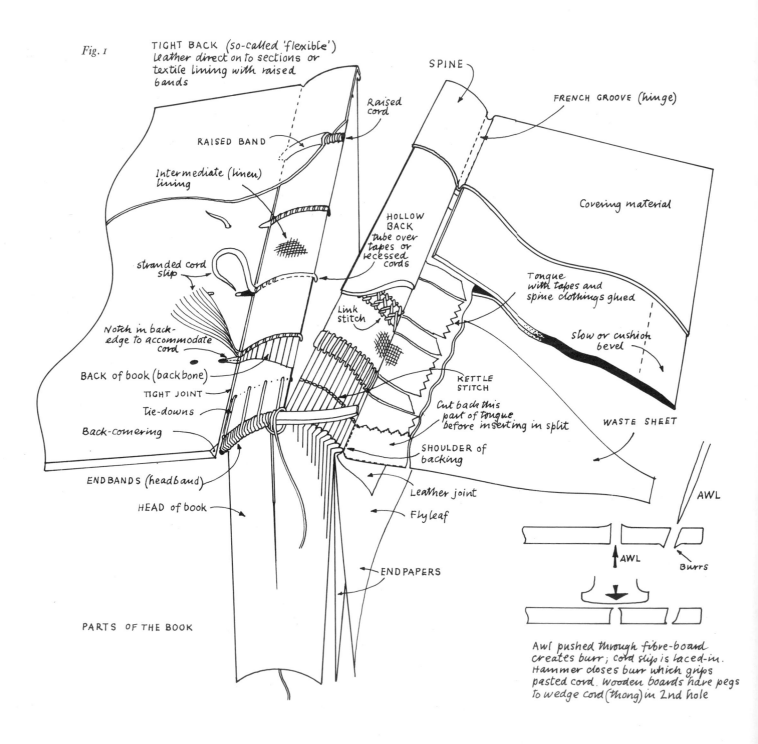

*Fig. 1*

TIGHT BACK (so-called 'flexible') Leather direct on to sections or textile lining with raised bands

SPINE

FRENCH GROOVE (hinge)

Raised cord

RAISED BAND

Intermediate (linen) lining

Covering material

HOLLOW BACK tube over tapes or recessed cords

stranded cord slip

Link stitch

Tongue with tapes and spine clothings glued

slow or cushion bevel

Notch in back-edge to accommodate cord

BACK of book (backbone)

TIGHT JOINT

Tie-downs

Back-cornering

KETTLE STITCH

Cut back this part of tongue before inserting in split

WASTE SHEET

SHOULDER of backing

ENDBANDS (headband)

Leather joint

AWL

HEAD of book

Fly leaf

AWL

Burrs

ENDPAPERS

PARTS OF THE BOOK

Awl pushed through fibre-board creates burr; cord slip is laced-in. Hammer closes burr which grips pasted cord. Wooden boards have pegs to wedge cord (thong) in 2nd hole

**Chart 2  The Principal Parts of the Bookbinding and notes on their functions** *(see Figs. 1, 2 and 3)*

| Part | Function | Requirements |
|------|----------|--------------|
| Paper (or leaf material) | Carries image | In selecting paper for new books, paper should function as Fig. 2. Preferably its substance should include long rag-fibres. Machine-made paper to have fibres running parallel to the back fold. Papers sized, for example, with one of the PVOH group have greater resistance to handling. Should be acid-free; pH 7 is neutral. |
| Sections | Form the main book-block. Made up from gatherings of several pairs of folded conjugate leaves | There should not be too many folds to a section. Thick sections tend to open in chunks creating more strain and friction on the sewing thread. Too many thin sections may adversely affect 'swelling' and lead to exaggerated round of the backbone. Sections and leaves must hold together withstanding repeated flexing and enable easy access to the contents, even when printed image occupies the back margins. |
| Boards (covers) | Protect book-block. Ease handling and stacking | Boards should be strong and inert; rope-fibre board and some containing plastics are best. They are usually more rigid than the leaves. Acrylic and other plastics, also light metals, are sometimes used. |
| Sewing and supports | Thread links sections (and leaves) together and to the sewing supports (cord, tapes etc.) | The thread is the most important connective element in a sewn book. It should be strong but not over thick, and resist tension and friction. Linen thread is often beeswaxed. The rest of the binding is constructed so that there is little or no movement against the thread. (Sewn unglued structures fail in this respect.) Ageing and acid rot are the main agents of destruction. The sewing supports link the book-block and boards via the sewing thread, which, to obviate excessive wear by friction, should be used in shortish lengths. |
| Adhesives | General bonding agents | For the 'fine' bookbinding these are mainly plasticized (animal) glues, (vegetable starch) pastes and synthetic resin emulsions (PVA). They should be protected against acids, moulds and insect pests. Glue or PVA is used to reinforce the bond between thread and sections and between backs of sections (or guards) and the back-linings, also in laminating boards, paper and book-cloth. Paste is used mainly in the leather work. |
| Coverings | Connective and protective | The covering material is the main substance of the hinge (or joint) connecting backbone and boards. It provides protection and finish to the outer surfaces of the boards and spine. It is the main vehicle of expression, decoration and book identification. Traditionally of leather, fine bindings may now be clothed in almost any relatively thin, flat material which may be provided with a hinge. |
| Edge features Squares | Protective refinements | Squares (the parts of the boards projecting beyond the book-block) are a feature of the book largely developed since the book was habitually kept upright in a book-stack. They prevent the tail edge scraping on the shelf, and support and protect the edges of the book-block. |
| Rounded and backed spine | Hooks sections together, consolidates them and provides an anchorage and support for the boards | Natural 'swelling' at the back folds created by accumulated sewing thread (and guards) causes the back to fall into a convex shape. Rounding is done to induce this shape which is 'set' by gluing up. Backing is the knocking over of the sections outwards from the centre to form a shoulder against which the back edge of the board is supported. Gluing up, rounding, backing and lining all help to create and preserve a sturdy shape to the backbone. The resultant concave foredge makes for easier access to a particular opening of the text, but this is defeated by deckle edges left without trim. |

| Part | Function | Requirements |
|------|----------|--------------|
| Gilding | Protective, 'decorative' | Both protects and decorates the edges of the leaves. Solid edges reduce the entry of injurious agents in the atmosphere and of light, and are sometimes underpainted and/or gauffered (tooled). Other edge treatments are possible, such as sculpturing. |
| Back-linings | Buffering, release and stabilising elements | Back-linings vary from none at all to many layers. Used to reinforce the inter-connection between the backs of sections and the covering material (and very often the boards). They help to stabilize and modify the flexing of the backbone. The tube hollow is a variation of the back lining to connect these to an independent spine covering. Other back linings are used to give a smooth finish to the spine. Materials: fine linen, lawn, organdie, calico, mull, leather, paper. |
| Endbands | End of spine finisher and strengthener | Endbands (now commonly called headbands) were originally used as the head and tail sewing supports, laced into the boards. Now usually consists of a single core or former (cord, gut or vellum-leather) encircled by a spiral of coloured silks tied down at regular intervals through the inside of the sections, preferably through a fine linen back-lining. They give added support to the covering leather (usually moulded to partly cover the top of the band at head and tail) where this functions as a finger catch for withdrawing from vertical stacking book-shelf. Also conceals the ends of the back linings and is used as part of the aesthetic finish. Double or triple tier headbands are also used constructed variously. Plaited leather thongs or thread have been sewn through the covering. *(38)* Restorers often use a primary sewing of linen thread with decorative secondary silk oversewing. |
| Endpapers | Buffering attachment and reinforcement at ends of book-block | In fine binding end-paper sections can be one of the most important structural elements. They act as a buffer between the book-block and the covers. They also conceal the sewing supports and linings at the inner hinge. They protect the end leaves of the text. A great many variations are possible with reinforcements giving secure connection between book-block and boards.* |

* Note: Ideally the covers of a book should not be attached directly to the book-block. Features such as loose guards round the backs of sections, the endpaper sections with joints, act as buffers or release agents preventing adhesives from touching the leaves.

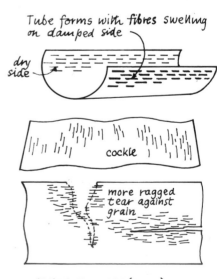

Tube forms with fibres swelling on damped side

dry side

cockle

more ragged tear against grain

CLUES TO FIBRE (GRAIN) DIRECTION

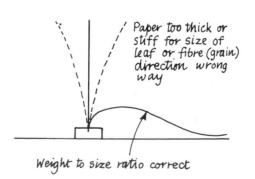

Paper too thick or stiff for size of leaf or fibre (grain) direction wrong way

Weight to size ratio correct

Fig. 3

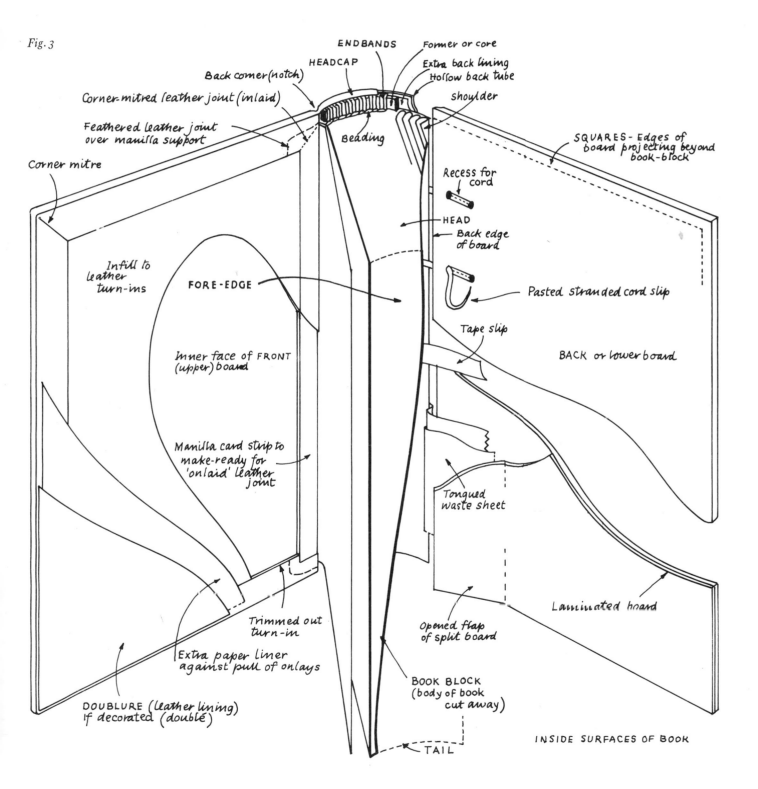

ENDBANDS

Former or core
Extra back lining
Hollow back tube

HEADCAP

Back corner (notch)

Corner-mitred leather joint (inlaid)

shoulder

Feathered leather joint over manilla support

Beading

SQUARES - Edges of board projecting beyond book-block

Corner mitre

Recess for cord

HEAD

Infill to leather turn-ins

FORE-EDGE

Back edge of board

Pasted stranded cord slip

Inner face of FRONT (upper) board

Tape slip

BACK or lower board

Manilla card strip to make-ready for 'onlaid' leather joint

Tongued waste sheet

Laminated board

Trimmed out turn-in

Opened flap of split board

Extra paper liner against pull of onlays

BOOK BLOCK (body of book cut away)

DOUBLURE (leather lining) if decorated (double)

TAIL

INSIDE SURFACES OF BOOK

## 4 Mechanical aids for the hand-binder. Adapted tools

Several new tools and adaptations of existing ones are mentioned in this book. Most of them arise because the craftsman feels the need to be freed from some restriction imposed by existing tools and skills, and time. The skilled hand-craftsman works not out of necessity but for philosophical reasons; it is a way of liberation for him, but we cannot here go into the ethics of his use of machines. These are not such that he ceases to subscribe to hand-work as a way of life and becomes mechanized. It is obviously part of the craftsman's ethic to improve his work and, if necessary for this, his tools and materials. He is no longer so doctrinaire that he will work laboriously by hand if a machine can do the job as well or better without losing that liveliness of touch associated with hand-work. Remember we are speaking of one-off objects, whereas machine philosophy concerns repetition of objects.

*Sydney Cockerell's 'ram'* (no photograph) was created perhaps for two reasons. It will put in large finishing tools requiring more pressure than a man can easily produce unaided, and put this tool down (easily) at any angle which would perhaps take a great deal more skill than an all-round craftsman can normally develop. The use of the conventional blocking press would be very cumbersome and time-consuming by comparison. Simply described the 'ram' is a pneumatically operated hydraulic aircraft undercarriage leg braced against a beam or ceiling, and poised over a bench on which the book is laid. The bench top is articulated to run on rails left and right and to and fro. Lays can be arranged on the sliding top. The ram is fitted with an electrically heated and controlled 'pin-vice' head for holding the shanks of the finishing tools. The ram may be poised at a slight angle or held in any position above the surface by two adjustable braces against the walls of a corner position. A foot-treadle switch operates the tool, bringing it down on to the prepared surface of the book. It may also be hand guided by an insulated arm projecting from the head and moved freely over the book-cover, depositing impressions where required.

*The Adana printing press* was adapted for similar reasons and also to permit a greater variety of type faces to be used at less expense than having them cut in bronze by the hand-engraver (Section 16).

*The adapted soldering-iron* (Fig. 4) is an admirable adaptation for repetitive tooling such as in the use of a short pallet line. If a finishing stove top is drilled with holes dozens of 'bits' may be kept heated and readily fitted for a change of unit in the design. As the tool is automatically temperature-controlled by a thermostat or rheostat (as is the 'ram') tooling may be continuous all day without the loss of time incurred in continual re-heating in the conventional manner. The polishing iron and the fillet can be treated in the same way.

Various paring machines are used for thinning leather for covering or onlaying and in the larger hand-bindery the Fortuna cylindrical-bladed model is popular. It needs practised handling to pare a skin all over and is mostly used for edging the covering rectangles. The Scharffix (another German tool) is a small non-mechanical scarfing

*Fig. 4*

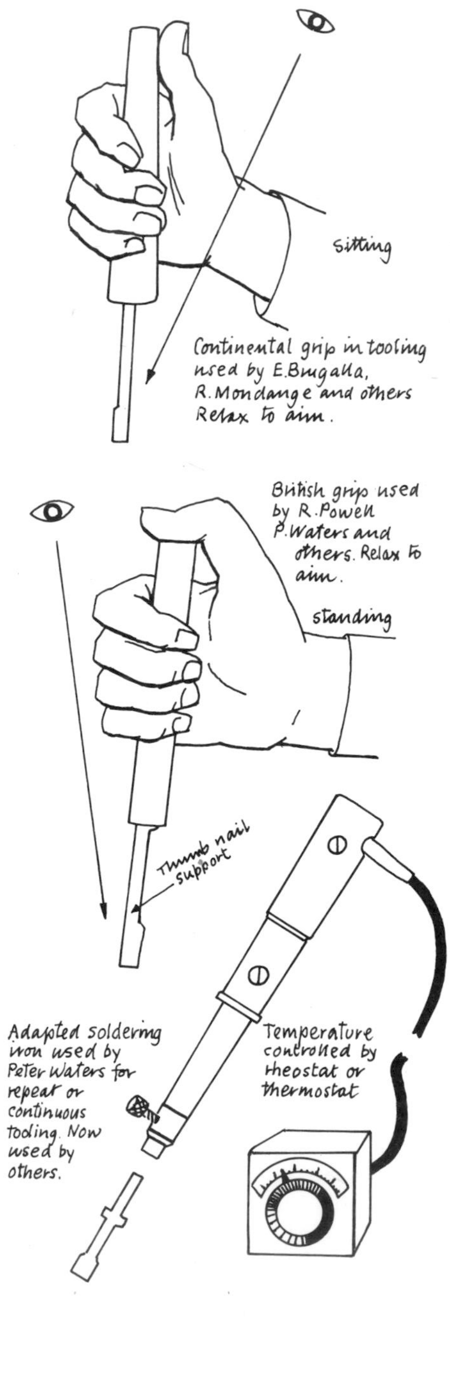

sitting

Continental grip in tooling used by E.Brugalla, R.Mondange and others Relax to aim.

British grip used by R.Powell P.Waters and others. Relax to aim.

standing

Thumb nail support

Adapted soldering iron used by Peter Waters for repeat or continuous tooling. Now used by others.

Temperature controlled by rheostat or thermostat

28

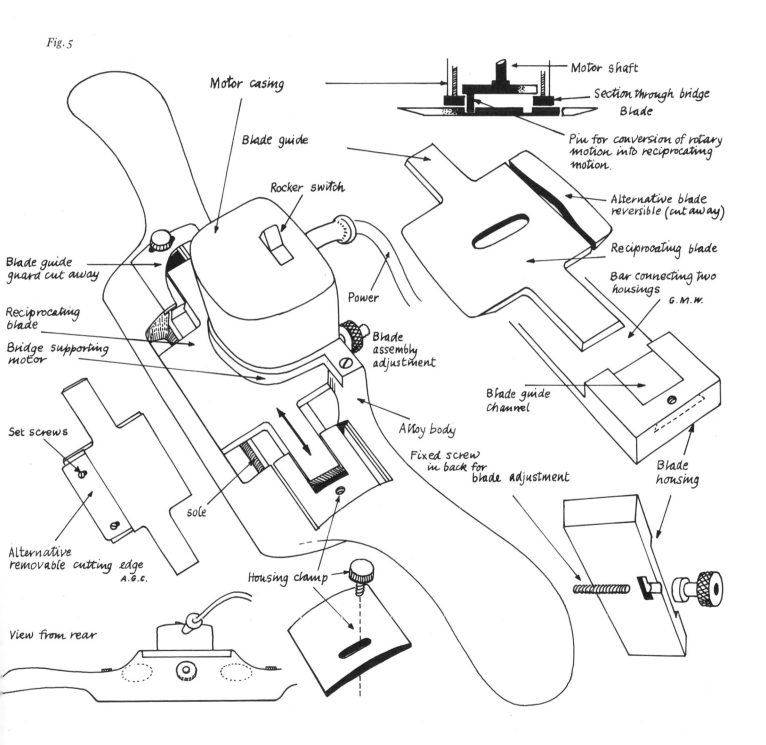

*Fig. 5*

Motor casing

Blade guide

Rocker switch

Power

Motor shaft

Section through bridge Blade

Pin for conversion of rotary motion into reciprocating motion.

Alternative blade reversible (cut away)

Reciprocating blade

Bar connecting two housings G.M.W.

Blade guide guard cut away

Reciprocating blade

Bridge supporting motor

Blade assembly adjustment

Alloy body

Blade guide channel

Blade housing

Set screws

sole

Fixed screw in back for blade adjustment

Alternative removable cutting edge A.G.C.

Housing clamp

View from rear

DESIGNERS IMPRESSION of the C P Paring machine

29

or edge paring tool; here the leather, vellum or paper is pulled between a small roller and a razor-blade.

*The CP Paring machine* (Fig. 5) is the answer I found – in a dream! – to the problem of cutting the very hard maril (Section 10). I was seeking an industrial (in-line) cutter for veneering maril blocks on a large scale; and also for a quicker method of paring a skin all-over by hand more efficiently than by the Fortuna machine. The design I have evolved resembles a wide spokeshave with a reciprocating blade. The tool may simply be pushed slowly across the leather (like a lawn-mower) and a collecting box for shavings may be attached to the front.

*The single-post sewing frame* is simpler to set up than a conventional type, and less obstructing to the operator. Most of these tools are invented 'on the job' by non-engineers and may lack sophistication.

2A-F   Philip Smith
Shakespeare *King Lear*
Build-up of image from feathered onlays
(Section 9)

3   Philip Smith
Shakespeare *King Lear*
Book-box in natural Sudanese cowhide. Lid with plastic templates under purple goatskin, tooled in blind. Press-stud fastening, felt lined
480 × 385 × 6omm (19 × 15⅛ × 2½in)

2A

2B

2C

3

2D　　　2E　　　　　　　2F

## 5 Hygroscopic materials and adhesives

Most of the materials with which the bookbinder works, such as paper, board and leather,[1] have hygroscopic or moisture-sensitive properties which cause fluctuations in the size of the fibres on the absorption and release of moisture. The simple test shown in the diagram will demonstrate the dimensional variability in paper and a similar procedure can be worked with card, cloth and leather before work is commenced (Fig. 6). This test not only shows the percentage of variation in size of the material on wetting but it also indicates the predominant fibre direction (*36*, pp. 225–8; *18*, pp. 30–33).

Leathers have pronounced hygroscopic tendencies and depending on the manufacturing processes some leathers are more vulnerable than others. The bookbinder is therefore working with a certain unpredictability in the behaviour of his materials, and the accuracy of his work will be affected by their dimensional instability. Whenever he is using moisture, that is, in all water-based adhesives such as starch and cellulose pastes, protein glues and vinyl emulsion adhesives (Appendix IV and *36*, Ch. 14), he must make allowances for hygroscopic variability.

Animal glues, because of their tendency to brittalize if over-dried (plasticizers are added to some glues), and to attract mould under humid conditions, have been largely superseded by internally plasticized polyvinyl acetate adhesives, which retain a high degree of flexibility and are stable under normal environmental conditions. Insect pests are not yet attracted to them.

Starch paste made from wheat, rye or rice flour is one of the most suitable adhesives in the covering of books with leather. By its penetrative nature it creates a greater malleability in the leather. It is advisable to include an anti-acid and fungicides in starch paste formulas.

*A Starch Paste Formula :* 1 pint (586cc) distilled water; 3oz (85·2 grams) white Canadian wheat flour. Fungicides: Topane (Ortho-phenylphenol); Thymol. Anti-acids: Magnesium acetate (lays buffer in paper); Disodium dihydrogen pyrophosphate (inhibits acid formation in leather).

Place the water and flour in a shaker or mixer; mix and allow to stand for a few minutes, meanwhile dissolving about 1 per cent (or a good pinch) Topane in some of the water together with an anti-acid or buffering agent. Add the protectives to the paste, put in a pan and boil while stirring for two minutes. Allow to cool to 49°C (120°F) and add two pinches of finely powdered Thymol crystals. (Thymol evaporates above 49°C.) Precipitated chalk (Calcium carbonate) is an anti-acid which also adds whiteness to paste. Crystalline phenol is a long-lasting fungicide but turns the paste a slight pink colour, as does Topane. Acid pastes tend to thin out (hydrolize) if kept too long. Alum is not recommended as a fungicide because of its acidity. Non-specialists should obtain the latest information from an authority before using chemical treatments.

PVA emulsion is highly viscous compared with paste and its tight long-chain molecular structure causes resistance to penetration into

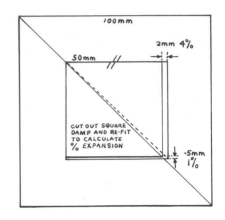

*Fig. 6*

*Fig. 7*

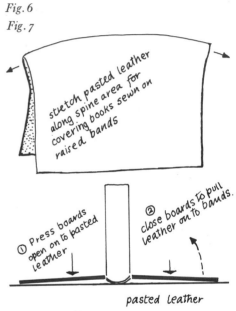

pasted leather

Use band-stick with rocking motion, then band-nippers and folder to sharpen bands

Tie-up with hooked boards if necessary - prevent cord marking leather with thick manilla card - torn edge

First stages in covering book with tight hinge.

leather (and other felted materials) so it is best used as a surface adhesive.

Prior to pasting leather a capillary reaction may be set up through the skin by damping the grain side with a sponge.[2] The paste is thereby sucked into the skin. Chrome-tanned and other water-repellant leathers require more prolonged and repeated pastings on the flesh side before they become suitably malleable.

*Application of paste or adhesive by hand.* The brush (Fig. 8) is held like a dagger and the adhesive is first brushed on to the material with strokes radiating from the central holding position.[3] This tends to leave minute wet ridges and dry valleys of adhesive on the surface. These ridges may be levelled and evened out by stippling with a stabbing action all over the surface, which helps the adhesive to penetrate between the fibres of the material. It also prevents the brush strokes showing through a thin material and causes the adhesive to stand up in minute pimples tending to retain the moisture longer. Use no more adhesive than is necessary.

With vegetable tanned goatskin – commonly called morocco – an initial heavy paste application is followed several minutes later by a further pasting. Surplus paste, which has not penetrated the fibres, may be scraped off gently with a piece of stiff card and immediately before covering a well stippled application of paste should keep the skin malleable for at least thirty minutes. Some native niger goatskins are particularly oily and require rather more damping. During the covering process (Figs. 7, 9) skins will remain workable for about one hour with judicious local damping of the grain side. Thicker skins will absorb more paste and moisture than thin or pared skins.

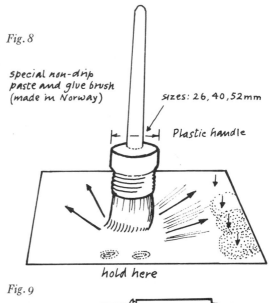

Fig. 8

special non-drip paste and glue brush (made in Norway)

sizes: 26, 40, 52mm

Plastic handle

hold here

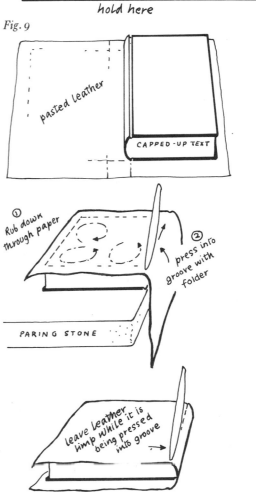

Fig. 9

pasted leather

CAPPED-UP TEXT

① Rub down through paper

② press into groove with folder

PARING STONE

leave leather limp while it is being pressed into groove

Turn book over and draw leather over spine. Put in second groove with folder, then rub over board through paper. Peel leather back from foredge to bring up grain, then rub down again.

First stages in covering book with groove hinge.

---

1 Vide: *The Restoration of Leather Bookbindings.* Mr Middleton devotes thirty-two pages to a definition of bookbinding terms: also twenty-five pages on basic equipment and materials.

2 When treating leather by washing in a protective agent, care should be taken not to over-wet or valuable salts may be washed out of the skin. Potassium lactate is hygroscopic and a bloom of mildew might form if the leather is badly stored. Disodium dihydrogen pyrophosphate (anti-acid buffer) can leave a bloom on the surface; this is harmless and may be eliminated when a varnish or wax polish is applied to a finished binding.

3 Under certain circumstances paste may be applied by roller or through a silk screen.

# 6 Plastics

This brief account of plastics is included here because these
materials are being explored by hand-bookbinders and are already
being used in industrial bookbinding. The scope for the creative
hand-binder is really enormous and the few directions suggested
below cannot be comprehensive. They are designed to stimulate
imagination in their possibilities rather than to give exhaustive
information on the subject. The binder who wishes to investigate
further should consult the three books listed below (*13, 19, 69*). The
use of plastics may demand a 'chemical' as well as a 'manual' attitude
in the artist/craftsman so that some knowledge of these materials
and their structure may be rewarding and excellent textbooks are
available on the subject.

> A plastics is an organic material, composed wholly or mainly of
> carbon compounds, which on application of adequate heat and
> pressure can be caused to flow and take up a desired shape, which
> will be retained when the applied temperature and pressure are
> removed (*19*, p. 29).

The carbon compounds are assembled from giant molecules, very
long chains of carbon atoms sometimes branched or linked
crossways in various configurations. These chains occur naturally
as in cellulose fibres or, from coal and oil products, can be built in
the laboratory using short molecules known as 'monomers' by
uniting them to give long chains or 'polymers'. The chemical process
is known as polymerization. When monomers of different kinds are
united the product is a 'copolymer'.

Copolymers can be alloyed or mixed by copolymerization, enabling
many combinations of properties to be tailor-made into the material.

An important property of plastics, which is unattainable in leathers,
is that nearly all of them are water-white in the pure state and most
are highly transparent. 'Perspex', for example, possesses the most
unique clarity of all solid materials and transmits 92 per cent of
visible light. It is inferior to glass in that it abrades too readily. Most
colours may be produced in plastics materials by the addition of
pigments or dyestuffs.

Although it is possible to process raw animal skins to evolve a great
variety of qualities in the final product, with the devising of
polymerization techniques an almost limitless permutation of
properties can be arrived at in plastics. The one vital property (from
a hand-bookbinder's point of view) not yet achieved in plastics is the
cold state malleability to form corners, head caps, etc., of a leather-
like goatskin, but a new material may stimulate a re-thinking of
methods and appearances.

Plastics are divided into two main classes known as thermoplastic
(thermosoftening) and thermosetting (thermohardening) plastics.
Thermoplastic materials may be softened and re-softened indefinitely
by applied heat and pressure without losing quality or strength – too
much heat would cause chemical decomposition. Thermosetting
plastics begin as thermoplastic material but undergo a chemical
change when subjected to the requisite heat and pressure and further

applications of these will not re-soften them or usefully change their shape.

At the molecular level thermosoftening plastics is a tangle of amorphous chains sliding against each other giving the effect of plasticity. When polymerization produces thermosetting plastics the molecular chains have cross-links between them bonding them rigidly together. Heating and solvents affect the loose chains but do not move the rigid chains.

Plasticizers can be added to cause internal lubrication in thermo-plastics thereby softening them. (Internally plasticized materials, such as PVA VJC555 adhesive, are plasticized by copolymerization and not by addition. Acrylics are often used as internal plasticizers in this way.) Thermoplastics materials may be machined almost like metals, by drilling, turning, abrazing, etc. Adhesion can be obtained between like materials by suitable solvents, or welded by hot-air jet, flame, or H.F. heating (diathermy) (*36*, Ch. 13).

To give leather a greater degree of resistance to wet and dry rubbing of the surface, plastics finishes are often applied to book leathers which must withstand a considerable amount of abrasive wear (*55*, Ch. 32). Sprayed plastics finishes, however wear-resistant, impart a certain monotonous artificial look to the grain surface. These finishes also make leather resistant to onlay adhesion and so inlays are more practical here. It is probably the mixture of these two basically different materials (although with features in common), together with associations from the days when plastics were thought to be a cheap substitute, which the hand-bookbinder, brought up on 'Oasis' leather, finds abhorrent, quite apart from negative effects on tooling impressions. Shellac varnish (a kind of plastics) has been used by bookbinders (mainly in the trade) for generations, but as a final protective coating after finishing the binding. Plastics have properties in their own right and with the solution to the hinging problem may be eminently suitable for book-covering. (Polypropylene binding is referred to later in this section.)

*Possible application to Bookbinding*

Rigid boards may be made by compression moulding, starting with a thermosetting powder which is placed in a mould and subjected to heat and pressure. A blocking-press might be adapted for this purpose, but a separate hinging material and attachment would have to be devised.

Covers or boards may also be moulded by injecting a heated granule-form thermoplastics into a two-part mould where it hardens.

Cases may be vacuum-formed. A thermoplastics sheet is held in a frame, softened by heating and drawn down into a mould by vacuum pressure.

Laminated covers may be fabricated by pressing layers of thermo-setting resin-impregnated material together with heat. Again a blocking-press adaptation with a heater plate on both platens would achieve this.

Although most plastics-forming equipment is large and expensive and beyond the scope of the small bindery, access to such methods may be possible through the goodwill of local industry or colleges of art and technology. Two of the simpler processes for the small binder in the making of plastics bindings would be in (a) using the domestic oven for tray-moulding of polythene covers, which could be inlaid in a manner analogous to leather bindings; and (b) in the exciting potential of setting in clear resins. The former method is fully described in (*13*) and the latter in (*69*). Many adaptations of these basic methods will occur to the bookbinder sufficiently interested to take them up.[1]

Many will be familiar with 'fresnel' plastic sheet (used by the manufacturers of picture postcard novelties). This effect, giving an optical illusion of three dimensions or the movement of an image, is created by cutting a series of two or three photographic images into narrow strips (by photographic means in the industrial product) and assembling them on a layer of paper which is then laminated to the back of a finely ridged plastic sheet. The ridges are tiny triangular prisms which allow light to enter and be reflected from the sides, so that from one angle the strips of one image are seen and from another angle the other image may be seen. By careful and accurate placing of the strips in relation to the prismatic sheet an illusion of movement is created by slightly moving the support. This optical device is possible on a larger scale and in principle is related to paintings by the Israeli artist Agam, and other Op artists.

Polypropylene sheet extruded or moulded to the thickness of the average hard cover of a commercial binding (say 1–3mm) is very hard and rigid and could not be bent without heating to case in a book. However, if the hinge part of this sheet/cover is reduced to 0·15–0·25mm a remarkably strong hinge is created. The author devised (Provisional Patent Application 27320/61) a method whereby transparent all-plastics bindings could be joined to the book body without conventional endpapers and adhesives, merely by bonding it by dielectric heating to a narrow plastics 'guard' attached round the first section. Variations of this method are shown in the sketches (Fig. 10).

Using a transparent cover would create interesting design possibilities while eliminating several processes from the conventional binding sequence. The endpaper would be printed on the outside with material usually printed on the title page and book-jacket, or the cover could be printed in reverse on the inside surface with this material. The spine-liner strip might also be printed to show through the transparent spine (which could alternatively be printed as an opaque to hide the structure). Objects could be moulded into the cover for special bindings or the cover could be printed with part of an image both sides and give an optical 'movement' because of the thickness of material between the two surfaces. Many possibilities for blocked and printed effects present themselves to the imagination. This kind of binding would withstand great wear. With a plastics

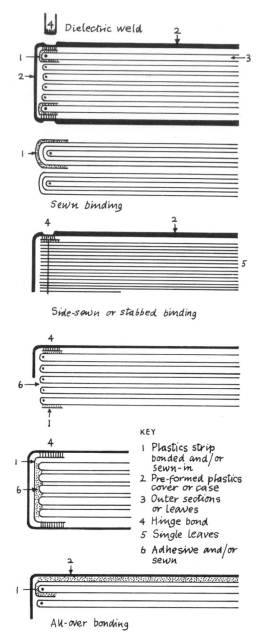

*Fig. 10*

KEY

1 Plastics strip bonded and/or sewn-in
2 Pre-formed plastics cover or case
3 Outer sections or leaves
4 Hinge bond
5 Single leaves
6 Adhesive and/or sewn

1 Materials may be obtained in England from Griffin & George Limited, Ealing Road, Alperton, Middlesex.

36

'paper', cover and leaves could be welded together onto the spine strip of the cover in one operation. Heat sensitive adhesives could be coated onto the inside of the cover and this laminated to the first section of the book (Fig. 10).

The hand-binder equipped with hot-bar welding gear could use a similar covering for fine binding treatment. Most plastics fine bindings require a separate spine covering and hinging material but the join may easily be incorporated into the imagery of the covers, where it could be camouflaged.

### *Plexiglas (Perspex) in hand-bookbinding* by Gotthilf Kurz (Translated by Anton Scheck)

Acrylic resin is a modern material which is suitable for use in the best fine binding. Its most successful applications take into consideration its natural properties, for as with every other material it has its own characteristics and laws.

The person whose imagination cannot stretch beyond traditional materials such as leather, vellum, fabrics and paper, would not find it easy to think about the use of new materials for bookbinding. It is difficult to understand why the editor of a bookbinding journal recently dismissed the use of Plexiglas (or Perspex) with the remark, 'It is beyond the limits of bookbinding.' If the bookbinder of the past had listened to such opinions we would still be using wooden boards – if the codex had been invented at all! Were the limits of any material to be defined, the creative, go-ahead person would still transcend them. Bookbinding critics would be well advised not to encourage the already slightly conservative tendencies of most bookbinders.

Plexiglas is available in about fifty colours as well as the common clear variety and it can be obtained in any caliper suitable for book covers. It may be cut, sawn, planed and worked in ways similar to those used for wood. It can also be glued, engraved and filigreed and different colours can be laminated to give remarkable colour effects. In the paler shades new expressions may be achieved by the underlaying of signs, print and type. It is also possible to encapsulate other materials in the covers, for example, gold leaf or very thin layers of stone (Plates 4 and 6) or wood veneers, film transparencies or negatives, paper, etc. This list indicates the almost unlimited possibilities of creation in Plexiglas by the gifted bookbinder.

Plate 6 shows fragile gold leaf encapsulated with all its natural beauty, fragmented and wrinkled in a random manner. This effect could only be achieved by using a rigid supporting carrier, and the transparent Plexiglas is just right for this purpose, as it would be for encapsulating any fragile material or object requiring support. Other materials such as leather of a certain size, do not require this kind of treatment.

It is not very easy for a bookbinder to work with liquid Plexiglas and he must find a workshop which deals with plastics. The liquid resin sets only under a certain artificial neon light and for this a special installation is required.

Plexiglas covers may be attached to the book-block in several different ways. In the two examples shown the end sections are made up with two folios the outer of which is laminated with suede leather as a flyleaf, and the sections sewn on reinforced leather straps (Fig. 11). The backbone was given a degree of stability by gluing leather strips between the sewing supports which also levelled it.

The covers were assembled separately from the book-block – a principle used in case-binding – but a strong and flexible linking material had to be developed. For this a piece of long-grain vellum was laminated to leather and press-dried for about seven hours. The straps (Fig. 12) were then cut out on both sides of the spine strip to a length of 40–60mm, long enough to slot through the Plexiglas 'boards'. The slots were drilled and smoothed so that relatively friction-free hinge movement was achieved (Fig. 13). The covers were connected together leaving sufficient space between to allow free articulation. The straps butt together in the centre of the back strip, which was then prepared and drilled to receive the book-block sewing supports, the slips of which are slotted through and glued one over the other on the spine (Fig. 11).

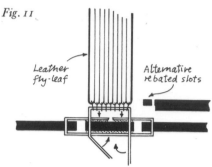

*Fig. 11*

Book-block sewn on straps laced through back strip

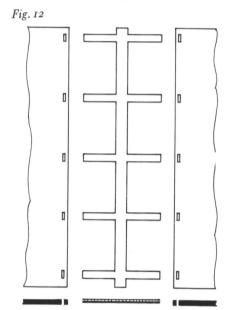

*Fig. 12*

Pierced boards and back strip of laminated vellum and leather

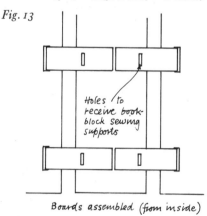

*Fig. 13*

Holes to receive book-block sewing supports

Boards assembled (from inside)

Back strip and hinge make-up with slots
(sketches after G. Kurz)

4   Gotthilf Kurz
*Guest Book*
Black Jura slate encapsulated in plexiglas (perspex), boards hinged on vellum straps.
Platinum coloured leather flyleaves
400×300mm (15¾×11¾in) 1972

*AA Book of the Car*
Automobile Association Drive Publications and Reader's
Digest Association (Plate 5)

This book was an experiment by the producers, designed to
withstand the kind of wear a book would get from use in and around
the car. The design concept began with a graphic designer liking a
sample of milled aluminium foil, known as Dufex. As an external
covering this foil was too flimsy and vulnerable to disfigurement.
It was decided that it would require a protective layer of transparent
plastic. Due to a whole series of technical requirements in achieving
the desired visual effect together with hard-wearing properties
– elimination of surface static in welding, exclusion of air in the
plastics 'envelope', seam welding vulnerability at corners, etc. – the
final make up seems complicated, and no doubt if the cost of
polypropylene, with its excellent flexing properties for the hinge, had
been lower, a technically simpler binding might have been adopted.

The Dufex foil was embossed with a milled texture to a key-line
drawing and an acetate film laminated to it to prevent marking (even
through the transparent PVC cover). The foil lamina was next stuck
to a greyboard with a wax adhesive and the outer corners round-
punched (a sharp corner would possibly have pried open the weld on
impact). The case was assembled by laying to a jig the three pieces
of board (back, front and spine strip) on a grey PVC sheet. The
back-board and spine stiffener were edge welded in an enclosure of
another grey PVC sheet up to the front hinge. The front-board was
edge welded in an enclosure of clear PVC sheet. The welding was by
a one-shot H.F. diathermal electrode (*36*, Ch. 13). The assembled
case is glued to the cloth-joint-reinforced endpapers with PVA
emulsion.

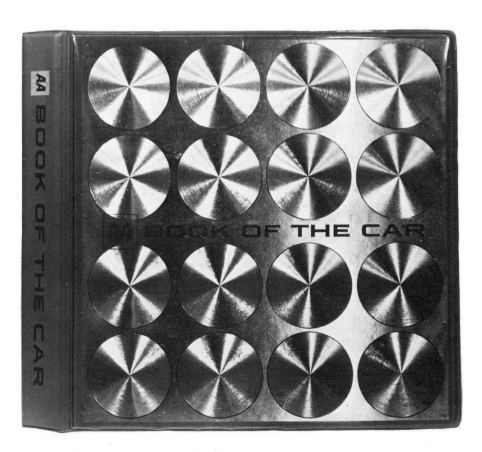

5   *AA Book of the Car* produced by Drive
Publications and The Reader's Digest
Association. (1970)
Grey and clear PVC. Anodized aluminium
foil (Section 6)
268 × 271 × 38mm (10½ × 10⅝ × 1½in)

6 Gotthilf Kurz
*Livre d'Or*
Gold leaf encapsulated in plexiglas (perspex).
Red-orange calf flyleaves
400 × 300mm (15¾ × 11¾in) 1970


7 Gerard Charrière
*XXXIV Drawings for Dante's Inferno*
illustrated by Robert Rauchenberg.
Black calf. Ribbed plastic panel over
multicoloured paper collage
290 × 280 × 30mm (11½ × 11 × 1⅛in) 1969

*opposite*

8A Philip Smith
Germain Bazin *The Loom of Art* Black
'Oasis'.
Multicoloured feathered onlays. White,
grey and pink angels. Gold, black and
blind stamping and tooling. Blue
morocco spine. Tongue and slot board
attachment
290 × 250 × 45mm (11½ × 9¼ × 1¾in)
1962–3
Private collection

8B Philip Smith
*The New English Bible* The New
Testament. OUP and CUP.
Scarf-joined black, grey and light-grey
'Oasis' with onlays of the same colours.
Orange and red onlays in spine area.
Gold and black tooling
230 × 50 × 28mm (9 × 6 × 1⅛in) 1961
Private collection

6

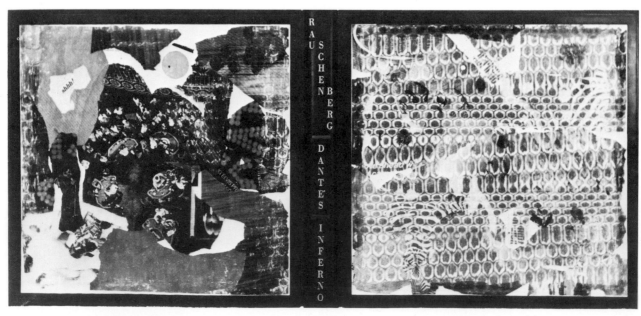

7

8A

8B

8C

8C   Philip Smith
*The Tibetan Book of the Dead* OUP.
Purple morocco. Feathered onlays and
coloured silks embroidered by Dorothy
Smith. Stamped and tooled in gold and
black
220 × 150 × 30mm (8¾ × 6 × 1¼in) 1960
Private collection British Museum

9A   Philip Smith
*New Testament and Psalms* OUP.
Dark green kid. Orange, white and grey
feathered onlays. Gold tooling
127 × 78 × 21mm (5 × 3 × ¾in) 1960
Private collection

9B   Philip Smith
*New Testament and Psalms* OUP
Purple 'Oasis' morocco. Feathered
onlays. Coloured silk embroidery by
Dorothy Smith. Stamping in black.
Recessed and varnished transfer
lettering
127 × 78 × 21mm (5 × 3 × ¾in) 1960
Victoria and Albert Museum

9A       9B

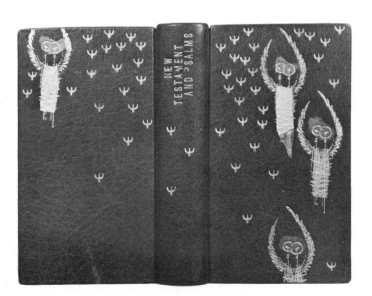

# 7 Leather

Leather is such a versatile material that after almost 2,000 years it is still the material most used for the covering of fine books. Not only is it still the favourite covering material but new ways of using it are being discovered.

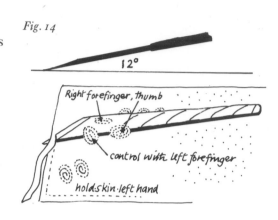

*Fig. 14*

Leather may be defined as the hide or skin of an animal which still retains its natural fibrous structure after being treated against putrescence by tanning. The term 'leather' covers a great variety of different 'materials' manufactured from the hides and skins of animals (including fish, reptiles and birds). It may be endowed with properties possessed by no other single substance, including the chemically structured plastics evolved by science and technology (Section 6).

The principal properties of leather are flexibility, strength, malleability, and resistance to water; all the properties of living skin except for malleability. Leather may be rigid or flexible, soft or hard, elastic or firm, loose or consolidated. The hide from a rhinoceros or elephant, for example, may be processed to produce a thick, bullet-proof slab or a soft velvety material. Various permutations of these properties may be imparted to a particular raw hide or skin by varying the methods of manufacture, many of which are listed in the chart (Appendix II).

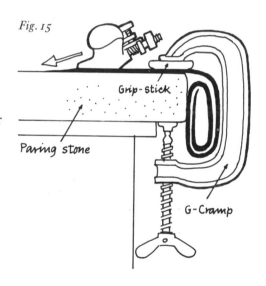

*Fig. 15*

Raw hide[1] or skin varies in the structure of the fibrous material of which it is composed. The raw skin consists of three principal layers (67, Plates 1–3). The outer layer is the *epidermis*, which contains hard surface cells, hair follicles, pores, etc. The middle layer is the *corium*, composed of cells and cell products in fibrous strands. The corium fibres of leather are composed of long-chain molecules of the protein, collagen, twisted together into micelle bundles or fibrils which are further bound together by reticular 'netting' to form the rope-like corium fibres. It is this hierarchy of threads and bundles, twisted together in a random three dimensional pattern, which gives leather its characteristic flexibility and strength. The lower layer of the skin is composed of connective *adipose* tissue, containing fatty cells. In the manufacture of leather the butcher removes the skin from the dead animal, and the tanner removes the epidermal and adipose layers. This leaves the central corium layer, consisting of the interwoven collagen fibres, to be converted into leather.

The surface of the corium, known as the *grain* side, varies from animal to animal in the pattern formed by the size and distribution of the hair follicles and other surface characteristics caused by the underlying muscular tissue. A calf skin is relatively smooth, for instance, as it has not developed very big follicles. The fibrous structure also varies in breeds of animals from different localities, and also in different areas of the same skin.

The manufacturing processes used by the tanner (Appendix II) ensure that the raw skin will be resistant to decomposition, putrefaction and solubility. This is brought about by more or less permanent chemical changes in the collagen content of the skin and which preserve the fibrous structure intact.

1 The term raw hide is given to the pelt of a large animal such as a horse or cow; the term skin is given to the pelt of a small animal such as a goat or sheep and also to that of the immature animal of the large variety, such as a calf.

The processing of skins to make leather may be divided into three distinct parts which are listed in the chart. These parts are the pre-tanning or curing processes, the tanning processes and the post-tanning or finishing processes. To produce good quality leather great care must be taken at each stage, especially in the balancing of acid and alkaline properties. For a greater depth of treatment of this subject see (55).

## Working with leather

Each bookbinding design concept includes within it the kinds of material which will best express it. If the binding is to be of leather several factors are considered in the selection of the skins. These are: (a) the type and physical characteristics of the skin, i.e. rough elephant, smooth calf, tear strength, resistance to acid rot, etc.; (b) the visual character of the skin in relation to the content of the book; (c) size of the book; whether a skin would be left full thickness or pared down, or matching skins if more than one is required; (d) colour; type of dye, light fastness, etc.; (e) 'decoration'; the use of the word 'decoration' does not mean only arbitrary patterning, but stands for functional and expressive markings designed into the covers. Decoration is an apt term where it implies something applied, not as part of the function of the binding, but as an addition. In *expressive* bookbinding the expression or imagery worked into the covers is considered part of the function of the whole in conveying the essential character of the literature.

The covering leather is cut from the skin as economically as possible taking account of the 'way of grain' in respect of hygroscopic effects. When wet the tanned skin tends to resume (remember) the shape of the original animal, where expansion and contraction in breathing was towards a greater circumference rather than greater head to tail length. This property is more pronounced in vellum. Normally a skin gains in width, the expansion being away from the backbone (spine) towards the belly of the animal. The corium fibres are looser, and the skin softer, the further from the spine they lie. Wherever possible the leather is cut to lie round the book as it lay round the animal. The spine area produces harder inflexible leather and this is noticeable in the colour and texture of the grain. Unless the leather is to be stretched over raised bands (Fig. 8) the spine of the animal may be aligned along the back (spine) of the book, where the change of the grain configuration is less noticeable.[2] An unavoidable placing of the backbone area on the covers may perhaps be disguised or otherwise lost in any subsequent 'decoration'. Sometimes it is desired to feature this 'rough' graining as part of the imagery; so the placing of it will be determined by the concept. Hygroscopic expansion/shrinkage factors are not of such great account where many small pieces of the skin are used in inlay and onlay work, but where several large pieces are scarf-joined to form a whole cover the lie of the fibre direction should be considered (Plates 42, 81C).

On an average sized book (260 × 180mm or 10 × 7in) it is usual to

2 Not advisable with tight or narrow spines, as this would increase the tendency to lift or to stiffen the hinge. The hardness would also affect the 'feel' of tooling.

*Fig. 16*

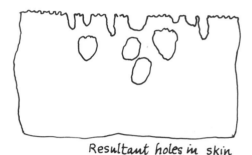

Paring with fragments of waste under thin skin

Resultant holes in skin

*Fig. 17*

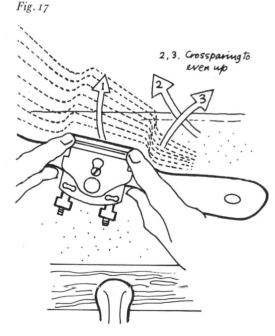

2, 3. Crossparing to even up

allow 26mm (1in) for turn-ins. A 6mm (¼in) edging bevel made with paring knife or machine eases subsequent spokeshave paring without snagging the edges of the skin (Fig. 14). All unevenness is lightly pared away all over the skin, to leave an even caliper (thickness). The book is now placed on the skin which is wrapped evenly around it. By running the fingers with pressure down the hinges and along the board edges an impressed line is left in the nap of the flesh side. These marks may be emphasized with a non-penetrative marker. The skin is now held to a paring stone by means of a G-cramp and grip-stick which has all edges rounded (Fig. 15). The leather is pared away along or towards the edge beginning about 13mm (½in) inside the marked lines. These lines are gradually pared away but may be renewed periodically.

After every few strokes of the spokeshave the leather edge should be lifted and any residue removed. Fragments under the paring edge can cause holes and tears in the skin (Fig. 16). The result of edge paring is a slow smooth bevel about 40mm (1½in) all round. The leading edge, or toe, of the spokeshave is pushed at a slight angle to the edge to give a shearing action (Fig. 17).

The sole of the tool is held flat and pressure borne on the toe to prevent scooping (Figs. 15, 17). For books with 'french' groove hinges the leather does not require thinning along the joint so much as for a 'tight' joint, because the flexing area is spread into the groove and not only along a thin line. In any style barely enough is pared away consistent with ease of opening of the boards, and bulge-free turn-ins at head and tail of spine (Fig. 18).

A useful means of thinning locally at the hinges is to cut two narrow strips of manilla card (same caliper as is required to be removed from the leather) and to scarf these off along both edges with glass-paper. Place the strips in position to the marks (head and tail of spine) under the leather and clamp in position with the grip-stick. Spokeshave the surplus leather along the strips (Fig. 19). Remove the strips and pare across the lines to eliminate sudden changes of thickness across the joints. Finish by glass-papering. The paring operation stretches the skin which is reduced to its original size by boarding to grain-up (Fig. 20).

Leather frequently reaches the binder in stretched and measured skins, and natural grain leathers such as 'Oasis' morocco or native niger skins have not been grained-up by boarding. Native crust leather coming into the tannery for re-tanning is rather stiff and board-like and boarding up tends to 'work-up' the natural grain tendency; it also eliminates the dead flat appearance produced by staking, which increases flexibility and softens the leather. Boarding by hand is performed by placing the dry leather flesh-side down on a flat surface and folding the skin over grain to grain side to produce a crease, which is moved about to and fro across the skin with a cork-covered board (Fig. 20).

Moving the crease about in one direction produces straight or 'willow' grain; in two directions at right-angles produces 'box' grain;

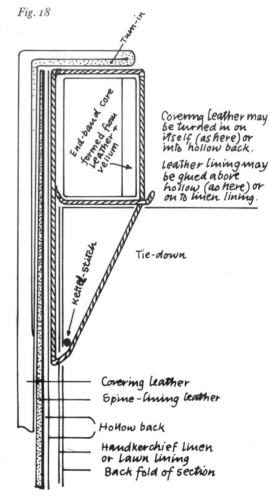

Fig. 18

Covering leather may be turned in on itself (as here) or into hollow back.

Leather lining may be glued above hollow (as here) or on to linen lining.

Tie-down

Covering leather
Spine-lining leather

Hollow back

Handkerchief linen or lawn lining
Back fold of section

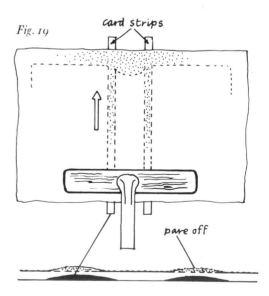

Fig. 19

card strips

pare off

working the crease in all directions breaks up the grain further. The leather tends to 'stuff' up with boarding and loses area. Localized graining can be achieved by the binder by moving the crease about with the heel of the hand or with a backing board. Natural movements in the grain pattern may be exaggerated by boarding with the fold along the interstices of the grain[3] (Plate 83B).

When the skin is fully pasted the combined swell of the fibres may increase the width of the skin by about 2 per cent, the length slightly less (Fig. 6). Allowance for this expansion should be made when cutting out and paring. Boarding up eliminates most of this expansion. On drying, the fibres of the leather shrink, the grain contracts and flattens slightly. When pasted to cover-boards this shrinkage pulls or wraps the board. This warping is balanced by the combined pull of all linings put down on the opposite face of the board. The aim in lining boards, of relaxing the leather by boarding and later 'fixing' by hot polishing, is to achieve as inert a board structure as is possible to withstand the various environments it may be related to during its life.[4]

The leather is boarded up and the skin is pasted for covering (Figs. 8, 9). Some of the conventional covering methods are shown in the diagrams and particular methods described in the case history (Section 19). The leather is drawn on to the book leaving a turn-in projection all round. A siliconed or waxed release-paper is laid over the board and the leather gently rubbed down with the block using a circular motion (Fig. 9). Before turning in the fore-edge peel back the leather in a fold grain to grain up to the hinge (Fig. 20). This brings up a fuller grain lost in drawing on the leather, which is again put down without any stretching and rubbed down gently as before. The corners are then cut for mitring (Fig. 21) and the edges turned in beginning with the fore-edge. The caps are formed (Fig. 22) and the joints or grooves set. The corners are finished, the caps set and tied up (Fig. 23). The spine covering is firmly rubbed down to ensure adhesion, especially carefully at the hinges, and at the corners and inner margins.

All rubbing down of surfaces should be done through a release paper to prevent marking and bruising of the tender damp leather. Should any marks or dents appear in the skin, these may be removed by inserting a fine needle point at an angle into the nearest grain interstice and lifting the leather from the board. Damp the 'pimple' so formed and rub down lightly. If the leather is smooth, such as box calf (so-called because it was used for covering boxes – not because it has a cross-boarded, box grain configuration), a blemish may be lifted out with self-adhesive tape.

The covered book is left to dry out between foam polyether or rubber sheets, between boards bearing about 15lb (6·8 kilos) weight. After about eight hours the boards are flexed open little by little (a touch with a damp sponge along the hinge helps) and the leather joints are put down (Plate 80D). Corner mitring the turn-in at the hinges takes away strength where it is most needed. A sounder method is to trim out the turn-ins through a narrow strip of thin card at least

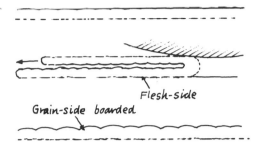

*Fig. 20*

3 The elasticity and strength of the skin lies in the corium fibres; it is essential that enough of this fibrous material is left to perform its function at hinges. The un-skived skin of a younger, smaller animal retains more strength than a split or pared skin of an older, larger animal reduced to the same caliper. In trade binderies much of the wearing quality and strength of leather is sacrificed to obtain a slick 'mechanical' finish. The trade, who are the largest consumers of leathers, order the production of thinner skins at the tannery, believing that this will economise on time and labour in paring. Many individual fine binders have great difficulty in finding skins in the UK suitable for first-class production. Most of such work has now passed to them.

4 The exact use and habitat of a particular binding cannot be fully known but the following should be taken into account in the construction of the binding, especially the covers: the bindery, the book-box and library storage, the open table, transportation from one environment to another, the museum or exhibition display case or room. (Hot lights should be excluded from display cases; windows of display rooms should be of the ultra-violet filter type; protection should be given against salty atmosphere; humidity and temperature controls should be installed; also air-conditioning.) I usually submit the finished binding (also at intermediate stages of board lining) to various reasonable extremes of temperature and humidity to test movement of the boards before parting with the book. Probably the most sympathetic conditions for fine books are a temperature of 17°C (63°F) at 63% humidity in moving air.

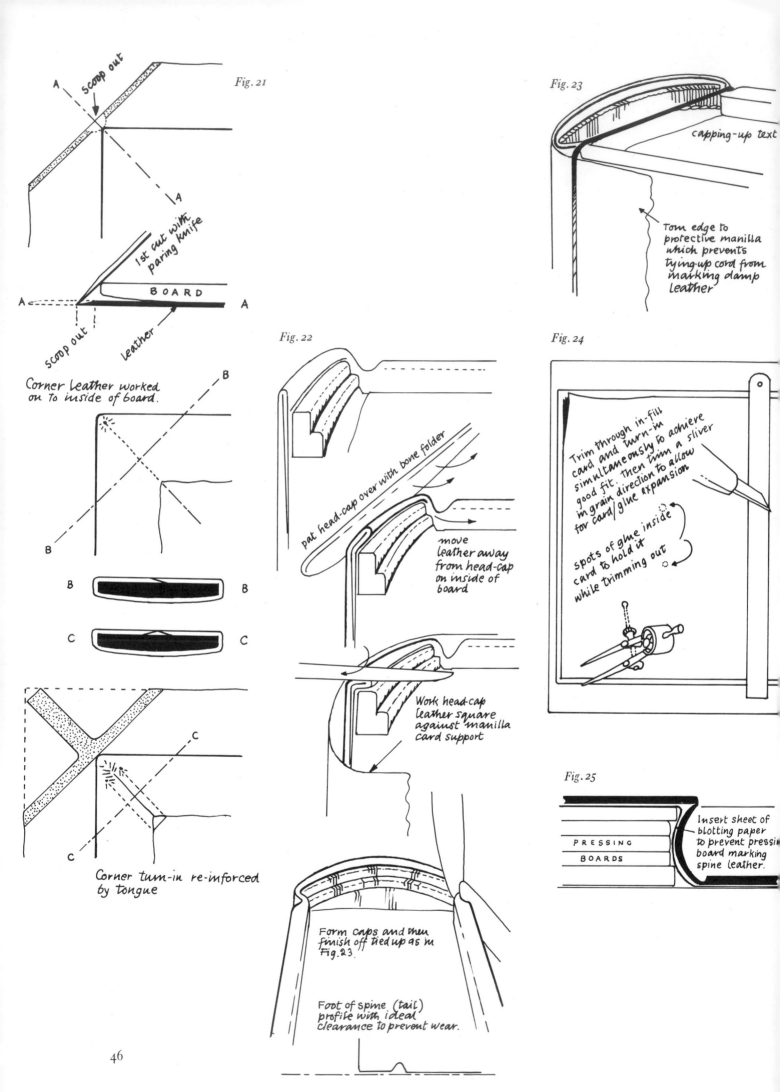

Fig. 21

Scoop out

A

A

1st cut with paring knife

A

BOARD

A

scoop out

Leather

Corner Leather worked on to inside of board.

B

B

B

B

C

C

Corner turn-in re-inforced by tongue

Fig. 22

pat head-cap over with bone folder

move leather away from head-cap on inside of board

Work head-cap leather square against manilla card support

Form caps and then finish off tied up as in Fig. 23.

Foot of spine (tail) profile with ideal clearance to prevent wear.

Fig. 23

capping-up text

Torn edge to protective manilla which prevents tying-up cord from marking damp leather

Fig. 24

Trim through in-fill card and turn-in simultaneously to achieve good fit. Then trim a sliver in grain direction to allow for card/glue expansion

spots of glue inside card to hold it while trimming out

Fig. 25

Insert sheet of blotting paper to prevent pressing board marking spine leather.

PRESSING

BOARDS

FORMATION OF CAPS.

12mm ($\frac{1}{2}$in) away from and parallel to the board edges. Glue down this card strip along the back edge of the board to level up with the turn-ins (Fig. 2). Feather the leather joint at the ends, either mitred or squarish, depending on the amount of border to be exposed beyond the paste-down or doublure. Damp the grain side of the joint and paste it on the flesh side. I use PVA for the final application to speed adhesion. Shut the board on the joint, and if a tight hinge, open immediately and adjust the leather, setting it carefully along the back edge of the board. After about five minutes trim out and fill the board with pasted card equal to the combined thickness of joint and card strip beneath it (Figs. 24, 25). Trim a sliver from the back edge of the infill card before fitting to allow for swell. The leather joint is less likely to 'wrinkle' into a 'pencil case' if the book-block is closed on the board rather than vice-versa. With a grooved hinge the board is closed on the pasted joint, opened to set and rub down before being closed again for pressing and drying shut with a barrier sheet – usually oil-board or a 'tin' with ('Photoprinto') water-mark-free blotting paper during pressing.

This completes the conventional covering process and leaves the binding ready for 'decoration'. If the board lining is to be of leather this is treated after the board has been stabilized with the necessary linings. When trimming out for leather doublures (linings) one adopts one of the procedures as for inlays where the piece of leather to be removed and the piece of leather to replace it are both cut through simultaneously, with the proviso that the inlay is well boarded-up so that it will butt to the edges without leaving a gap on drying. Some binders line both their inlays and the doublures to stabilize before inlaying (Fig. 26). On some modern French bindings a change of colour along the narrow edge of the board is obtained apparently by continuing the doublure to the centre of the edge and tooling it down with a line. This can be done by first onlaying a narrow strip of very thin leather (usually box calf) to the half way mark along the edge and bringing it over on to the inside turn-in; the doublure being onlaid over an infill and covering turn-in to the extreme edge of the inner board surface. If the extra thickness of doublure or fly-leaf are to be added at a later stage the book should be forwarded with a compensating card of an equivalent caliper between the board and book-block to prevent gape (Figs. 27, 28).

Before you begin a process know *why* you are doing it; if you know what result you want to achieve and why, you will discover a way to achieve it. This means you have to pre-plan your sequence of operations before each stage.

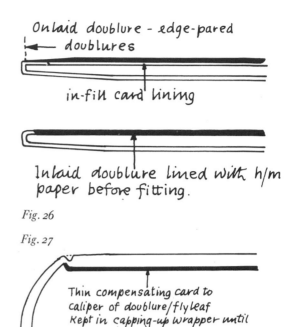

Onlaid doublure – edge-pared doublures

in-fill card lining

Inlaid doublure lined with h/m paper before fitting.

*Fig. 26*

*Fig. 27*

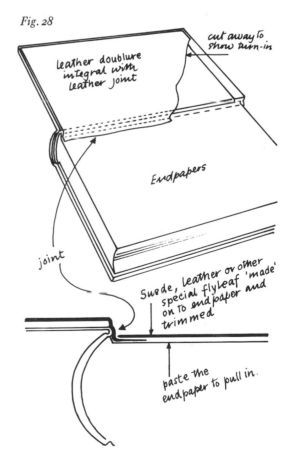

Thin compensating card to caliper of doublure/flyleaf kept in capping-up wrapper until flyleaf / doublure are attached

Loose strip of card at back edge of board if no leather joint sewn-in.

*Fig. 28*

Leather doublure integral with leather joint

cut away to show turn-in

Endpapers

joint

Suede, leather or other special flyleaf 'made' on to endpaper and trimmed

paste the endpaper to pull in.

## 8 Building images with leather

There are a good many ways of building images with leather, and many of the standard methods are ably described in his book *Modern Design in Bookbinding* (35) by Edgar Mansfield.

Most of these methods involve the cutting away of the underlying ground and replacing it with other pieces of leather of a different colour or surface configuration; or with the placing of pieces of leather on the surface to cover parts of the underlying ground. The operation is of course not confined to leather, for other materials may be treated in a similar way. The methods are termed respectively inlaying and onlaying, and include variations such as inset onlays, inlaid onlays, and both inlays and onlays raised and recessed. The permutations are endless and all these techniques may or may not be accompanied by tooling, stamping and modelling (Figs. 29, 30).

Less widely used methods of 'decoration' include building and modelling the underlying board structure (Plate 35), insetting of ivory, metals, jewels and semi-precious stones and shell (mother-of-pearl) (Plates 73, 48, 96); modelling of the leather over structures attached to the boards, such as string, plastic and wood (Plate 1). Recent innovations with leather imagery are feathered onlays, maril (marbled inlaid leather), puckered leather using the ground leather, inlays or onlays created by inducing the grain and developing this technique up to the positive folding and modelling of the leather (Plates 19, 18).

Several other methods of bookbinding 'decoration' are cut-outs in the boards (Plate 20), moving parts (manually, by gravity (Plate 61) or mechanically/electronically triggered), insetting of miscellaneous objects (Plate 13), collages, fresnel optics, plastics, metal and papier mâché; shaped books (Plate 46), colouring, staining, marbling and photographic derivations. Some of these techniques are illustrated here in the photographs, where these were obtainable. I may have included a particular photograph perhaps because it exemplifies a particular technique and not because it is necessarily considered the best, or even a good example of design, in that technique. Whatever the technique, it should always be considered the servant of the creative process and of the author's intention embodied in his text.

The shallow paring of leather produces a broken edge, especially with the well-boarded grain of Levant and Niger moroccos. Traditionally it was the practice to tool in the edges of the onlays over any slight feathering to prevent their picking up and to obtain a hard edge between areas (Fig. 29). The craftsman tends by nature to be precise and pernickety, and abhors inaccuracy and blemish in his work. It is not surprising therefore that 'randomness' is rare in craft-work. If it appears it is usually interpreted as carelessness or lack of control.

Under the influence of modern movements in painting, certain bookbinders tried out techniques which gave a 'soft' edge to shapes. On the continent of Europe these bookbinders produced 'torn'

*Fig. 29*

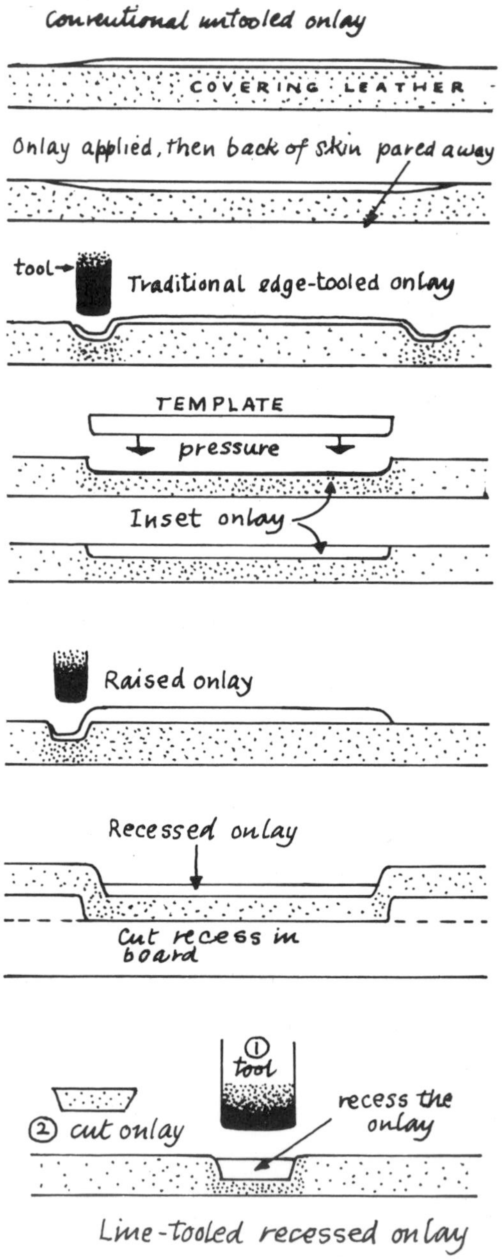

Conventional untooled onlay

COVERING LEATHER

Onlay applied, then back of skin pared away

tool → Traditional edge-tooled onlay

TEMPLATE
pressure
Inset onlay

Raised onlay

Recessed onlay
Cut recess in board

① tool
② cut onlay    recess the onlay

Line-tooled recessed onlay

onlays, i.e. Claude Staly, Coster-Dumas. This kind of onlay stands proud of the surface and is deliberately cut and shaped to look 'torn'. Images are usually balanced mirror-image-wise on both boards, and indicate a decorative approach, as does the repetition of the same design on both boards.

A hand-binding with decoration on the front board only suggests that a book is considered as a display surface, and not three-dimensionally 'in the round'. Very often such bindings have other features unrelated to the cover design, such as the position, scale and treatment of the titling.

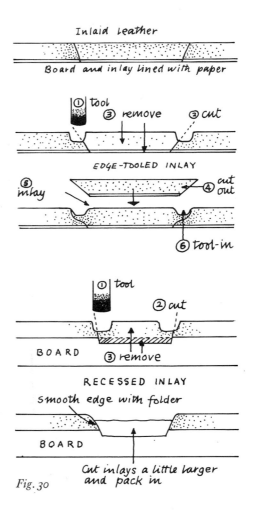

Fig. 30

10A

10A   Philip Smith
Trs. E. Kadloubovsky and G. E. H. Palmer *Writings from the Philokalia on the Prayer of the Heart* Faber and Faber.
Dark-green 'Oasis' goatskin. Multicoloured feathered onlays. Black and gold tooling. Recessed and varnished transfer lettering
$223 \times 152 \times 30$mm ($8\frac{3}{4} \times 6 \times 1\frac{1}{4}$in) 1961
Private collection

10B   Philip Smith
Detail 15

10C   Philip Smith
Detail 8C. Blocking over feathered onlays

10D   Philip Smith
Detail 23. Tooling and feathered onlays

10B

10C

10D

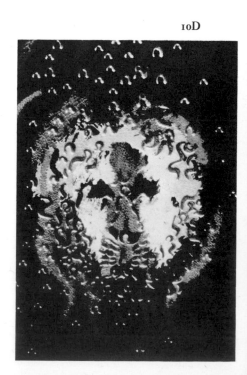

11    Philip Smith
J. R. R. Tolkien *The Lord of the Rings*
Three volumes bound as one.
First design. Violet and purple 'Oasis'.
Feathered onlays. Black and gold stamping.
Gauffered illustrations on gold edges
230×153×77mm (9×6×3in) 1962
Private collection

12    Philip Smith
Winston S. Churchill *The Island Race*
Cassell
Black 'Oasis'. Multicoloured feathered
onlays over acrylic impasto. Recessed
leather-covered plastic figures
315×235×40mm (12⅜×9¼×1½in) 1965
Private collection

## 9 Feathered onlays

Feathered onlay makes use of a natural effect of paring the edge of a piece of leather at a shallow angle. I noticed this effect quite by accident one day in 1959. I carried out tests to ascertain its power of adhesion in withstanding normal handling of the book. At first the feathered onlays were applied to the already covered book in the traditional manner (Plate 10). It occurred to me later that a smoother and more functional finish could be obtained by assembling the pieces on the loose covering leather and paring away an equal amount on the flesh side (Fig. 29). This greatly increased the possibilities inherent in the use of leather as an expressive medium.

The exact feathering and shape of a specific cut cannot accurately be known in advance although each fragment may be shaped further (Fig. 16). The method demands an intuitive approach to image building and attempts by designers to produce the feathered onlay 'look' through an intermediary tend to produce a stilted effect.

The techniques I use are described below, and follow on a close appraisal of the book during the reading of which pen and ink sketches and notes may be made (Plate 31). Sometimes the colour is described in a half-scale sketch (Plate 67), but to keep rigidly to a precise design would be inimical to this way of working. A more lively and truthful result is produced by a spontaneous handling of the medium. The sketches are used as aide-memoires, and are developed in their detail in the handling of the leather.

With reference to the sketch and to the colour sample card of available leathers many pieces of leather are pared off for use as onlays. These pieces are at first cut 'as they come' off the many waste pieces of leather which I have accumulated over the years. The different colours are arranged in order of size and colour on a large white board, which is used as a kind of palette (Plate 2A).

A frame of white card is cut to the size of the double spread of the book covers and placed over a sheet of toned card similar in colour to the covering leather (Plate 80C). The pieces of feathered onlay are selected from the large palette and laid loosely in position within the frame as the composition is built up.

An area measuring about 250mm (10ins) square on a sheet of stiff plastic is pasted with a brushful of starch paste into which a brushful of PVA emulsion adhesive (Spynflex 232–1720[1]) is mixed. The paste component penetrates and wets the onlay and the PVA component acts as a surface adhesive and prevents the onlay drifting off when the skin is pasted on the flesh side for covering at a later stage. The PVA is relatively insoluble in water after drying.

Several pieces of leather are selected from within the card frame and placed flesh-side down on the adhesive mixture and after a few seconds are picked off with mounted needles (Fig. 31) and placed in position on the loose covering leather, which has been damped lightly with a sponge. Care must be taken that every fragment of feathering receives adhesive and that none of it is turned under. As

*Fig. 31*

shaped dowel

MOUNTED NEEDLE *for handling small onlays etc.*

1 National Adhesives, Slough, Bucks, England.

52

it is positioned on the skin each onlay is rubbed down through a piece of release paper, and any surplus adhesive removed with the finger or a damped cloth. The pieces of onlay are placed side by side with perhaps the feathering of two adjacent pieces overlapping. When several pieces have been assembled a sheet of release paper is placed over the skin and the whole is nipped in the press. From time to time the card frame is placed over the growing composition and this is compared with the initial concept. There is a three-way reference between the selection of feathered onlay pieces, the ground leather with the growing design, and the definitive sketch. Any pieces of onlay which are considered particularly interesting are selected for inclusion in the design if they will further promote the meaning and beauty of the finished work. A piece of leather, which had some spottings due to some fault in the tanning process, was noticed and retained for possible incorporation when the occasion presented itself, and is shown in Plate 100C.

Any title lettering or title piece is always taken into account as part of the total expression and not something added as an afterthought. At this stage of near completion the whole surface of the skin is dabbed with a damp sponge, the surface allowed to dry and the skin pressed for about half an hour.

The dried assemblage is pared on the flesh side to level up. (This process often leaves an interesting configuration in the nap. A deliberate use of this could be made by temporarily attaching paper shapes to the grain-side, paring over and covering the book with the flesh side (suede) out.) The edges and hinges are now pared (Figs. 17, 19), the leather pasted and the book covered (Figs. 8, 9). While the leather is still damp after covering the binding is appraised and any aesthetic or functional adjustments made, perhaps by adding small onlays, re-setting any fragments disturbed during covering and attention to any fragments which cross the joint areas. It is always advisable to allow a break in any 'decoration' which may be disturbed or crack where it crosses the joint, especially on books likely to receive heavy use, because repeated flexing of the joint may lift the onlay. It is however a simple matter to slip a needle point carrying a spot of PVA into any 'pencil case' so formed!

Even minute pieces of leather may be used with this technique. The use of 'waste' is an attitude of mind, stemming from a parsimonious outlook and a necessity to exploit possibilities. Leather may be feathered in a variety of ways; using a paring knife, a spokeshave or other instrument. The leather is feathered by removal of the grain-side or the flesh side of the leather. It is often less laborious with thick leather to pare away the surface grain to produce an onlay. The grain pattern is best retained by making a fine skim with a sharp blade on the grain side, when it may be 'snuffed' off in a fine network (Plate 81G). This feathered onlay is the 'positive' result of the operation, but the remaining snuffed surface is also used expressively in the design (Plate 81F). The finished grain-side of leather has a harder, more impervious structure than has the relatively porous underlying corium. On some skins the dye is concentrated at the surface and becomes paler as it penetrates through the corium, giving a shaded effect in cross section (Plates 14, 16). When the surface is snuffed the corium is barely exposed and the deeper parts of the grain interstices show as a 'negative' veining. This veined area is pared off, the woolly corium fibres are compacted and sealed by an application of PVA emulsion. The final waxing of the covers makes an impervious finish.

## King·Lear inset onlays

The making of the binding for *King Lear* demanded the innovation of several new techniques. The design also makes use of several levels of visual ambiguity. The two factors are inter-related. First the colour effects: the orange and grey are of equal value (tonally) and towards the centre of the image the visual conflict is strongest and both focuses attention of the eyes of Lear and puts him behind bars: the strongest hues are situated around the edges of the image, and serve as a decoy to distract the eye. This movement around the perimeter is reinforced by the multiple ogee curves of the hair. The second visual ambiguity is created by the face being composed from the letter forms of the name; a statement of Lear's inner conflicts. The face is completely static and relies for its power on the subtlety of the expression. The total visual effect is one of stillness in movement. The image attempts to sum up in one statement the whole psychological situation confronting Lear. Thus is one able to rationalize something of the products of unconscious forces!

Special techniques were devised for the accomplishment of the visual effect. The images are built up from feathered onlays (Plates 2A–F) on to a grey 'Oasis' skin; when completed the flesh side was pared over-all to the thickness of impressions left in the orange leather base-board. The boards are covered in a well-grained Cape goatskin using a tongue and slot style. Plastics template letter forms were impressed in the damp leather immediately after covering and filling in the boards. The templates were used in cutting out the letter forms from the sheets with the onlaid images. These leather sheets were temporarily supported by pasting lightly to thin blotting paper to prevent distortion during cutting. (Either a scalpel or the stencil knife (Fig. 32) may be used.) The leather letter shapes were then damped and glued into the recesses in the stamped orange background. The whole board was subjected to great pressure to level the feathered onlays and the inset cut-outs (Fig. 33). The whole procedure was thought to be more effective than inlaying the cut-outs in the traditional manner. The spine strip was first onlaid with fragments of coloured 'Oasis', pared level and to shape, then a thin piece of gilding tissue was pasted in position on the flesh side to support the area where the 'Chemac' etched block with the title lettering was to be stamped (Fig. 34).

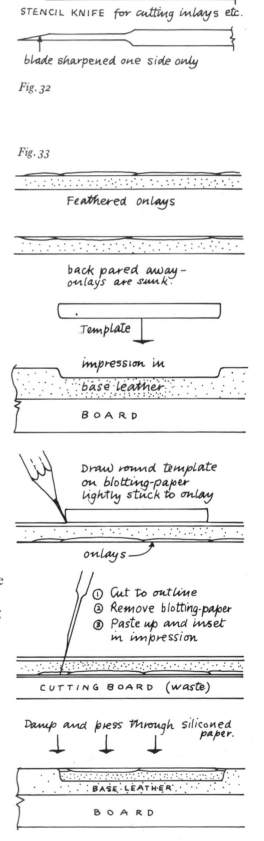

STENCIL KNIFE *for cutting inlays etc.*

*blade sharpened one side only*

*Fig. 32*

*Fig. 33*

Feathered onlays

*back pared away – onlays are sunk.*

*Template*

*impression in*

*base leather*

BOARD

*Draw round template on blotting-paper lightly stuck to onlay*

*onlays*

① *Cut to outline*
② *Remove blotting-paper*
③ *Paste up and inset in impression*

CUTTING BOARD (waste)

*Damp and press through siliconed paper.*

BASE LEATHER

BOARD

54

The titling was darkened by printing ink and varnished with 'Vinalak'. The spine was later covered on to the waste sheet to form a tongue (Fig. 35).

The plastics templates were later used as titling on the box lid, covered to make a leather relief (Plate 3). A fuller case history of this binding is recorded in (56).

*Fig. 34*

*Fig. 35*

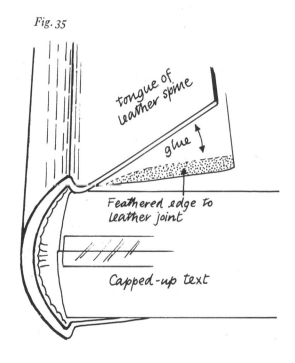

13   Philip Smith
Jaquet and Chapuis *The Swiss Watch*
Scarf-joined white alum-tawed pigskin, grey and black 'Oasis' goatskin. Feathered
onlays and inlays. Inset watch movements (Fig. 67)
305 × 225 × 40mm (12 × 8⅞ × 1½in) 1963
Collection: Don Bartolomeo March Severa, Spain

56

**14**

**15**

**16**

14    Philip Smith
J. R. R. Tolkien *The Lord of the Rings* First paper-back
edition.
Light blue 'Oasis' with sectioned onlays (first use on a
binding). Book side-sewn. Limp manilla boards with
fore-edge and end-cap flaps. Gauffered gold edges
$207 \times 135 \times 42$mm ($8\frac{1}{8} \times 5\frac{1}{4} \times 1\frac{3}{4}$in) 1969
Private collection South Africa

15    Philip Smith
Ed. Douglas Cooper *Great Private Collections*
Spine and back board covered in orange 'Oasis'. Front board
(tongue and slot) black 'Oasis'. Feathered onlays in greys,
white and various greens. Gold, black and blind stamping
and tooling
$318 \times 273 \times 48$mm ($12\frac{1}{2} \times 10\frac{3}{4} \times 1\frac{7}{8}$in) 1963–4
Private collection

16    Philip Smith
Trs. Kadloubovsky and Palmer *Unseen Warfare* Faber
and Faber.
Red and dark-brown scarf-joined 'Oasis'. Orange and violet
along join. Sectioned onlays and maril. Gold kid. (Second
maril binding)
$215 \times 140 \times 25$mm ($8\frac{1}{2} \times 5\frac{1}{2} \times 1$in) 1964 and 1969
Collection: E. Greenhill

57

## 10  Sectioned onlays and the development of maril

The waste pieces from the template cut-out lettering in the binding for *King Lear* were retained as are all my trimmings of leather. In January 1969 while working on the binding for the *Seven Pillars of Wisdom*[1] I selected a piece of this leather in building up the imagery. This waste leather was already in two layers and in paring it thinner for a feathered onlay fragment, an interesting colour-change effect of the shallow cross-section through two different coloured leathers was revealed. Dye often takes more strongly on the surface and the colour gets lighter as it sinks through the corium; cross-sectioning exposed this effect. It clearly had expressive possibilities. Having sought more fluid and subtle effects and the creation of soft-edged forms[2] this discovery was a God-send. I immediately postponed work on the binding for the *Seven Pillars* (which bears the first evidence of pre-maril) and in two days of continuous experiment explored a whole range of effects possible to sectioned onlays and *maril* (named later).

My first experiment consisted simply of gluing up a sandwich of half a dozen layers of leather, pressing them and slicing through them at different angles, and of making 'v'-cut incisions in the surface to get the effects of incised forms. The next step of laying strips of leather, butted together in sheets with several sheets cross-aligned, revealed interesting chequer-board effects in the cross-sections. This led on to variations in cross-stripping; shaping the section of the strips which were sandwiched together. One effect was obtained by layering flat pieces and cross-layering with 'boot-lace' sections of white leather. Cross-sections had wavy stripes with white dots, like beads.

I began to shape the layers by paring to different thicknesses and varying the thickness along the same strip. This led on to assembling dozens of scraps of skiver-thin leather in layers at random. The next step was the result of layering the leathers and then rolling them up giving a spiral cross-section. The random patches of onlay became more random as the number of pieces multiplied with each make and then it occurred to me that it would speed the experiments if I were to place a handful of fragments in a bowl and mix in some adhesive. I stirred the mixture like porridge, squeezed it out and compacted it as before in the nipping press. Many slabs of the leather composition were made up in this way; some of them were mostly one-coloured scraps; others a selection of two or three colours; some a random mixture of many colours. Different grades of mix were tried; some were composed of large fragments, some of smaller ones; and many intermediate variations. One could see the possibilities of controlling the configurations by placing mixtures of different single-colour fragments together to create different shapes when the slabs are surface shaved. Another variation was obtained by sinking rolled and twisted layerings into the random mixes. One could even compose specific configurations by layering to form human figures, faces, etc. This is done by working from the 'end-grain' or cross-section. One of my last developments with the slabs of fragments was to plane some smooth and make a solid book cover of it.

1 Collection: Lt-Colonel P. L. Bradfer-Lawrence.

2 The chemistry of painting with stains and dyes seemed to me too complex for a non-specialist (see Section 15).

The first book on which experiments with early maril were tried was a copy of *The Lord of the Rings* (Plate 14). The design is composed mainly from strip cross-sections. A name had to be found to describe this material. I wanted a short word, something English-sounding, unlike the term 'repoussé', for example. I was working on the above-mentioned binding, which also has other unconventional features, and decided that its name must be a word from this, my favourite book, whose author is a philologist. I contacted Professor Tolkien, but he admitted to insufficient knowledge of his invented Tengwar to find a name which would have the connotation 'open-ended' (open end of the section through the material, and configuratively ambiguous). I remembered the name Silmaril in *The Lord of the Rings* and thought that the word had the right 'ring' to it, especially the 'maril' part which was short.[3] Six months later, after I had been advised by an architect friend to apply for Patents[4] on the material (subsequently having done so) I was considering the word 'maril' when it occurred to me that it could stand for *mar*bled *i*nlaid *l*eather.

At this period I had designed the first Book-wall and was half-way through the forwarding. This set of books presented an opportunity for testing maril in many different ways and each volume reveals one or other facet of feathered, sectioned and maril onlays, as well as different sewings and hinges. But of course, as always in using new materials, one has to bear in mind that one is developing them for a definite purpose. My purpose was to find the means of opening up my work in bookbinding to give it a greater range for expressing insight triggered by the books, for I had found the traditional methods of tooling-in onlays and inlays too restricting for the achievement of this goal.

3 Professor Tolkien told me that names and words from his books have been used for many things including features on the moon!

4 The material is registered under British Patent No 1288 939. US Patent Application No 252,942.

Edgar Mansfield discovered the expressive possibilities of such a natural effect in leather as its tendency to crease up if pushed about in covering a book.[1] Where a less imaginative user might have tried to smooth out wrinkles caused perhaps by clumsy covering, an imaginative mind sees the expressive potential. As long ago as 1952 we can see the beginnings of his awareness of this tendency in leather, which in 1959 reached its most expressive effect in combination with tooling in the binding for *Behold this Dreamer* (Plate 37). The 'discovery' of wrinkles in leather is a good example of the use of 'errors'[2] (cf. also Plate 34F).

Many bookbinders in the past must have seen – but not noticed – the natural feathering of the edge of leather when bevel-cut, or the cross-section of the cut edge of leather, or that leather naturally puckers into folds as does the skin of the face in expressing thought and emotions; conventional 'craft-attitudes' have tried to correct errors rather than see their positive side. It is evident that mistakes can lead to fresh discoveries. Every student of bookbinding knows that if any fragment of leather finds its way under the edge being pared it will cause a hole to be torn in the leather. Many of the features in feathered onlay bindings may be produced by deliberately placing pieces, shaped to requirement, under the skin when paring. Broken edges and shaped holes result (Fig. 16). Another device for paring leather making use of this principle is described in Fig. 19, and also in levelling the flesh side when onlays (or card templates) have been stuck to the grain side (Fig. 33).

The effect of puckering the skin when covering may be controlled by judicious paring. The skin will tend to form wrinkles where there is a thinning in the corium; so the lines of creases can be induced along these lines pared in the leather. The leather pushed up into folds must be allowed for when measuring the leather for covering. The leather is cut larger, more area being allowed where more pronounced creasing is required (Fig. 35). When using this technique it is essential to a rigid finish of the folds that the leather (either in direct covering or as thin or thick onlays and inlays) be given thorough impregnation with paste. This enables one to work the damp leather more freely and causes it to set very hard when dried out.

Several other binders make use of the folding in leather. Trevor Jones in his binding for *Finnegan's Wake* (Plate 50) uses grain creases – over raised (lino) elements with tooling – in the Mansfield manner. Anthony Cains was using puckered leather during his period with Sydney Cockerell in 1961 and he has exaggerated the folding and modelling as a feature in its own right (Plates 18, 19). Sally Lou Smith has also adopted the technique, usually using it as an arbitrary decorative feature with gold tooled edges (Plate 17) in the form of thinly pared onlays. A further use of it has been made in my work on the binding of Poe's *Tales of Mystery and Imagination* (Plates 28, 36) where the leather is first onlaid and then puckered to define the silver kid onlays. I have also

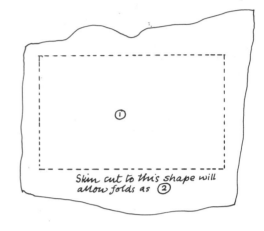

*Fig. 35a*

1 I am told that an African student of W. Matthews puckered his covering leather in the 1930's.

2 I use the word 'errors' advisably; not 'chance' which is an entirely different aspect of cause and effect.

used it expressively to create a more 'spiritual' effect with silver kid, both full skin and as puckered onlays, in the bindings for *The Lord of the Rings* book-wall (Plate 43), and in the board recesses of the binding for *Pilgrim's Progress* (Plates 46, 47). Vulnerability to scuffing of the surface must be allowed for in the design concept so that in time the exposed natural under-surface continues to express the movements in the leather (cf. unworn cover modelling Plate 1). Strategically placed folds would act as 'bosses' and take all the wear thereby protecting the rest of the cover.

17   S. Lou Smith
*Torah* Koren Publishers Jerusalem (1963).
Black Cape Levant morocco. Tan 'Oasis' onlays puckered and recessed.
Gold tooling
349×235×65mm (13¾×9¼×2½in) 1972
Private collection

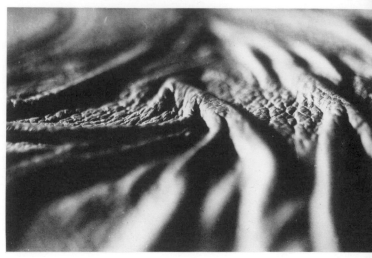

18   Anthony Cains
*The Pergamon World Atlas*
Details of puckered leather and wooden stamp

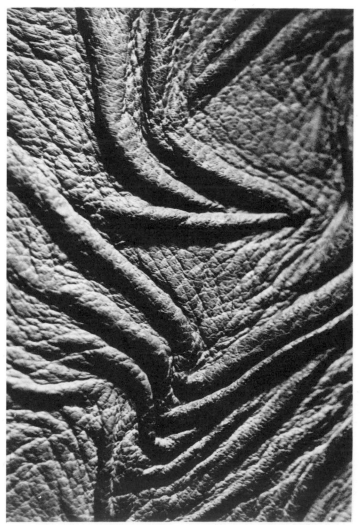

19   Anthony Cains
*Pergamon World Atlas* Pergamon Press (1968).
Puckered undyed goatskin. Blocked in blind from a wooden stamp. Green
goatskin doublures
405 × 317 × 45mm (16 × 12½ × 1¾in) 1969
Private collection

## 12 Cover boards

The best hand-made rope-fibre millboards (binder's boards) are no longer made (except perhaps in limited private production). Several types are made by machine and some, like best Dutch greyboard, are used in quality commercial production. Strawboard is rather too brittle but is not so prone to atmospheric pollution (formation of sulphuric acids). Many types of chipboard and pasteboard and mounting boards are available which are flexible and lightweight (qualities to recommend them) but the strongest and most compact, but heaviest in substance, is millboard. This is considered the best available foundation for fine book covers.

All boards cockle and warp if left in a humid atmosphere and the bookbinder's task is to construct a board which is as inert as possible for a fibrous hygroscopic material in a range of different atmospheric conditions, which may range from below 10°C (50°F) at R.H. 70 per cent to 32°C (90°F) R.H. 25 per cent (in hot light exhibitions).[1] Some binders are using plastics and light metal supports which are not so susceptible to atmospheric changes, but they often use them for aesthetic, not 'functional', purposes. It is the gain and loss of moisture which is the main cause of movement in boards and a finished cover board which is sealed against this fluctuation (perhaps by a varnish or wax polish) would be more stable. Achieving and controlling stability is one of the most difficult tasks facing the hand-bookbinder, most of whose materials are unpredictable. One solution is a board made up from several layers with the balanced opposition of pulls from within and without. A typical finished cover board can consist of nine or ten layers as in Fig. 36. Laminating with hand-made paper between millboard layers and again on both sides,[2] and leaving the board to dry both in air and in the press for several days before use creates a good foundation to covering. After covering with leather and being given their penultimate inside linings the boards should again be allowed to dry and mature by alternate standing open and pressing.

Common problems are those occurring in exhibition conditions or in centrally heated libraries, where the atmosphere will dry out the outer surfaces of a closed book. Those which are intricately applied with onlays will suffer most (other things being equal) because the combined shrinkage of the thin onlay leathers and the underlying ground will increase the 'pull'. The last lining (doublure) should not be put down or tooled until the binder has made sure (perhaps by playing a warm-air fan on it) that the outer face has contracted fully.

One way to pull back a board is to relax one side by dampening and playing the fan on the other side so that it dries out first and more quickly. Points to note: paste or glue the thinner of two laminas, which should be nearest to the book-block, as this will pull the board towards the book. It is vital to have a flat board before the inner hinge lining (joint) is put down, otherwise strain will be applied to the hinge joints and an unsightly shoulder ridge will appear on the outside. This unwanted shoulder ridge may be caused in several ways; the inner leather joint being too thick; by closing the board

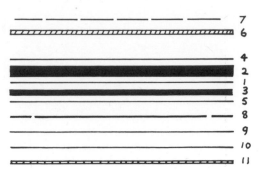

Typical BOARD MAKE-UP numbered in order of application

1. Hand-made paper stabilizer
2. Machine-made black millboard
3. Thinner m/m millboard
4, 5. H/m paper liners (parts of 4 lift away when inlaying)
6. Covering leather
7. Thin onlay leather
8. In-fill card (turn-ins)
9. M/m paper leveller (sand-papered)
10. H/m paper liner (feathered)
11. Leather doublure (onlaid)

*Fig. 36*

1 A simple way of determining relative humidity is by using a wet and dry bulb psychrometer and referring to psychrometric tables.

2 The paper lining is useful during inlay procedures, the paper peeling off leaving the board surface intact.

20　Philip Smith
Lewis Carroll *Alice's Adventures in Wonderland* illustrated by Dali. Maecenas
Press New York
Feathered onlays and maril. Rayon gold-stamped flyleaf (Dali signature). Cerise
suede doublures. Hand-painted flyleaves and box
$432 \times 286 \times 50$mm ($17 \times 11\frac{1}{4} \times 2$in) 1971–2
Collection: Mr and Mrs Peter Minton

21 Philip Smith
Shakespeare *King Lear* illustrated by Oscar Kokoschka. Ganymed Original
Editions. OUP.
Orange Cape morocco with inset feathered onlays (Section 9)
457 × 362 × 40mm (18¾ × 14¼ × 1⅝in) 1967–8
Collection: Colin Franklin

Fig. 37

when the joint is too dry and stiff; by the backing shoulder being too high, and combinations of these faults.

Boards are fitted to the book in several ways. The book is prepared for boarding (perhaps by trimming, rounding and backing) and the boards are measured to fit the book giving parallel 'squares' (Fig. 2) and cut by hand with steel straight-edge and knife (light stroking cuts) or by board-cutter. If it is a valuable book previously not cut square, and not to be trimmed again, boards may be made square (with uneven 'squares') or cut to fit the un-square book. A mutual decision should be agreed by binder and client on this and any other uncertainty of procedure of this nature.

To ensure accurate and parallel 'squares' the boards may be ploughed with the book-edges. Book and boards are knocked up square to the head edge, which is ploughed square to the spine (the fore-edge having first been ploughed parallel to the spine folds). The boards are lowered two squares and ploughed with the tail edge. It is usually more convenient to shape and bevel the boards before lacing-in or attaching.

*Board attachment variations*

Figs. 37, 38 show some common board attachments. These may be used for various reasons but very often personal preference will dictate the choice of style, with the binder balancing one requirement against another. Thick books are usually sewn on double raised cords or recessed cords, which are then laced in with a tight joint giving support against the shoulder.[3] The supported groove attributed to Thomas Harrison (Fig. 59) gives the same advantage as the support of a tight joint, together with the use of thicker leather of the grooved style. Many designer-bookbinders prefer to use the tight joint because the slighter hinge-line does not break the continuity of surface or imagery round the spine on to the covers. It is advisable to interrupt the flow of gold lines at this point because flexing the board hinge in opening will cause a ragged crack in the gold (see Plate 85). Because of the much earlier breakdown of the hinge with a tight joint I use some method of extra reinforcement. One of these is to bring the linen lining from the spine over on to the inside of the board (Fig. 37C).[4] (A layer of hand-made or blotting paper may be glued over the whole of the outside of the board over tape slips, linings, etc., and sandpapered level.) Other devices which reinforce a joint at the vulnerable head and tail ends are the insertion of linen in the turn-in (Fig. 39) or by providing a short groove at the head and tail with the rest of the hinge tight. This may sometimes be a useful aesthetic device with shaped and modelled boards. The

3 When fitting for a tight joint make allowance for any stuck-in leather joints, doublures or extra fly-leaf linings (Figs 27, 28).

4 Joints in Figs 37A, B, D and E are used in the book-wall.

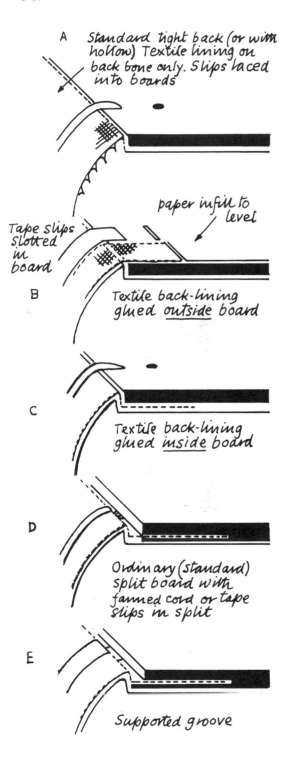

A  Standard tight back (or with hollow) Textile lining on back bone only. Slips laced into boards

Tape slips slotted in board

paper infill to level

B  Textile back-lining glued *outside* board

C  Textile back-lining glued *inside* board

D  Ordinary (standard) split board with fanned cord or tape slips in split

E  Supported groove

Some board attachments. Coverings and inner attachments (endpapers, joints etc.) not shown board attachment method is not chosen in isolation; endpaper make-up is an important consideration and both will be dictated by the requirements of function, use, aesthetics and economics in a particular situation. (Figs. 40–55A give several different treatments of differing bulk and strength.)

The tongue-and-slot board attachment (aspects of which are shown in Figs. 35, 65, 68, 69, 91, 94, 97, 98), one of the strongest methods, is a development of the method shown at Fig. 56 but has the advantage that it is relatively easy to remove the board (or book) for future repairs or re-binding. The variation in Fig. 57 also permits a narrow separate spine and full board-covering and can be blocked (off the book) and treated as a case-binding (like Fig. 58) but has in effect a 'library' split board structure (Fig. 59).

The 'opening' of the book is its most vulnerable mechanism. Breakdown occurs along the hinge of the cover and inside joint, the stress points (Fig. 58). Another breakdown point should the boards be attached too rigidly is the connection to the first sections of the book. Fig. 60 shows a method of overcasting the joint which prevents a breakdown there. This method does, however, prevent the first few sections from opening out to the back folds. A loose guard (S.C.) round the first and last section prevents drag on these when the board and end-paper sections are opened, as do some of the 'gusset' endpapers (Figs. 49–55).

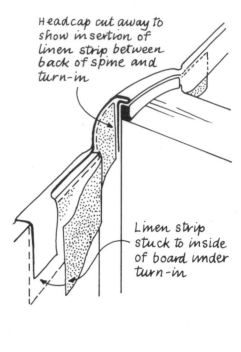

Headcap cut away to show insertion of linen strip between back of spine and turn-in

Linen strip stuck to inside of board under turn-in

Position of linen in spine turn-in (cross-section)

REINFORCED HINGE ENDS

Fig. 39

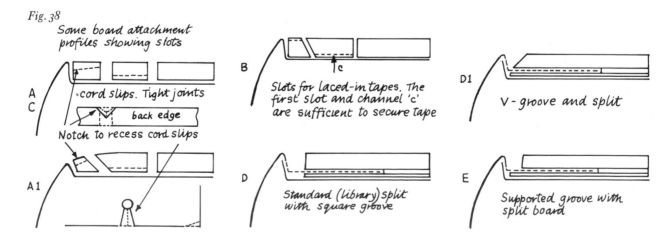

Fig. 38

Some board attachment profiles showing slots

A
C · cord slips. Tight joints
back edge
Notch to recess cord slips

A1

B
Slots for laced-in tapes. The first slot and channel 'c' are sufficient to secure tape

D
Standard (library) split with square groove

D1
V - groove and split

E
Supported groove with split board

68

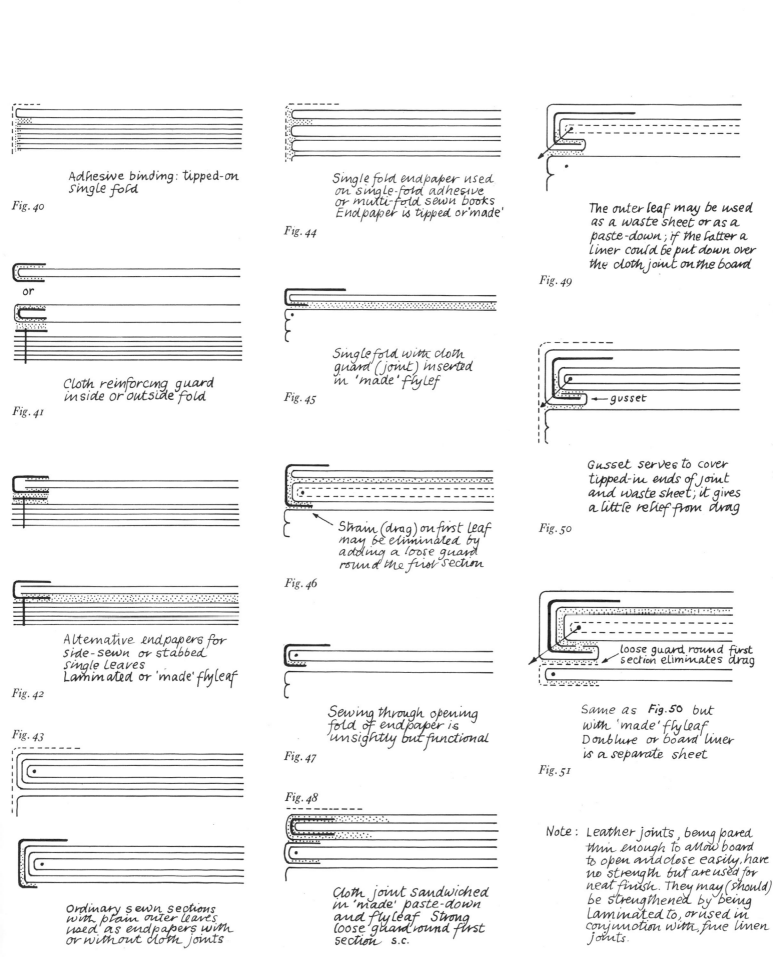

Adhesive binding: tipped-on single fold

Fig. 40

or

Cloth reinforcing guard inside or outside fold

Fig. 41

Alternative endpapers for side-sewn or stabbed single leaves
Laminated or 'made' flyleaf

Fig. 42

Fig. 43

Ordinary sewn sections with plain outer leaves used as endpapers with or without cloth joints

Single fold endpaper used on single-fold adhesive or multi-fold sewn books
Endpaper is tipped or 'made'

Fig. 44

Single fold with cloth guard (joint) inserted in 'made' flylef

Fig. 45

Strain (drag) on first leaf may be eliminated by adding a loose guard round the first section

Fig. 46

Sewing through opening fold of endpaper is unsightly but functional

Fig. 47

Fig. 48

Cloth joint sandwiched in 'made' paste-down and flyleaf Strong loose guard round first section s.c.

The outer leaf may be used as a waste sheet or as a paste-down; if the latter a liner could be put down over the cloth joint on the board

Fig. 49

← gusset

Gusset serves to cover tipped-in ends of joint and waste sheet; it gives a little relief from drag

Fig. 50

loose guard round first section eliminates drag

Same as Fig. 50 but with 'made' flyleaf Doublure or board liner is a separate sheet

Fig. 51

Note: Leather joints, being pared thin enough to allow board to open and close easily, have no strength but are used for neat finish. They may (should) be strengthened by being laminated to, or used in conjunction with, fine linen joints.

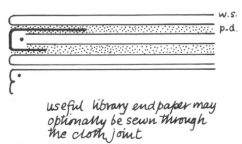

w.s.
p-d.

useful library endpaper may
optionally be sewn through
the cloth joint

Fig. 52

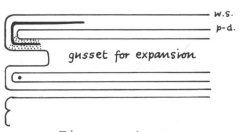

w.s.
p-d.

gusset for expansion

Zig-zag endpaper

Fig. 53

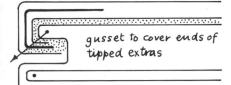

gusset to cover ends of
tipped extras

zig-zag with 'made'
flyleaf

Fig. 54

Fig. 55

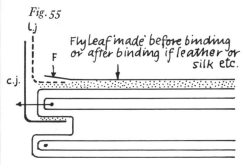

l.j

F

c.j.

Flyleaf 'made' before binding
or after binding if leather or
silk etc.

zig-zag used with leather
joint put in after binding;
first flyleaf may be 'made'
with end section and left
with loose flap F. linen
joint is sewn in

Fig. 55a

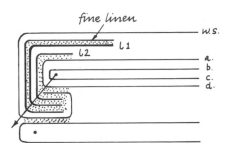

fine linen

w.s.

l2   l1

a.
b.
c.
d.

Endpaper with reinforced
leather joint (l1) Grain
surface leather edge (l2) on
outer flyleaf fold (a.- d.) used
for all-leather or silk flyleaf
put down after binding.
(This l2 could be extended to
become all-leather flyleaf
'made' before sewing book)

Flyleaves fold d.
waste sheet    Leather joint, grain side    glue out

Fence of waste paper

A

waste sheet

B

fold over
a.
d.
w.s.
fold over

C

Leather, grain-side: backed to linen
very thin leather, flesh-side
a.
d.
w.s.

Make-up of 'universal' endpaper

① Laminate linen to leather strip
② Edge flyleaf with thin leather
③ Lay out and glue up as A. Press.
④ Fold up as B or C. Press.
⑤ Trim to size and sew.

Fig. 56

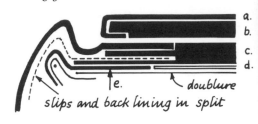

a.
b.
c.
d.

e.    doublure

slips and back lining in split

a. Board covering material; back-
edge turn-in and outer
board covering only pasted down
at first stage

b. Main board with turn-in
recess (p1) inside back-edge

c. Thin supported split board; spine
covering recess at back-edge

d. In-fill for leather joint and
turn-ins from a.

e. Standard sewn-in leather joint

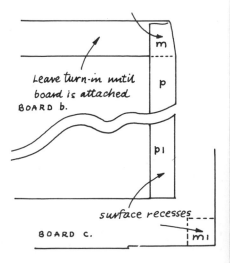

m

p

Leave turn-in until
board is attached
BOARD b.

p1

surface recesses

BOARD c.    m1

Cut away edge in split board to
accommodate spine covering at
turn-in

Components and make-up of
pre-'tongue-and-slot' board
structure.

*Fig. 57*

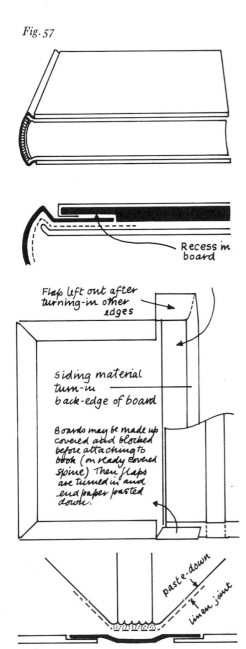

Recess in board

Flap left out after turning-in other edges

Siding material turn-in back-edge of board

Boards may be made up covered and blocked before attaching to book (on ready covered spine). Then flaps are turned in and end paper pasted down.

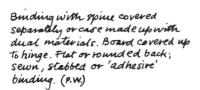

paste-down

linen joint

Binding with spine covered separately or case made up with dual materials. Board covered up to hinge. Flat or rounded back; sewn, stabbed or 'adhesive' binding. (P.W.)

*Fig. 58*

S

stress points

Publisher's hard-back (flat-back) covers and back-strip made up as case off the book-block. Attachment is between cloth and paper only. Anchorage is strengthened at hinge when tape slips are included at S.

*Fig. 59*

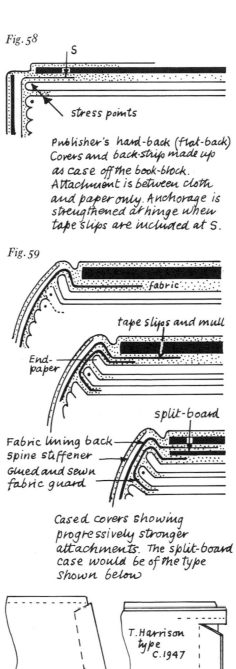

fabric

tape slips and mull

End-paper

split-board

Fabric lining back
Spine stiffener
Glued and sewn fabric guard

Cased covers showing progressively stronger attachments. The split-board case would be of the type shown below

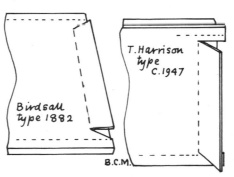

Birdsall type 1882

T. Harrison type c.1947

B.C.M.

*Fig. 60*

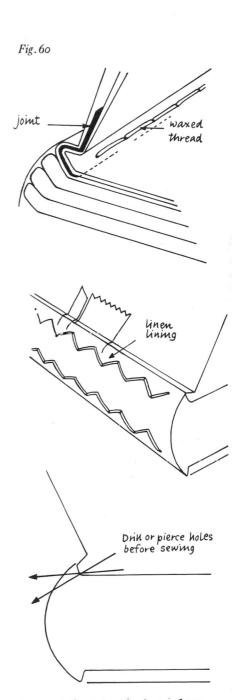

joint

waxed thread

linen lining

Drill or pierce holes before sewing

A method of overcasting to re-inforce the opening of a book. This method is preferable to one where the thread is made vulnerable to friction by passing round and over the point of the shoulder.

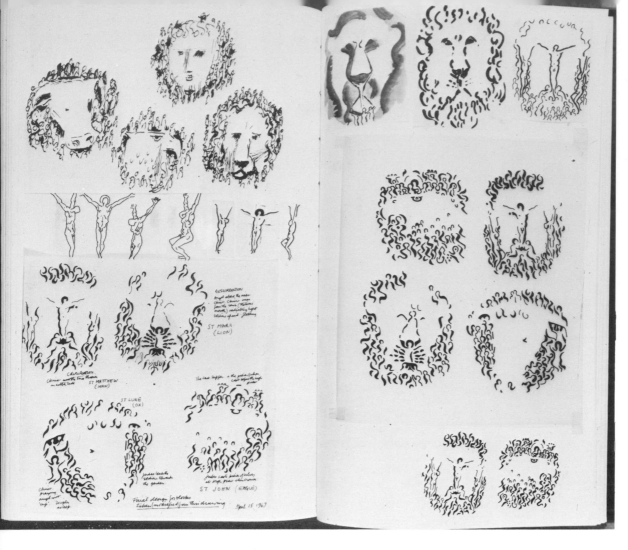

22   Philip Smith
*The Holy Gospel*
Drawings for head-scenes
Page size: 385 × 245mm (15⅛ × 9⅝ in)

23   Philip Smith
*The Holy Gospel* Officina Bodoni Press.
Royal blue 'Oasis'. Feathered onlays. Gold tooling
300 × 205 × 45mm (11⅞ × 8 × 1¾ in) 1966–7
Collection: Colin Franklin

23

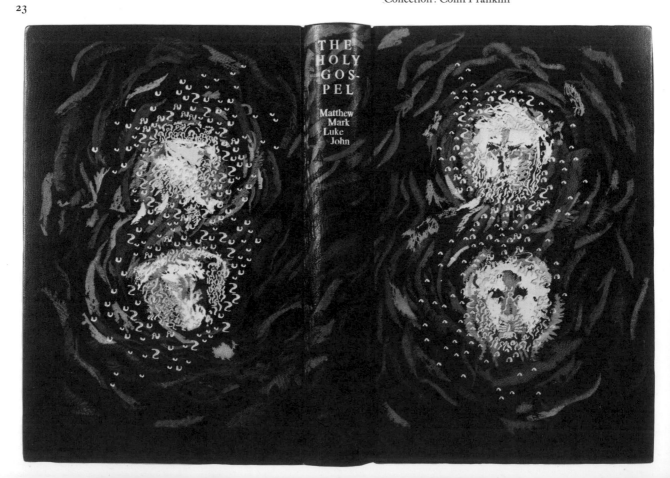

**24**
Work chart (and author) in studio. Daily
activities are marked in colour code

**25**
(left to right) Philip Smith, J. R. R. Tolkien,
HRH The Duke of Edinburgh. Presentation to
His Royal Highness of a copy of *The Lord of
the Rings* signed by Professor Tolkien, at the
Victoria and Albert Museum exhibition of The
Craftsman's Art, May 1973 (*Photo: Design
Council*) (See Plate 96)

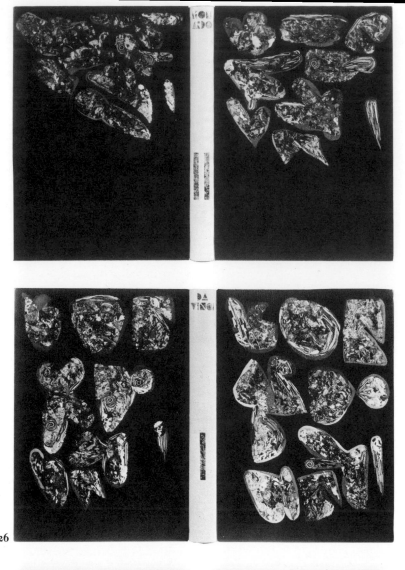

26

27

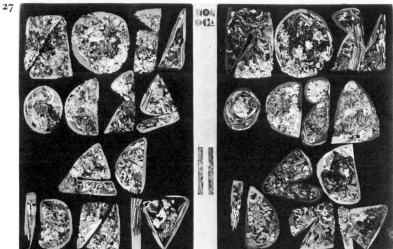

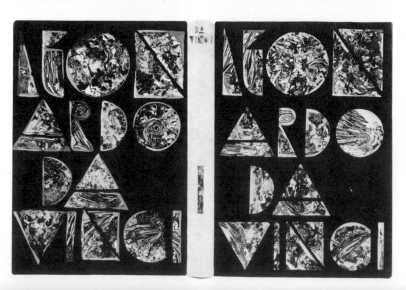

26 & 27    Philip Smith
*Leonardo da Vinci* Milan Memorial
Exhibition Edition. Leisure Arts English
Edition. Volumes 1 and 2. 1969
Vellum spines. Tongue and slot boards
covered in black 'Oasis'. Maril onlays
edged with coloured onlays changing
across eight boards. Sequence metamor-
phosis of letter forms. Awarded Gold
Medal, São Paulo Bienale,
$370 \times 260 \times 40$ and 35mm
($14\frac{1}{2} \times 10\frac{1}{4} \times 1\frac{1}{2}$ and $1\frac{3}{8}$in) 1972

28A   Philip Smith
Edgar Allan Poe *Tales of Mystery and Imagination* Harrap (1919).
Scarf-joined black and grey 'Oasis'. Feathered onlays and maril. Part of cover
puckered with silver kid and onlays. Acrylic 'windows' in transparent black and
neutral plexiglas (perspex)
272 × 218 × 50mm (10¾ × 8½ × 2in) 1971–2
Private collection

28B   Philip Smith
Detail. Onlays

28C   Philip Smith
Detail. Puckering

28B

28C

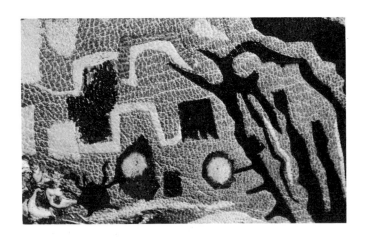

29A

29A    Philip Smith
Lewis Carroll *Alice's Adventures in Wonderland*
Brown 'Oasis'. Spine (tongue and slot) crimson 'Oasis'. Plexiglas-reinforced
(perspex) cut-outs

29B    Philip Smith
Detail. Head(s)

29C    Philip Smith
Detail. Queen of Hearts

29B                    29C

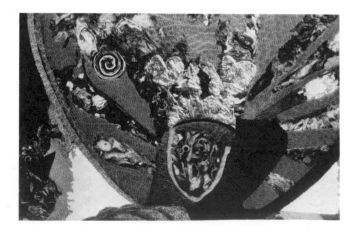

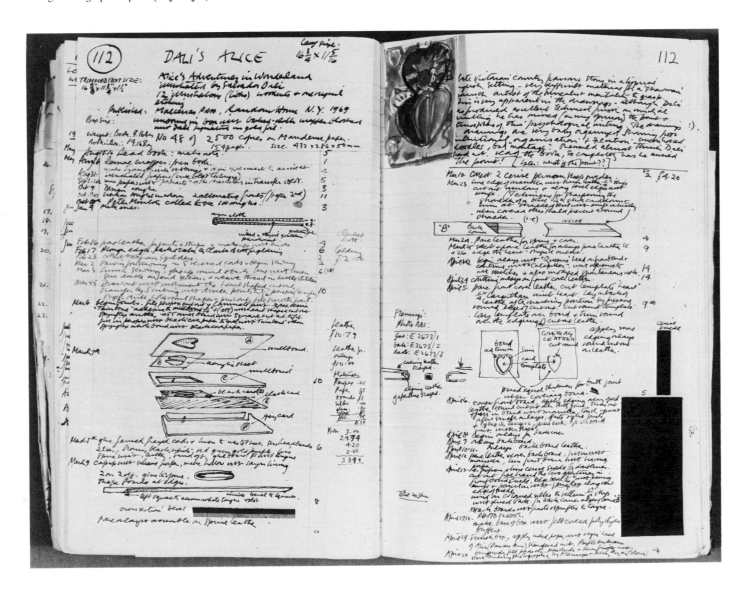

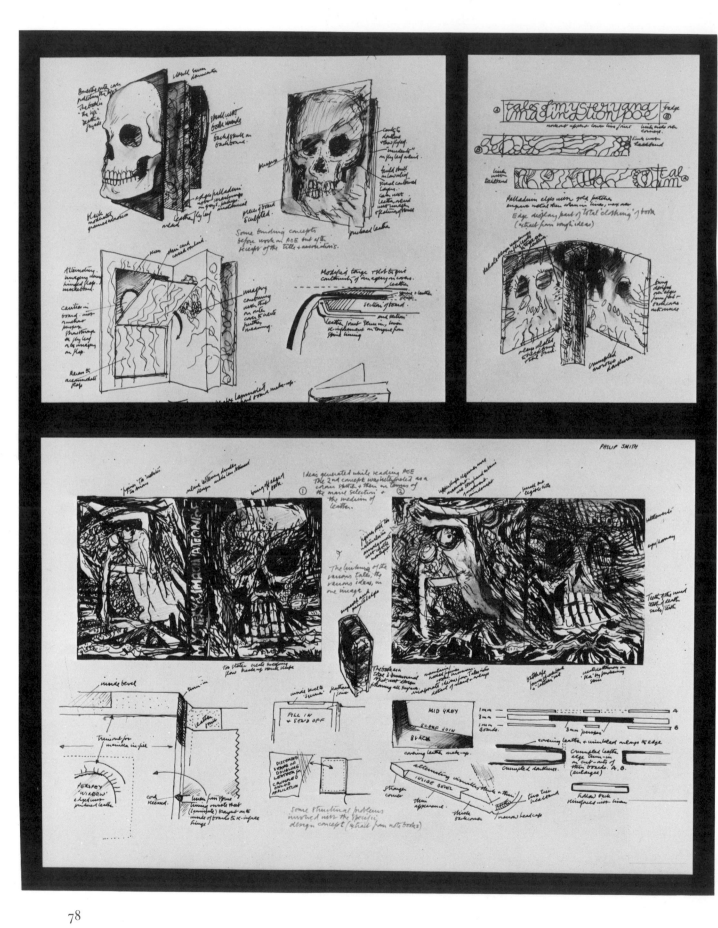

32    Philip Smith
Poe. Definitive colour sketch full size. Drawings for edge treatment: greys and
mauves on palladium

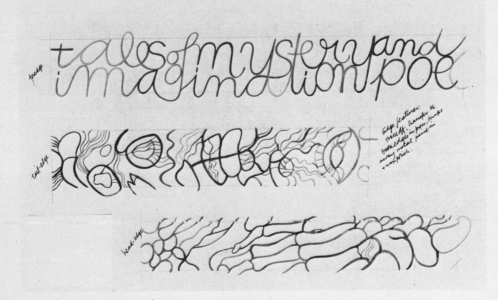

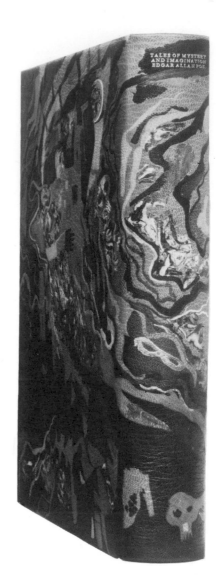

33A

33A   Philip Smith
Poe. Book-box with morocco spine and cloth sides, covered with images
hand-painted in coloured inks, similar to flyleaves

33B   Philip Smith
Poe. Edge treatment and shaped board edges

33B

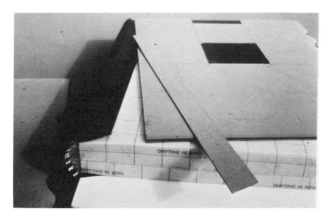

34A          34B

34C          34D

34E          34F

34A   Philip Smith
Detail. *The Pilgrim's Progress*
Two-tier end-band (Fig. 92)

34B   Philip Smith
Detail. *The Pilgrim's Progress*
Leather spine tongue. Board with
slot cut-out shaped edges

34C   Philip Smith
Detail. *Alice*
Head-band and board edge

34D   Philip Smith
Detail. Poe
Fore-edge title design engraved
and coloured

34E   Philip Smith
Detail. *Alice*
Hand-painted box lid

34F   B. N. C. Florence
Book damaged in flood
Shrunken and puckered leather

## 13 Design for use

The special problem given below is used as an example of the kind of thinking leading to a design solution where a detail of the typographic design posed a difficult structural problem in a book commissioned as a modern 'fine' binding.[1] (This is usually associated with full leather, highly decorated rigid boards, gilt edges, silk end-bands, etc.)

It is commonly assumed that fine or creative bookbinding provides merely a pretty packaging, and sometimes it is treated as such by both binders and collectors. To be an integral part of the book both the structure and 'decoration' should be 'functional', that is, designed with special regard to use in a given context.

This particular problem was to produce a binding for a facsimile of a large anatomical 'atlas' by Vesalius, *De Humani Corporis Fabrica*. This was a limited edition from the fifteenth century Belgian anatomist's original edition and woodcuts, reproduced by the Bremer Press in 1934. The following is an extract from a project still in progress at the time of writing, and a sketch of the proposed covers is shown in Plate 94. The book was presented as a collection of large folio sections, size 560 × 390 × 50mm (22 × 15¼ × 2in) thick, weighing 17½lb (7·9 kilos) and made up from 184 leaves in thirty-seven sections. The book was foliated on receipt at the bindery. At first glance it seemed to call for a straightforward binding on webbing tapes, linings and hollow back with a tight joint in the backing shoulder. A closer inspection revealed that there were tiny key numbers to the diagrams almost hidden in the back folds on both sides of the leaves. This meant that conventional gluing up, rounding and backing of the sections would probably lose these clues to the diagrams. The book must therefore be constructed to open to the back fold at each spread. Glue could not be applied directly to the folds of the leaves because, penetrating between the section backs, it would obscure the numbers. Three possible solutions to this part of the problem occurred to me. (1) To sew the book on a loose zig-zag guard (Fig. 61) which would both prevent the sections from being glued directly and also conceal any 'opening' between the sections which might show the back linings; this would add to the swelling at the spine but at the same time encourage it into a natural round, lessening the likelihood, almost inevitable in an unbacked (or flat-back) book, of the fore-edge becoming convex. (2) To extend the back margins beyond the key numbers by slitting the folds throughout and scarf-joining on to new paper guard folds (Fig. 62). This would change the original format of the book and also entail a great deal of extra working time, but the book could then be completed in the conventional manner. (3) All the sections could be thrown out on 'meeting guards' (Fig. 63). This would provide free opening of the sections to the back folds but is inherently a weak structural method, especially on a large book with heavy (½lb or ·227 kilo) sections; all the hinging is taken by the first sewing on to the guards, unsupported by glue or linen hinge guards (Fig. 64) (not possible because the small numbers would be covered). The thread would soon break down with the continual friction of swinging on the stubs. An advantage is that the book could be rounded and

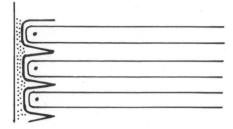

Loose ZIG-ZAG or CONCERTINA guard prevents any adhesive from direct contact with backs of sections. Useful for valuable mss or flat-opening spreads

*Fig. 61*

*Fig. 62*

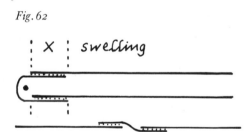

Joining two single leaves on the verso
If a large number of leaves in the same book has to be treated, x may be reduced by scarf-joining

SCARF-JOINED Guards. Stagger the join line if many leaves or plates are to be treated

1 At the time of the original edition the style of binding would have no shoulder.

82

35A & B   Faith Shannon
George Moore *A Monograph of the Genus Crocus* (1886)
Green Italian goatskin. Relief inset of balsa wood, papier-mâché and plaster.
Miniature watercolour painted on vellum.
Domed plate glass. Velvet-padded box
$320 \times 260 \times 55$mm ($12\frac{1}{2} \times 10\frac{1}{4} \times 2\frac{1}{4}$in) 1973

36    Philip Smith
Edgar Allan Poe *Tales of Mystery and Imagination*
Front board. Hand-painted flyleaf visible through 'window'. Doublures of
onlaid puckered goatskin. Palladium edges engraved and coloured
272 × 218 × 50mm (10¾ × 8½ × 2in) 1971–2
Private collection

backed and support heavy boards (or alternatively the stubs could be stab-sewn).

A large book such as this is not normally kept upright (on its tail edge) in the book-shelf, but laid flat. In use it is laid on a table or desk. There seemed little reason to consider hard inflexible covers apart from the conventional appearance these give. Heavy boards on an unbacked book put considerable strain on the joint area and tend to 'ride' back, tearing away from the back edge and going out of square (see Fig. 58). One method of overcoming this tendency is to give the book a kind of 'stationery binding' spring-back, but this is usually clumsy looking and 'round-shouldered'. With sufficient lining from the backbone continuing on to the sides, and the right balancing of the jointing materials, a built-up shoulder would allow the book to open flat to the back folds and also impart a 'fine-binding' finish besides giving some support to the back edge of the boards. My own conclusion favoured treatment 1 (Fig. 61) for the sewing structure, and the built-up shoulder hinge for the boards (Fig. 65).

The method of making the built-up shoulder is to soak a length of hemp cord in paste and PVA mix (stretched out between anchor points like a line), allow it to dry and then wrap it inside a strip of leather thoroughly pasted. When almost set the shoulder piece is formed into a flattened triangular section, cut to length and made up in the endpaper section as Fig. 65. The strength of the cover attachment depends on the linen reinforcements and the over-sewing through the joint (and shoulder piece), and the linen back lining. The stiff leaves help to give rigidity to the whole assembly. I decided to make the boards 'hard' but as slender as possible consistent with stability against warp, and to attach them by the strong 'tongue and slot' method (Fig. 65).

As I had to allow for maximum use of the book, this included the distinct possibility of the backbone becoming flat, if not actually concave. To preserve the 'modern fine binding' look I decided on a hollow back which would keep its round. With eventual concavity of the backbone under this round spine something had to be devised to conceal the 'pencil case' down the hollow spine which would then have developed. Fig. 66 shows my structure against this eventuality, and consists of a pair of end-flaps lying on the leaves at head and tail of the spine. Various shapes are possible depending on taste or ingenuity. Mine are quite simple flat pointed ovals each with an additional 'square' strip round the back edge to continue the line of the boards. They are not intended to function as end-bands as this is a stack-flat book, and in any case it is provided with a protective book-box for storage. These end-flaps also provide a convenient site for the book title, or may carry other expressive markings.

In my discussion with the client on the structural problem posed by the numbers in the folds I had given a further alternative should he wish to have a conventional binding structure. I suggested that we could side-step the problem by neatly pencilling in the numbers further out in the margins away from the sewing folds.

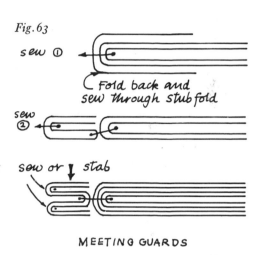

*Fig. 63*

MEETING GUARDS

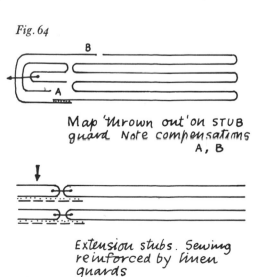

*Fig. 64*

Map 'thrown out' on STUB guard. Note compensations A, B

Extension stubs. Sewing reinforced by linen guards

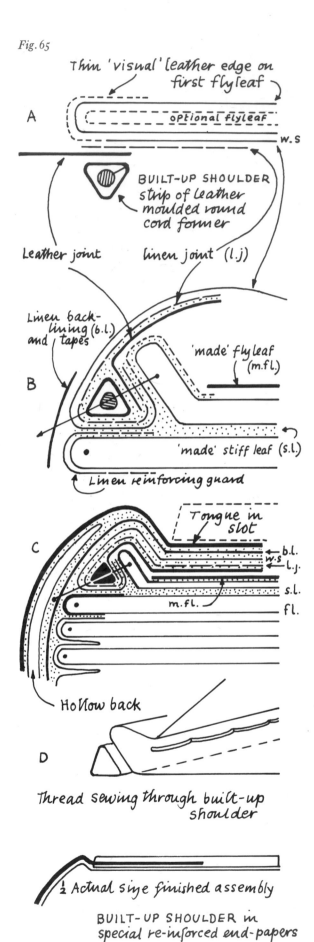

Fig. 65

A

Thin 'visual' leather edge on first flyleaf

optional flyleaf

w.s

BUILT-UP SHOULDER
strip of leather
moulded round
cord former

Leather joint

linen joint (l.j)

Linen back-
lining (b.l.)
and tapes

'made' flyleaf
(m.fl.)

B

'made' stiff leaf (s.l.)

Linen reinforcing guard

C

Tongue in
slot

b.l.
w.s
l.j.
s.l.
m.fl.
fl.

Hollow back

D

Thread sewing through built-up
shoulder

½ Actual size finished assembly

BUILT-UP SHOULDER in
special re-inforced end-papers

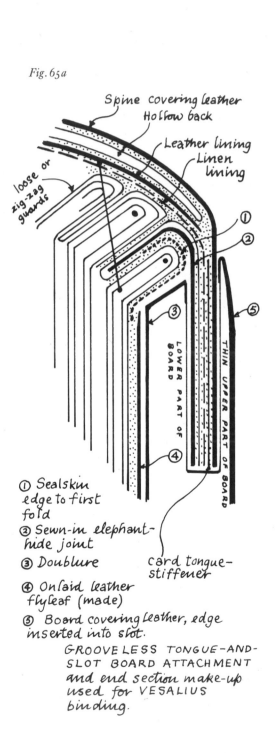

Fig. 65a

Spine covering leather
Hollow back

Leather lining
Linen
lining

loose or
zig-zag
guards

①
②

③

LOWER PART OF
BOARD

④

THIN UPPER PART OF BOARD

⑤

card tongue-
stiffener

① Sealskin
edge to first
fold
② Sewn-in elephant-
hide joint
③ Doublure
④ Onlaid leather
flyleaf (made)
⑤ Board covering leather, edge
inserted into slot.

GROOVELESS TONGUE-AND-
SLOT BOARD ATTACHMENT
and end section make-up
used for VESALIUS
binding.

This method appealed to him because it seemed to allow a more robust backbone and board support and concessions to the printing were minimized: so in the end this conventional method was adopted but I incorporated several of the re-inforcing features because it was such a heavy book. I include the above account because it indicates several approaches to one special problem amongst many which continually appear in this work. The actual structure finally used is shown in Fig. 65A. Naturally an explanation of the reason for the pencilling-in would be included in a binder's note bound in to the last section of the book.

## Surface design

Surface design composition is the visual ordering of the elements, lines, colours, forms, and the spaces between; which may be described by using such terms as direction, weight, emphasis or stress, movement, perspective, proportion and the rest (35, p. 99 et seq.). In learning how to design, the binder must master all these elements, but bear in mind that each arrangement, each relationship of parts, is creating 'meaning', that is, it contains all the above factors. His sensibility alone will tell him whether he is projecting the 'design meaning' which will communicate the intended experience. For the bookbinder, the relevant composition is not an arrangement of masses or colours designed for visual comfort (symmetry, balance, tastefulness), but is determined by the inner necessity of the original insight, idea or purpose aroused by the book he is binding.

This is not to say that abstract style surface decoration cannot be a means to the essential projection of the book within, but in the light of the ethos postulated in this book arbitrary surface decoration neglects or evades the main issues relating to the evolution of the modern fine binding, which render obsolete the use of the covers purely as a display surface, where a wall panel would be more appropriate to that kind of 'free expression' (Vide: Chart 1. Section 2).

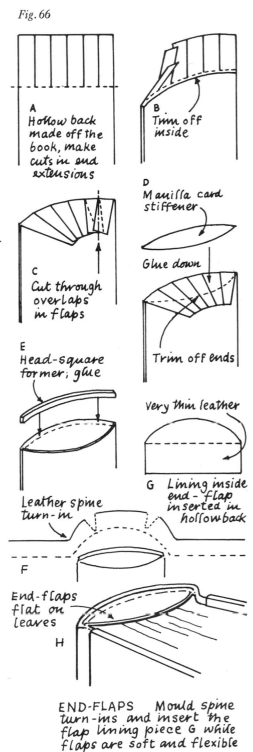

*Fig. 66*

A Hollow back made off the book, make cuts in end extensions

B Trim off inside

C Cut through overlaps in flaps

D Manilla card stiffener

Glue down

Trim off ends

E Head-square former; glue

Very thin leather

G Lining inside end-flap inserted in hollowback

Leather spine turn-in

F

End-flaps flat on leaves

H

END-FLAPS Mould spine turn-ins and insert the flap lining piece G while flaps are soft and flexible

## 14 Building surface structures

Relief effects are created by shaping of the boards; by applying objects and other materials to the board surface; by onlay and inlay of leather of different thicknesses.

Examples of relief work may be seen in many of the plates.

In the binding for *Jane Eyre* (Plate 20) the letter forms are assembled in ·75mm ($\frac{1}{32}$in) black board by cutting away and adding to make a relief in three levels. The board is then covered with leather and a negative template (from the discarded pieces of board) pressed into this assembled and covered board. The base leather is scarf-joined from grey, black, olive and purple skins (as Plate 81C and Fig. 67) with the onlays applied afterwards, the whole of the assembly being pared to ·75mm before covering.[1]

The binding for *The Island Race* (Plate 12) is an experiment derived from a memory of Graham Sutherland's portrait of Churchill and Peter Blake's Pop-art paintings, included here only to show an example of mixed media, including leather-covered 'Airfix' plastic figures recessed in board cut-outs, acrylic impasto paint, allowed to harden in relief, applied to the boards before covering, and feathered onlays. The design is an intellectually constructed one but it allowed various techniques to be tried out.

In the binding for *Don Quichotte* (Plate 106) illustrated by Dali, Henri Mercher achieves a remarkable effect of floating forms with the molten tin shapes stuck to the boards in actual relief, and given a *trompe l'oeil* effect by the black box-calf shadows, and coloured tooling. This designer's binding for *Promethée* includes the use of red tooling on a bright green morocco with relief forms in coloured plexiglas (Plate 107).

The total thickness of the boards in the binding for *The Swiss Watch* is 4·5mm ($\frac{3}{16}$in) to allow for the complex layering and leather turn-ins into the recesses over the acetate windows which protect the Swiss watch movements inset in the cavities (Plate 83A, Fig. 67). The covering leather is scarf-joined white pigskin, grey and black 'Oasis' moroccos with the same colours applied as feathered onlays. The circles are achieved partly by cutting out in one place and inlaying in another place and partly from onlays. The 'XIII' is an onlay recessed into a tooled impression flush with the surface (Fig. 29). The boards are cambered to produce a 2·5mm ($\frac{1}{8}$in) edge. Various ideas for board structures are shown in drawings (Plate 70). Other board structures are exemplified in the bindings of Edgar Allen Poe's *Tales of Mystery and Imagination* (Plates 31, 33B, 36) which is described in the drawings showing the integral designing of structural and visual elements, and *Alice in Wonderland,* illustrated by Dali (Fig. 68, Plate 20), which incorporates a cut-out enabling part of Dali's gold-stamped signature on the flyleaf to combine with the letters 'ce' on the cover and also with other visual elements in the design.

This book presented several problems. The major one was Dali's own illustrations which were free-style combined with elements such as caterpillars and butterflies painted in a *trompe l'oeil* manner,

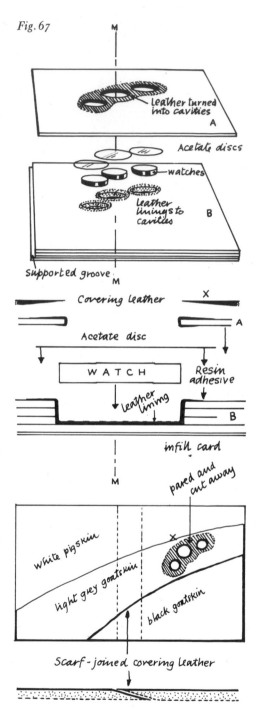

Fig. 67

'THE SWISS WATCH' Board structure

1 The imagery makes visual sense and is significant looked at vertically or horizontally.

*Fig. 68*

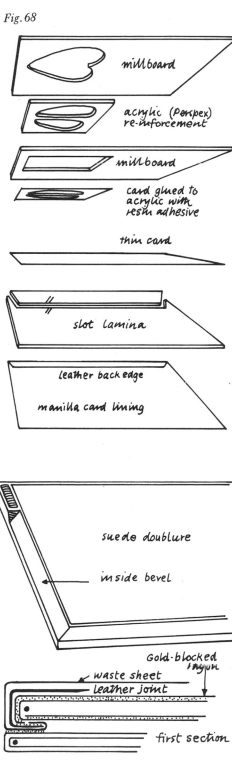

millboard

acrylic (Perspex) re-inforcement

millboard

card glued to acrylic with resin adhesive

thin card

slot lamina

leather back edge

manilla card lining

suede doublure

inside bevel

Gold-blocked layout

waste sheet

leather joint

first section

'ALICE...' Board structure and end sections

*Fig. 69*

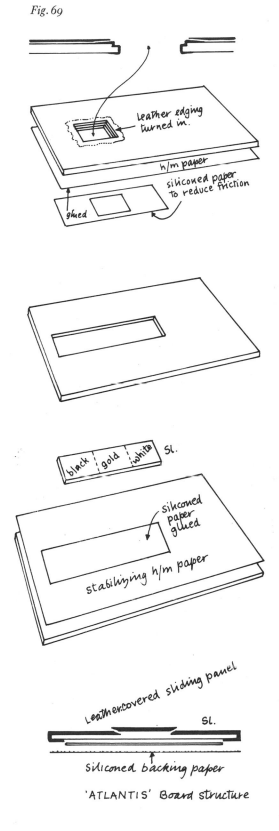

leather edging turned in.

h/m paper

siliconed paper to reduce friction

glued

black | gold | white   Sl.

siliconed paper glued

stabilizing h/m paper

leather-covered sliding panel

Sl.

siliconed backing paper

'ATLANTIS' Board structure

naturalistically. In the original edition of the story an integral
mental image is created which is strongly associated with Tenniel's
illustrations. Dali's interpretation conflicted with this mental image.
One method of interposing an intermediary between Dali's style and
the more universal visual associations with Tenniel would be to
make an illustration combining the two elements, which is now
laminated to the second flyleaf. The illustration combines the free
'ink-resist' technique (Plates 33A, 34E) with 'set-off' transfers from
images of cats and queens selected from magazine colour
supplements. A further link with Tenniel is made in some of the
images used in feathered onlays on the covers, mainly the back cover.
The result is a design mixture of Dali, Tenniel, Carroll and Smith,
in which technical considerations dominated the expression. The
board incorporates a perspex reinforcement of the cut-out, sharp
narrow bevels on the inside of the board (Figs. 68, 70), and the
end-band patterns which continue on the inside of the head and tail
board edges (Plate 34C) where these change to full thickness to
accommodate the tongue in the slot. The binding of *Atlantis* (Plate
70) incorporates a device for altering the mood of the image in the
small sliding panel, lower centre (Fig. 69).

A book-binding with a powerful formal quality – of being 'an object'
– is the one designed by Marcel Duchamp for a copy of *Ubu Roi* by
Alfred Jarry and bound by Mary Reynolds (Plate 104). The tan
morocco covers are each cut out in the shape of a bold letter 'U',
with a gold crown on the black-silk flyleaf showing through the
counter-space when the book is closed. The lower end of the spine
finishes short and the book-block is round-cornered there to follow
the shape of the 'U'. The letter 'B' is onlaid on the spine. The simple
symmetry of the short word has been turned to sculptural advantage
by the inventive Duchamp. The binding is physically related to the
title; the binding *is* literally the title.

Projections and relief work on book-covers have been historically
fairly common, but some collectors view its non-functional use as an
abuse of the medium. Whereas the relief work on the 'Churchill'
binding is negligible with the more pronounced projections
counter-recessed, the 'eye' on Faith Shannon's book-cover (Plate 35)
rises mountainously 15mm ($\frac{1}{2}$in) from the surrounding plain board
surface. This structure is built from papier-mâché over a balsa wood
foundation and domed smooth with a plaster/PVA mixture. The
visual pun is just missed in the crocuses growing from the pupil of
the eye. Protecting the watercolour miniature on white vellum is a
specially blown plate-glass 'cornea'. The covering leather is cut out
and turned in on the 'eyelids'. The rest of the binding, including the
title style and position, is treated in a traditional manner.

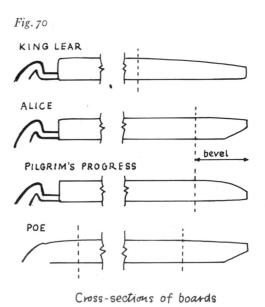

*Fig. 70*

KING LEAR

ALICE

bevel

PILGRIM'S PROGRESS

POE

Cross-sections of boards

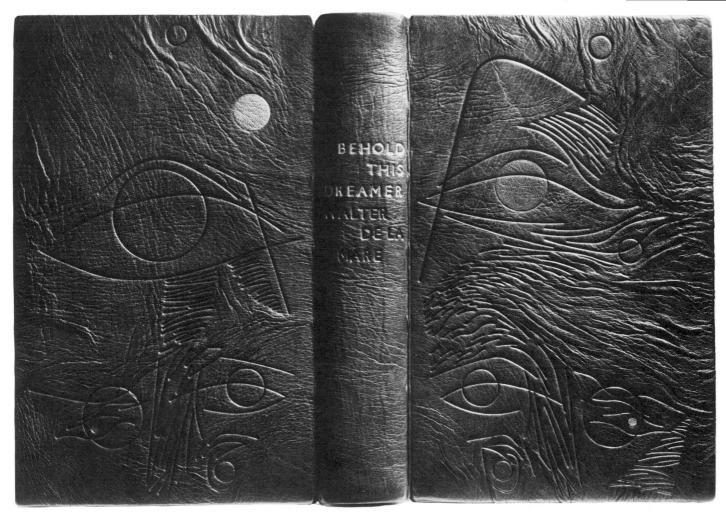

37

38

37    Edgar Mansfield
Walter de la Mare *Behold this Dreamer*
Native dyed dull purple morocco with tan and
brown variations. Inlaid and tooled. Puckered
covering. Title in palladium and blind
230 × 145 × 45mm (9 × 5¾ × 1¾in) 1959

38    Edgar Mansfield
Pierre Reverdy *Le Chant des Morts*
Deep red morocco. Inlaid native dyed
dark-blue with heavily induced grain creases.
Recessed onlays in red, natural and black
435 × 325 × 40mm (17 × 12¾ × 1½in)

39

39    Edgar Mansfield
Edith Sitwell *Five Poems* (1928)
Chrome-yellow morocco. Inlaid lemon-yellow,
natural, dove-grey and black. Black and blind tooling
280 × 205mm (11 × 8in) 1961

40    Edgar Mansfield
H. E. Bates *Through the Woods* Gollancz (1936).
Native dyed yellow morocco. Induced grain creases.
Blind-tooled in various tones
265 × 190 × 27mm (10½ × 7½ × 1in) 1952
Collection: British Museum

40

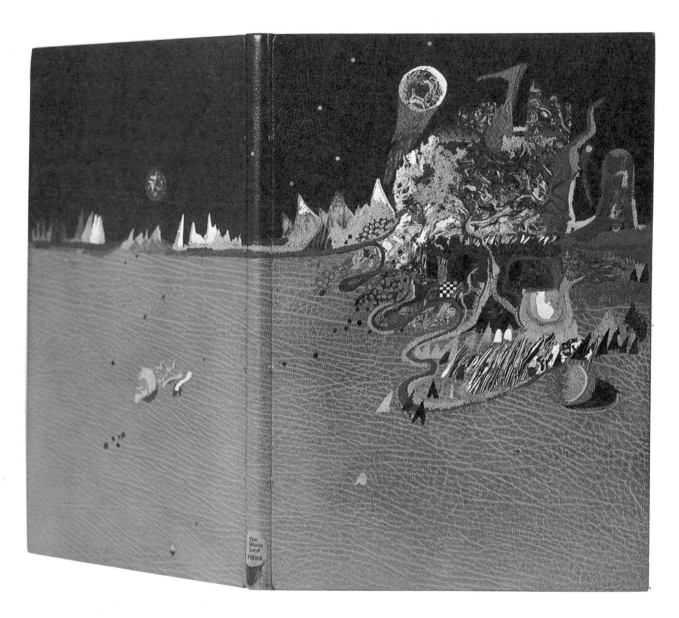

41   Philip Smith
T. S. Eliot *The Waste Land* Officina Bodoni Press.
Scarf-joined 'Oasis' morocco. Feathered onlays and maril. Hand-painted
doublures and book-box
295 × 205 × 15mm (11½ × 8 × ⅝in) 1971
Collection: Duncan Houx Olmsted, USA

42    Philip Smith

Charlotte Brontë *Jane Eyre* illustrated by Ethel Gabin.
Scarf-joined moroccos, feathered onlays and maril, laminated boards cut in
relief. Tongue and slot board attachment
375 × 290 × 35mm (14¾ × 11½ × 1⅜in) 1970
Private collection

43    Philip Smith
J. R. R. Tolkien *The Lord of the Rings* 1970-71
Front of 6-unit book-wall. Walnut, aluminium and Perspex case made by Desmond Ryan. Scarf-joined 'Oasis'
goatskin. Feathered onlays and maril. Lower centre book covered in puckered silver kid. Palladium and gold
edges and titles. On removable feet. 575 × 539 × 75mm (22⅝ × 21½ × 3in) Collection: Colin and Charlotte Franklin

44    Philip Smith
*The Lord of the Rings* Front of book-wall

44

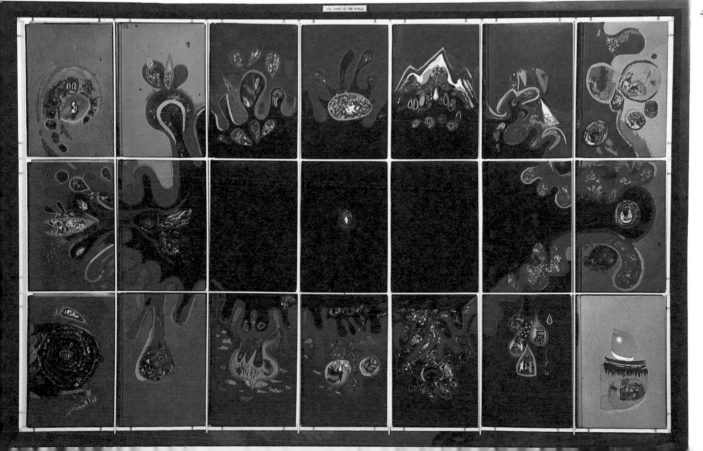

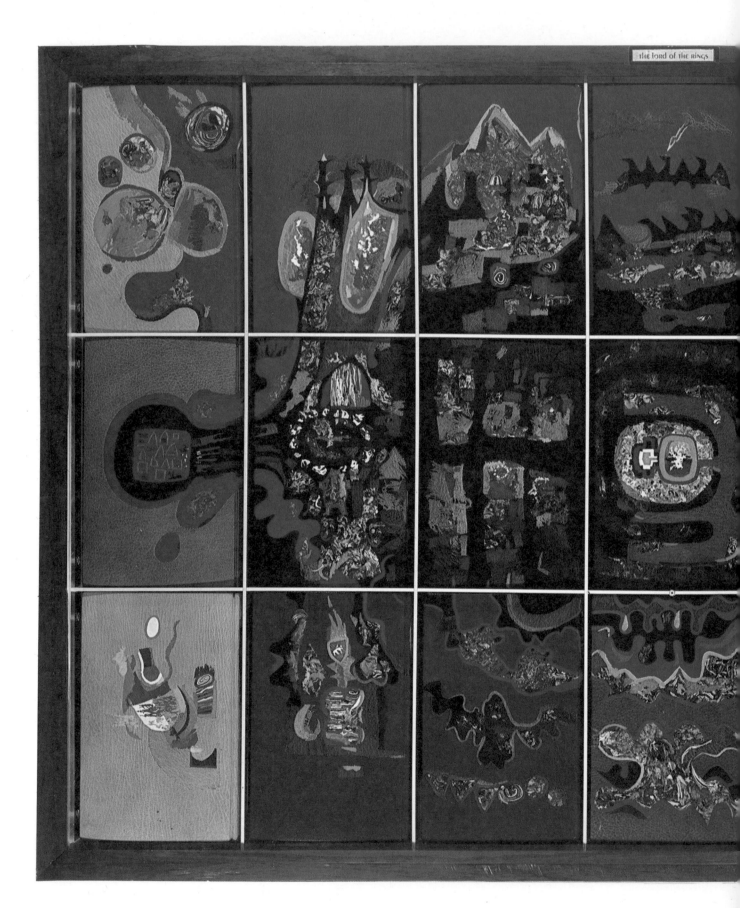

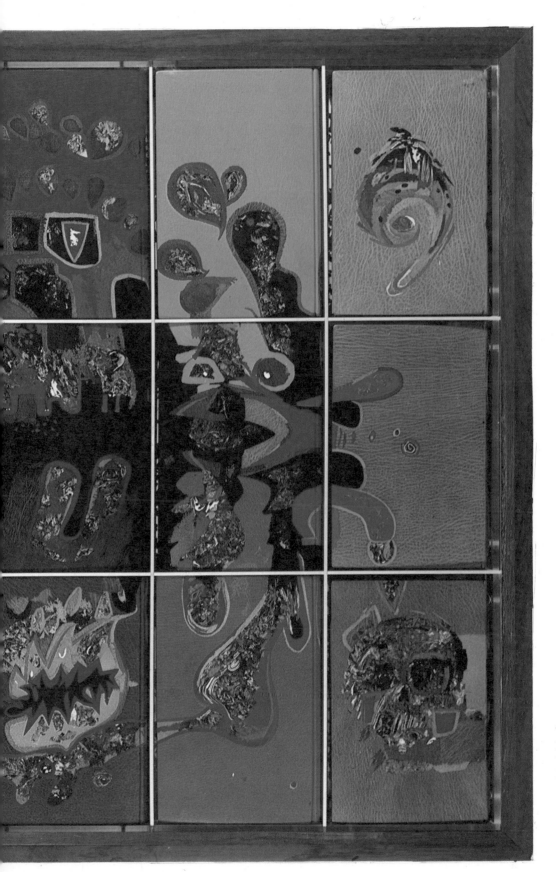

45  Philip Smith
J. R. R. Tolkien *The Lord of the Rings*
 made 1968–9
Book-wall. Seven sets of the three-
volume edition. Upper row is Vol. 1;
centre row is Vol. 2; lower row is Vol. 3.
Bound in scarf-joined moroccos, with
feathered onlays and maril; some blind
tooling; titles and edges in gold and
palladium. Rosewood, aluminium and
perspex case made by Desmond Ryan
1172 × 770 × 76mm (46¼ × 30¼ × 3in)
Collection: Colin and Charlotte Franklin

46    Philip Smith
John Bunyan *The Pilgrim's Progress* Cresset Press. (1928)
Black 'Oasis' goatskin over recessed and profiled boards. Gold puckered kid in
recesses (Section 19, Figs. 91, 99). Back board. 1972

47    Philip Smith
*The Pilgrim's Progress* Front board
365 × 273 × 50mm (14⅜ × 10¾ × 2in)
Collection: Major William Spowers

48 Philip Smith
J. R. R. Tolkien *The Lord of the Rings* 1973
Deluxe India paper single volume edition. 'Dual landscape' design in puckered
and modelled silver kid and maril; figured mother-of-pearl insets. Hand-painted
endpapers. Palladium and gold edges
230 × 150 × 30mm (9 × 6 × 1⅛in)

49 Philip Smith
Pietro Bembo *On Etna* Officina Bodoni limited edition (1969) 1974
Scarf-joined 'Oasis' feathered and punched onlays and maril. Hand-painted
endpapers
235 × 160 × 22mm (9¼ × 6¼ × ⅞in)
Collection: Tony Appleton

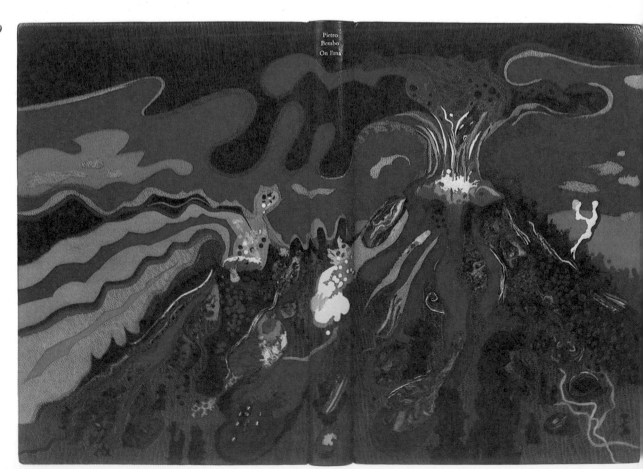

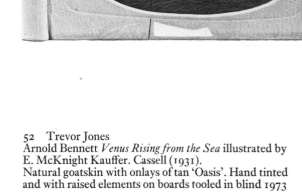

50    Trevor Jones
James Joyce *Finnegan's Wake* Faber and Faber.
Black niger morocco modelled over raised elements. Blind
and gold tooling 225 × 150 × 40mm (8⅞ × 6 × 1½in) 1958
Collection: Victoria and Albert Museum

51    Trevor Jones
Herman Melville *Benito Cereno* illustrated by
E. McKnight Kauffer. Nonesuch Press (1926).
Natural morocco. Recessed and raised inlays. Blind tooling
and stamped background texture
310 × 195 × 22mm (12¼ × 7¾ × ⅞in) 1961
Collection: Maggs Bros

52    Trevor Jones
Arnold Bennett *Venus Rising from the Sea* illustrated by
E. McKnight Kauffer. Cassell (1931).
Natural goatskin with onlays of tan 'Oasis'. Hand tinted
and with raised elements on boards tooled in blind 1973

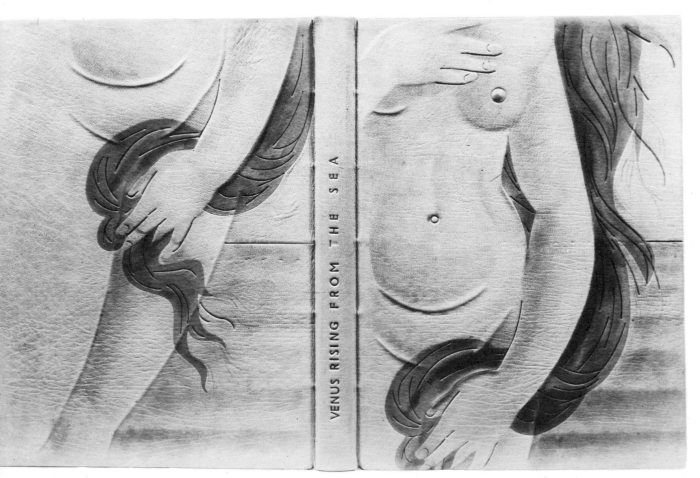

## 15 Illustrated and painted bindings

Faith Shannon creates exquisitely accurate botanical illustrations often used in an advertising context. In two bindings representing her recent work she applies her gift for delicate craftsmanship with the brush to padded silk and linen. The inspiration in both cases was the illustrations in the books, which are interpreted with painstaking care as padded forms grafted on to the surface of the cover.

In the binding for *The Fruitist* (Plate 53) the method used was to paint the silk which was then embroidered, filled with kapok and quilted on a fine stretched linen base. The padded-silk illustration was at first placed directly against the green leather but later removed and sewn to a velvet panel which was inset in the board. This second attempt achieves more sympathetic relationships. Narrow strips of marbled paper matching the endpapers were glued to the cut edge of the hexagonal recess.

The binding for *Alice through the Looking Glass*[1] was commissioned as an exhibition piece and the quilted figure entering the front board and emerging from the back board has something of the pop-art doll-like quality of Jan Howarth figures. It is an accurate transcription (although with added colour) of the Tenniel illustration. This figure is hand-painted on fine linen and the softly padded embroidery is glued for rigidity to a shaped 'hoop'. The figures are then glued with PVA to the silver kid which has been recess-pared over a template (method as in Fig. 19).

Painting designs on leather with dyes is one method of avoiding the difficulties and limitations usually imposed by traditional techniques, such as tooling, onlay and inlay, in the spontaneous expression of ideas. The binder does, however, need to know the chemistry of dyes and the chemistry of the particular leather he is treating if the effects he creates are to remain stable. Dyes on leather have been notoriously fugitive to light and to chemical change due to pH properties and salts in the skin. Once these factors are understood (*41*, *55*), the scope will be limited only by the creative sensibility, ingenuity and skill of the bookbinder, without which even the most fantastic techniques will not create an art form.

Several bookbinders have occasionally used dyes simply painted on to the leather (usually combined with tooling); for example, Arthur Johnson and Trevor Jones in England (Plate 52). Used in this way, compared with the deep, rich, full-bodied finish of onlay from the tannery-dyed skin, the dyes leave a thin-bodied, faded and 'hairy-edged' shape, due to creep into the interstices of the grain. The use of a resist is a method which would prevent the accidental spreading of the dye.

Ursula Katzenstein, a Brazilian bookbinder, uses a Japanese version of batik, called Roketsu Zome, on leather. She paints (in a bold folk-art manner) the slightly damped leather with a hot wax resist, brushes the dye over the surface, removes the wax selectively and re-paints to obtain simulated transparent, craquelé and other effects. The Sumerians and ancient Egyptians used a wax resist batik on

1 See Plate 2, p. 10 *Aspects of Modern British Crafts*, Royal Scottish Museum, Edinburgh, Catalogue 1973.

cloth many thousands of years ago. Painting and staining
bookbindings was a technique used on early European bookbindings
before the invention of onlay and inlay techniques.

53   Faith Shannon
B. Maund *The Fruitist* London (1880)
Green hard-grain morocco. Inset panel of dark-green velvet with hand-painted
embroidered and quilted silk. The hexagonal panels are edged with the marble
paper used for the flyleaves and doublures. Title hand-written on hand-made
paper label. Padded velvet-lined book-box
234 × 184 × 25mm (9¼ × 7¼ × 1in) 1972

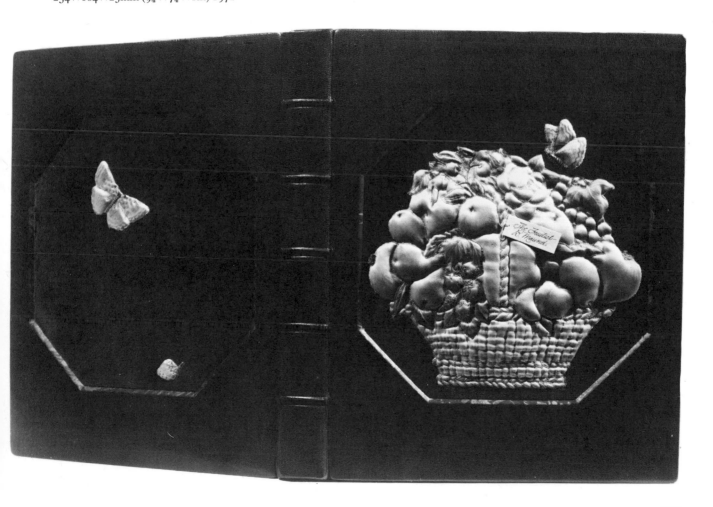

There are differing opinions about titling a 'one-off' binding. Any owner will distinguish it by the uniqueness of its imagery or design. He will know what he has and from this point of view a title is superfluous. Tradition dies hard however, so that titles are sometimes demanded by a collector. A series of volumes or a set requires some other distinguishing mark, even if it be a volume number only. Whatever the outcome the titling of an expressive binding should integrate with the general idiom and movement of the rest of the design (Plates 42, 10A). The spine is the traditional position for a title, but titles have also appeared on foredges (a recent version is shown in Plate 34C) and commercial practice is to advertise the title on the front cover (Plates 5, 58; see also Plate 53).

Several bindings illustrated herein make use of the title as a means towards expressing the character of the book (Plate 21) or as its only imagery (Plate 17). If type is used in titling then it should relate to the typographic style of the title page or text type faces. Built-up lettering should relate to the rest of the built-up tooling in weight and character. I have used all these methods although my inclination now is to make the title out of leather (Plate 68A); in this way no other medium is brought in. One typical method I have used is type-set and stamped titling (and other data such as author, editor, publisher, date).

A piece of leather is onlaid with fragments which will connect it to the other movements in the imagery, or left plain, and pared to a caliper which will take an impression. The impression area is stabilized by gluing a piece of torn gilder's tissue to the flesh side. The piece of leather is then held by self-adhesive tape to a piece of blotting paper (to take the impression) mounted on a piece of card (Fig. 34). The card is inserted up to lay edges in a converted Adana printing press[1] (or blocking press) and a blind impression is made. The impression is glaired in and gold leaf or palladium, etc., applied (Fig. 71). The title piece is now blocked, cleaned out and removed from the support. The leather is pared to shape and glued in position on the spine and linked up with further onlays (Plate 81A). As the title piece made in this way is normally applied after covering the extra thickness of the onlay may be accommodated by reducing the leather lining over the hollow back in that area with glass-paper. I usually work in any 'separate' title piece as the last part of the imagery, after the doublures or other board linings have been put down. Special first fly-leaves are usually put down (made) over the unsewn leather joint when this is integral with the board lining (Fig. 28). The finished binding is then pressed between polished plates or formica-lined pressing boards. After pressing, the whole of the leather surfaces may be polished with heated polishing irons; heavier grains may be rolled with a box-wood roller, special attention being paid to the cushioning or bevels which will have escaped pressure from the plates.

The final operation with a leather binding will be application of a varnish, or preferably an invisible micro-crystalline wax. Varnishes tend to discolour; the wax is colourless. Both varnish and wax should

1 I first saw this adaptation used by Mr S. Cockerell. An electric smoothing iron element is screwed to the fixed platen to heat the type.

be applied with a soft cloth or chamois with circular movements. The last two operations protect the binding from hygroscopic movement; the heated iron hardens and 'fixes' the grain and the wax seals it against handling and against harmful gases in the atmosphere.

## Gold and tooling

Gold tooling has great decorative power, but it has rarely been used for its expressive qualities. There can be no doubt that gold tooling on leather is an ideal means of decoration (Fig. 71), for its richness, untarnishing permanence and light reflecting quality, but it has a 'pretty' as opposed to an expressive effect.

Some of its most handsome effects have been achieved with the massing of small units in an all-over texture as in the seventeenth-century English 'cottage style' bindings or in Raymonde Mondange's massed gouge configurations to Paul Bonet's designs. Here the play and swirl of light is that of a virtuoso. Gold needs contrast and a domed, faceted or angled surface, a surface which changes direction, curves as in the Bonets, doming as in Sydney Cockerell's binding for *Comus* (Plate 5 Catalogue of *Modern British Bookbindings, Designer Bookbinders*, 1971) where pressure to put in large domed dots at an angle is achieved by means of one of the most interesting mechanical aids of the hand-binder, adapted from a hydraulic aircraft undercarriage strut: his 'ram'. William Matthews, another exponent of gold tooling, creates a textured reflection from his massed gold by engraving the tool surface with small 'V'-cuts and all surfaces are pressed in contact with the leather (Fig. 72). The use of gold leaf is traditionally associated with religion. Gold backgrounds in icons, mosaics and panels on jewelled bindings signified heaven, or eternity. They also symbolized the power and wealth of the Church. The use of gold for tooling appears to have originated in the Middle East, perhaps Persia, where liquid gold painted in impressions can be seen on bindings before the twelfth century AD (*38*, p. 173).

The whole ethos of modern design, especially abstract, and abstraction (which begins from natural or everyday objects) runs counter to the idea of prettiness in art, and in bookbinding, one of the last strongholds of conservative art, there is a definite movement away from gold tooling. Decorative designers, however, are reluctant to give up this medium and it often happens that in an intermediate stage in the evolution of an individual's work there will be a mixture of, say, incrustations of plastics or wood together with gold or blind tooling. This often indicates artistic indecision and inconsistency, but there is no rule against a sensitive artist relating such a mixture of media. Gold blocking (Plates 10C, 15) (or tooling) can be used with the quality of the surface reflectance varied from rough to smooth (dull to brilliant) and from deep yellow to almost white gold. Palladium, platinum and anodized aluminium foils of many colours are also used by bookbinders to create special effects.

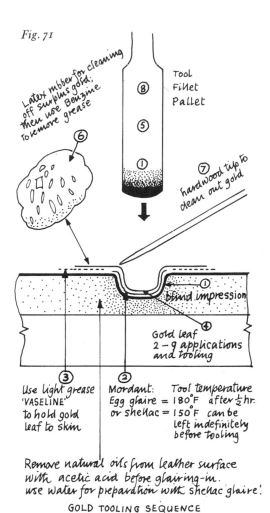

Fig. 71

GOLD TOOLING SEQUENCE

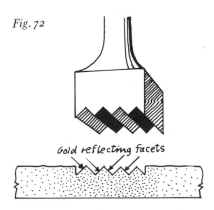

Fig. 72

Gold reflecting facets

Schematic representation of William Matthew's technique

Metallized edge treatment continues to be used by all schools of bookbinding both for its handsome quality/opulence effects and for its protective function, but these edges can be treated expressively by painting, gauffering, engraving, chiselling and sculpting, and colouring in different ways (Plates 11, 14, 34C) (*38*, Ch. VIII). In conjunction with colour on expressive bookbinding gold (and to a lesser extent 'silver'), is extremely difficult to harmonize because it retains its mystic associations even today, and it is probably sensible to use it where the evocation of these emotions is required.

Gold, for the expression of 'meaning beyond the decorative' is probably too powerful (in the sense of the invisibility of means which the book typographer aims at), to get beyond the stage of 'blinding' the viewer – 'Oh! isn't it beautiful – or – incredible.' The main aim of the typographic design of book texts is to draw attention to the meaning of the words, not to obtrude the earmarks and quirks of individual letter forms. The blend of elements in a book/binding is ideally designed to draw attention to meaning, not means.

The composite drawing (Fig. 71) describes by numbers the sequence of operations in preparing and tooling an impression. Fig. 4 shows the different holding and sighting methods in the British and Continental traditions. (The Cockerell cylindrical handle is formed from rolled asbestos.) To obtain greater solidity (without minute cracks) in the tooling several layers of gold leaf may be laid and tooled in. Check the results through a watchmaker's eye-glass! If the gold does not take it should be cleaned out (where loose) and prepared again and the procedure repeated until the required perfection is obtained. Normally a design is measured out on thin hand-made bank-paper and adapted to available tools, the pattern may be darkened in for clarity by tooling warm and picking up colour from carbon paper (touching the latter with the warm tool). The paper pattern is fixed to the book-cover with self-adhesive tape (cutting holes in blank spaces may be convenient for fixing down); the pattern is tooled through the paper on to the leather. After removing the paper the leather may be tooled blind again, prepared with mordant and re-tooled several times with gold leaf. For small detailed tools it may be thought more convenient to mark in main directional guide lines with a folder, glaire up the whole area or cover and lay gold leaf. The tooling is then done direct and freehand through the gold leaf. Another method is to dab the tool face lightly on a greasy pad, pick up the leaf on the finishing tool and make the impression. This is often done with dots or small-line pallets when mending, or when using ribbon gold on a roll or fillet.

*Gold tooling* by Emilio Brugalla

The finishing tool has a deeply engraved bronze face on a shank, with a long tang set into a handle. The wooden handle should be smooth and slightly pear shaped (Fig. 4) so that the hand will not slip when putting in the impression on leather. The sensibility of the hand and the suppleness of the fore arm should not be neutralized by nervous tensions. It is not necessary to curl the fingers right round the handle nor to fold the thumb over the top end of the handle; it is a mistake to think that one will impress the tool better this way. In doing so, he who vigorously presses it on the leather with more than necessary force creates a muscular contraction consequently cramping the wrist and fore-arm. This noticeably affects the sensitivity of the hand so indispensable in feeling the amount of pressure on the tool face. The skilfully controlled 'touch-down' registers the tool in the impression previously made in the leather by the same tool. The hand is relaxed quite perceptibly on the handle without actually letting go of it. These operations should be made in a perfectly relaxed manner.

Immediately the tool is felt to be in the impression one slowly but firmly grips it without tensing the nerves, and at a stroke an adequate impression is made. Just enough pressure is applied without overdoing it, and taking into account the nature of the engraving; whether it is solid, hatched, or hollow (outlined); engraved boldly, finely or in pointille.

Wrist articulation easily permits a light rotary or rocking motion enabling all the edges of the engraved drawing, starting at the centre or heart of the tool, to be impressed. At this moment the heat in the tool, passing through the gold leaf laid over and into the impression, coagulates the glaire or shellac previously painted in, and holds the gold in its trace. One simply removes the surplus gold and the tooling is complete.

Small tools are those which have a face area of under two square centimeters over-all as well as being delicately figured. It is not necessary to have a concentrated pressure in order to obtain neat, clean and brilliant tooling. The secret of good tooling lies in the natural sensitivity of the hand that acts instinctively. The hand should never make gratuitous movements. The violin virtuoso does not take the bow tightly in his hand; on the contrary it is held lightly by the finger tips. It is the same with hand tooling.

With large tools one uses a totally different technique. In this case the strength of the hand is not sufficient. So one leans heavily with the flat of the shoulder against the wrist; at the same time with the left arm under the bench one exerts a vertical pressure upwards.

## Some blocking procedures

A drawing is prepared in black ink on white card or a transparent base such as Tri-acetate film, preferably $\times 1\frac{1}{2}$ actual size. The drawing is photographically reduced by the blockmaker on to a sensitized metal plate (8 gauge or 5 gauge). This can be of zinc alloy (zinco) or brass (partly hand-engraved) but a very satisfactory metal is the one known as Chemac (a patent non-tarnishing copper alloy) of a quality and hardness between the two former metals.[1] The

1 The Chemac block is made by Mackrell & Co, Industrial Estate, Colchester Road, Witham, Essex, England.

design is etched to a required depth for blocking on leather, routed and cut to the edges of the image.

The block is pressed into a piece of thick blotting paper; the impression area is cut out and temporarily fixed in position to the book cover with self-adhesive tape. A piece of newsprint is glued to the back of the block with PVA, the block set in the impression on the paper template and the back of the block (on the newsprint) applied with more PVA. The book-board is opened and jigged up to lay edges under the heated blocking platen (180°F or 82°C). The platen is lowered to pick up the glued block (held down for about three seconds) from the paper impression, the book removed and the paper pattern taken off the cover. The book is again jigged to the lays and a blind impression made in the leather. This is prepared as for tooling gold leaf and blocked in two or three times until satisfactory. A 'worn' and polished block gives a livelier impression than a sharp-edged one; if the gold leaf is allowed to remain slightly up the sides of the impressions it also takes away a little of the overall flat look of blocking. I myself tend to design blocks so that hand tooling can be added in places to give a less mechanical look and prefer not to 'clean-out' too severely on blocking. The impression may be left natural blind or inked in. If one has no access to a blocking press good work may be done using a wide daylight iron nipping press. The block is heated on the finishing stove and placed manually in the prepared position on the leather. The book-block and back board is draped so that it falls clear of the upper platen over a built-up pile of pressing boards. Pressure is applied over the centre of the block by screwing down the top platen. The block (cooled) may now be rolled with a quick-dry printing ink and carefully registered in the blind impression and gently nipped. The inked impression is allowed two days to dry out before painting in a varnish (e.g. Vinalak).

The separated board (tongue and slot attachment) was developed partly to simplify blocking procedures on larger books. Plates 8A and 15, for example, are treated in the above ways. The block impressions which are partly gold and part black were achieved by preparing part of the impression with glaire and laying the gold leaf to a determined edge (say half-way across the impression) then later inking up the other part of the block to fill in the rest of the impression.

Plate 8C shows another variation where onlays were made on a loose covering leather which was then run through a sewing machine, covered and then blocked part gold and part black, with tooling added. Plate 9A shows blocking off the edge of the board; the book and lays being moved about under the press with the block stuck under the pressure centre.

54A

54B

54A & B
*The Foret Apocalypse* Bronze coffer. Lid designed by Dali,
cast by André Susse, gems and stones set by Sterle. 1958–61
860 × 780 × 150mm (34 × 30¾ × 6in). Weight 200 kilos (440lbs)

55   Hugo Peller
Jeremias Gotthelf *Gesammelte Werke*
18 volumes with tooled lines linking across all the spines.
Brown morocco, crimson title-piece 1958

55

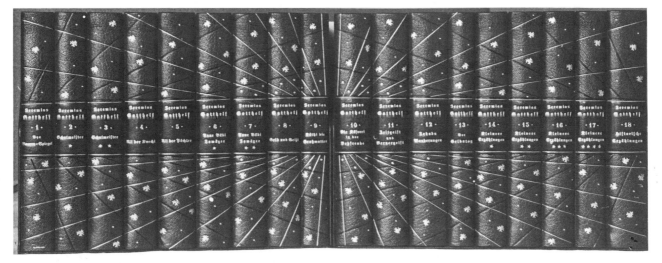

56

57

56   Peter Waters
*Chinese Calligraphy and Painting in the Collection of
John M. Crawford Jr*
Black goatskin. Multicoloured onlays, printed
stamps and gold tooling
325 × 240 × 45mm (12¾ × 9½ × 1¾in) 1964
Private collection

57   Peter Waters
*French and Italian Collectors and their Bindings*
Native red niger goatskin. Gold and blind tooling
(elongated lettering)
330 × 280 × 58mm (13 × 11 × 2¼in) 1964
Private collection

58   K. G. Pontus Hulten *The Machine* Museum of Modern Art New York 1968
Exhibition catalogue. Cover designed by Anders Österlin from photograph
by Alicia Legg. Printed and pressed tin. (Section 17)
245 × 217 × 13mm (9⅝ × 8½ × ½in)

## 17 Metal bindings

*The Foret 'Apocalypse'* (Plate 54)

In 1958 Joseph Foret, the Paris publisher, had the idea of bringing together into one work of art all the disciplines required in the production of a book, in order 'to leave to the world a testimony of our time before the end of Craftsmanship and Printing'. Writers, artists, designers, illustrators, printers and craftsmen were all to be represented and were commissioned to participate in this ambitious venture. The subject of Monsieur Foret's inspiration was the last and most enigmatic book of the Bible, *The Apocalypse* or *Revelation of St John*, a work of great poetic power and psychological insight into the nature of man.[1]

Joseph Foret views the book (combining several arts) as a greater vehicle of art than painting. Seven painters of various schools, seven writers and seven illustrators joined forces to illustrate the book and each other's comments on 'the End of the World'. It appears that all these artists and writers viewed the meaning of the Revelation of St John in temporal and spatial terms.

The original illustrations are on carefully selected sheep's parchment not yet assembled into codex form. The book will be kept in an enormous coffer shaped to imitate a book. On the lid of the coffer, which weighs 440lbs, is a bronze panel designed and partly executed by Salvador Dali. This design was contrived with typical Dali enthusiasm and intellect, beginning with a stroke of an axe into the original wax tablet and ending with a nail-bomb explosion! The prosaic knives and forks are a gesture to contemporary art mixed with some official Biblical symbolism in the jewels and semi-precious stones set by master jewellers.

It took calligrapher Micheline Nicolas 2,000 hours to write; and a further 4,000 hours for the gilding.

By producing an object of this size and weight Monsieur Foret was ensuring that this work, like some of the heavy chained medieval manuscripts, would not easily be stolen, and at the same time affording Dali one more opportunity to immortalize his personality. The above example is of course not strictly speaking a bookbinding, but the concept was probably evoked by certain medieval works. Metal spines, hinges, bosses and corners, clasps and metal 'findings' for the insetting of precious stones, are common features of Byzantine and other early liturgical books. Metal was similarly used in some Victorian bibles and albums. On the whole they proved too rigid and heavy for the attachments to the book-block and soon pulled away. Henri Mercher and other designers of hand-bound books in France are already using light metal supports for their binding decoration. The following example shows a direction in which light-weight metal covers might be explored by hand-binders.

1 For full details on this work see Joseph Foret's catalogue *The World's Wonder Book*, rue de La Fayette, Paris.

*The Machine*

Exhibition Catalogue, Museum of Modern Art, New York, 1968.
Produced in Sweden (Plate 58).

This is a catalogue of works by artists who make some comment on
technology and the machine. In spite of the wealth of ideas
demonstrated by the exhibits the producers of the cover have
missed an incredible opportunity to use this different medium
imaginatively. Notwithstanding its weak design, both functionally
and visually, it is included here, not because it is the only existing
metal-covered commercial book, but because no other example has
come into my hands; and because it might give bookbinding
designers some ideas which would really exploit the medium.

The art-paper book-block is adhesive bound with a hot-melt PVA.
The cover is riveted and hinged to a rather wide box-spine and is of
printed pressed steel. The colours are greenish-greys and black
with a yellow car and lettered 'The Machine' in red. The stamping
of the tin-plated steel has caused the front cover to buckle and
although the rest of the edges of the thin metal have been turned in,
the rounded corners are dangerously sharp. It does not appear that
a bookbinding designer was consulted!

Sets of volumes offer interesting possibilities to the artist. They permit work on a larger scale than is usually possible with single volumes. In the past books in sets have been bound uniformly, in the same colour leather and with title pieces and spine panels linked in horizontal bands across several volumes. Some bookbinders, notably Hugo Peller (Plate 55), and also, I believe, Paul Bonet, have linked their spine designs so that a different part of an overall design occurs on each volume, analogous to the collating marks on signature (section) backs.

The concept of the book-wall includes functional and rational purposes although it was originally conceived emotionally as an art object. The book-walls made to date are displayed in cases designed for exhibition security, but there is no problem in having cases made up with sliding or hinged panels for easy access to the books. The book-wall can be purpose-built for the library or the drawing room, where it could conceivably be used as a room-divider. A special non-reflective ultra-violet filter glass could be incorporated in the case. If one has elaborate bindings the sensible way to display these treasures is to show the whole of the covers, not just the small area of the spine in a shelf. It is possible to present sets of volumes from two upwards as free-standing objects and even one volume may be shown standing in a transparent display container. A development in hand is the use of separate slotted book-containers making possible variations in the shape and arrangement of a set of linked bindings.

The design problems involved in the book-wall are considerable if amorphous designs are to be unified into one object. Only one book can be read at a time and each individual binding must convey a feeling of completeness and unity in its design as well as combining to form part of a larger whole in the book-wall, and the imagery should be significant of the volume it encloses.[1] A set of forty-two volumes of Shakespeare's works would present a considerable challenge from this point of view. In the next section the way the book-wall was conceived and designed is discussed.

A series of books in which there is a development of images rather than one over-all image is shown in sequence in Plates 26, 27. The *Leonardo* bindings reveal their 'message' (i.e. give the complete experience) only if one possesses all the volumes. This design is based on the idea of a gradual discovery of order out of chaos in Leonardo da Vinci's life and work, and thus only indirectly bears on the actual contents of the books. Allusions to the contents are hidden in the maril letter forms.

In 1973 Peter Weiersmuller, a young Swiss bookbinder, arranged a set of four volumes of Novalis *Works* – with leather spines and sculpted wooden covers, partly painted, gilded or polished with freely drawn abstract configurations – spaced out like shelves in a slotted Plexiglas container. This enabled the painted book-edges to be displayed. This artist also is interested in the book as sculpture, with cut-outs, modelling, and Plexiglas insets, displayed in transparent slipcases and other containers. I discovered this work while going to press and was unable to include an illustration.

1 Other aspects of the book-wall are considered in (56) together with structural specifications.

## The book-wall

Bookbinders of different persuasions use different approaches in evolving a decorative or expressive bookbinding, and most of the issues bearing on this are listed in Chart 1. I have chosen my work on the book-walls to describe some of those which are involved in creative bookbinding processes. The main differences between kinds of bookbinding lie in the inception stages, and depend on the binder's concept of the book, i.e. whether design is a vehicle for the expression of 'pure' formal elements (in the abstract) or for the use of these in one of several ways relating to the book. Apart from motivating forces, all bookbinding involves some kind of planning and some method of making up, but not all bookbinders are interested in, or have the ability, inclination or special skills required to relate the image to the book content other than by title or general subject matter, which, although integrally deficient, may be sufficient for most binders and collectors. In the large book-wall (Plate 45) several concepts are involved and a more ambitious project is attempted. The small book-wall (Plate 43) is the expression of a simpler theme; it contains fewer elements, which results in an easier and more direct appeal.

I have often chosen *The Lord of the Rings* by Professor J. R. R. Tolkien as a subject for binding, because this offers a complete world with its landscapes, its different psychological types (expressed as elves, dwarves, men, hobbits and other creatures) and its archetypal symbols of man's quest for goodness, truth and individuality. It is one of the most moving accounts of endurance, dedication, fortitude and self-sacrifice in imaginative fiction. It is not possible to represent this world in a single image even as it is not possible to express Shakespeare's work in one image. The large book-wall was the result of several factors coming together at an appropriate moment. One was my love for this epic tale. The second was the need to find some form which would do justice to the scale of the writing and give expression to more than a small part of it. The third factor was the invitation from Josef Stemmle to exhibit my work at Ascona. For this exhibition I needed to find about forty works, and I had over two years' grace to prepare it. I had already read *The Lord of the Rings* several times and thought that I would order several copies of the book for individual bindings. I had to find a centre piece to hang the exhibition around. I had made no large bindings at that time but bindings for this book were much in my thoughts. I remember I was clearing some space in my studio and paused to rest for a moment. Suddenly I saw what I had to do to answer these problems. There was to be a wall of books containing seven sets of three volumes with images both sides representing the major opposing forces in the tale. I saw the black eye of Mordor on one side – a simple image of black on red; and a plan of the seven-walled city of Minas Tirith on the other – a complex image of many colours.

I quickly noted down on a scrap of paper all the details which came with this moment of insight. Each book was to contain a part of the design from the front and the back of the wall, linked by the spine.

It was analogous to the hierarchy of the world, with wholes composed of parts, and again those parts composed of lesser parts, but all contributing in many ways to the working of the whole. The idea that the book is read in time, goes on in time, but is all there, was to be represented by the series of individual images linked from one book to the next in three rows of seven books as a kind of story-board sequence. Each set of three volumes, of which this edition of the book is made up, should contain something of the macro-images and, distributed vertically, could be made to contain parts of that image conveying the mood from the beginning, the middle and the final parts of the book. Having synthesized the large scale problems and worked out the concept of the book-wall, it remained now a matter of designing for the structural requirements, and of discovering how each tri-partite binding image (front, back and spine) would compose when the complementary parts of the image from the back and front faces of the wall were juxtaposed, with the spine areas being used for adjustments to individual image linkage.

Having a 'given' scheme already on paper the next step was to draw out the front and back macro-images in rectangles calculated in size from the arrangement of the twenty-one books in a frame. Two scale frames were drawn out and each individual back and front micro-image (in a simple line form) was tried for linkage, and the various compositions were adjusted as units (Figs. 73, 74). A play between the two scales, the macro-images and the individual tri-partite micro-images, by assembling and taking apart, resulted in the making of the colour sketch at a later stage. Before this, however, there was the systematic work of reading, and making charts of events and thematic ideas and moods which had to be worked into the larger scheme in the frames. From these charts and tables the smaller details of colour and all incidental forms would be worked in.

I calculated the number of chapters in the epic and their division into twenty-one parts. This worked out at three chapters per cover or unit of the book-wall. Colour was no problem because one of Professor Tolkien's talents lay in the clear colour descriptions which created a background mood throughout the epic. I had made out several charts with twenty-one 'boxes' in which to make comments, to note colours, events and characteristic moods during the readings. Each 'box' represented the chapter groupings and their designation into set, book and chapter numbers. Anything stimulating my imagination was also noted in the appropriate box. I use this technique whenever I have a creative work to bind. I also made small colour sketches as anything occurred visually, and all this accumulated material was tested against the original insight images, and incorporated without altering these. It was a matter of clarifying visual detail. The result was the two finished colour sketches indicated in Plate 80A. Incidents which seemed to be outside the main conflict of the protagonists were depicted on the corner books of the wall, because owing to the circular and oval shapes of the macro-images, the corner books lie outside them, but are included in the 'story-board' sequence. In the two grids given in

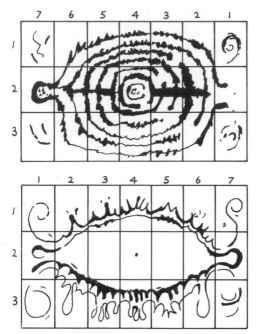

Main compositional movement of front of book-wall at an intermediate stage. Based on subject matter of book. Above: back of book-wall.

*Fig. 73*

*Fig. 74*

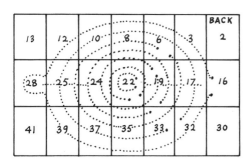

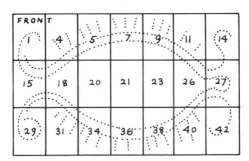

The numbers represent the approximate incidental sequence of frames (subject matter)

Figs. 73, 74 the sequence numbers are written inside the boxes, set numbers along the top and the volume numbers down the side.

My method is to make 'final' sketches to a small (perhaps $\frac{1}{3}$) scale so that detail is vague and allows for more spontaneity in handling and interpretation through the medium of onlay. With feathered onlays and maril designing often comes directly out of the materials[2] to produce a more fluid and spontaneous expression. The images are crypto-figurative, that is they are based on abstraction from the so-called naturalistic reality. Often several images are combined within each other to create a visual ambiguity.[3] There is an uncertainty about these images which allows an open-ended situation for the viewer, but the artist's insight will nevertheless lead him in a predictable direction. This kind of surrealistic expressionism seems to me the best means of creating visual expressions from literary expression. It should not be so abstract that it becomes an exercise in arbitrary 'basic design'.[4] At the same time it should not be too 'literal'. If it is too obvious the viewer will say to himself, 'Ah. That's what it means', and look no further. The image should contain enough toe-holds[5] to prevent the spectator asking, 'What does it mean?' – the sort of question which blocks the mind in front of an art object.

> If one looks at a thing with the intention of *trying* to discover what it means, one ends up no longer seeing the thing itself, but thinking of the question that has been raised.
> – René Magritte

The communication must be so subtle and cleverly arranged – this is given by the original insight – that it by-passes the chatter of the mind, with its prejudices, theories, pre-conceptions, associative thoughts and literalness.

One may ask, 'How is one to receive insights?' These are obviously not under the direct control of the artist, otherwise every man-made thing could be inspired. My experience and observation lead me to believe that insight is encouraged by a certain kind of 'priming' of the mind. It is certain that an unhappy or pressurized mind (one continually 'full' of conflicts) cannot operate efficiently. The following brief outline of my method is essential to any consideration of the book in relation to its expression in the binding – which is the main new direction the craft may take further, and which is essentially the theme of this book.

*Visual expression from literary expression : method*

Read the work. Take notes of main features in the subject matter, with attention to colour evocations and other striking features. Chart a summary of the book; assess its themes and character. If not clear, repeat the above, but as far as possible without previous associations. (Note-taking is of course optional during any of the readings, as this may disturb the continuity.) Researching into the author's work may be helpful, since he may have constant thematic concepts.

2  This depends on the preparation, sorting through and selection from hundreds of pieces of maril and feathered onlay leather.

3  An obvious example is seen in Plate 28A.

4  i.e. being interested purely in the arrangement of line and form (design meaning) without disciplining oneself to the central requirement of this medium.

5  The perfect visual image contains ingredients from each level of reality. If familiar reality is omitted no birth of art is possible. All great art makes a reference to our physical reality in its image abstraction. Imaginative communication depends largely on the skilful blending of the familiar and the unusual (cf. *26*, pp. 262–3).

Make a thematic record, stating the ideas in the book. A literary analysis is not necessary and would intellectualize the result, which is to be in visual terms.[6] The aim is to achieve a feeling for the book. Now apply the method of contemplation to the book. To explain: sit comfortably (with eyes closed) and use a technique which will quieten the mind, that is, put everything aside from it by an act of disengagement (63, 64). Bring some thematic quality to mind (that is, the experience of the book) and hold it before the mind's eye, without thought or analysis. Keep it in the present moment before the imagination, letting go of everything else. For me, the pure and perfect image must arise out of the silence; mental static and 'noise' would impose a 'dis-figurement' on this image.

Images float before the mind, and these one merely observes. If extraneous things intrude turn the attention back to a predominant image of the book. It is the concentration of attention which steers the mind back to a relevant image, and in this way one keeps to the present moment, crucial to contact with the creative imagination, which is allied to the dreaming mind (26). Contemplation may occupy five or ten minutes, after which one makes a concrete reminder on paper (the aide-memoire). This discipline is an alternating play between active and passive attention.

> The procedure may not bring direct insight, but one just continues with other work on the project. Even with a clear visual insight one may, on attempting to set it down, find that the image is more elusive than one assumed; so allow intuition to rule the pen, brush, etc., in finding the way back to it. The artist cannot avoid some psychological discipline if his work is to have any significance, and it is only significant if it comes from the right place in him; from '. . . the still point of the turning world' (T. S. Eliot).

Once the sketch has been finally formulated, the next step is to prepare the materials for its transformation into the actual bookbinding. Much of the forwarding work will have been undertaken once the original plan has been conceived and it is now a matter of relating such items as colour of endbands, edge treatment and board structures to the final sketch idea. The four stages of the programme do not always occur consecutively and some of them may even take place simultaneously. With the large book-wall, which I envisaged as figured with feathered onlays, I had ordered seven sets of the three volumes in folded sheets. The publishers were prepared at that time to allow me only six sets and so one triad of volumes is a book-shop purchase, taken down and re-sewn; already trimmed it is somewhat smaller than the other six triads. During forwarding of the volumes I had in the meantime discovered maril (Section 10) which would allow me to interpret the work in a much more fluid and detailed way. Plates 80, 81 show the general idea of assembly of onlays in relation to colour sketches. I folded the two coloured sketches along the grid-lines vertically and, putting two covers together, isolated them in the card frame. The prepared leather (usually with at least two coloured pieces scarf-joined) was then onlaid with reference to the framed sketches.[7] All the covers were made up in this way. Work with onlays usually began by measuring out with dividers the

6 In reading the book, which may be the first step in the process, only simple attention is required to register the words. But deeper applications of attention are necessary to grasp the implied meaning of sentences, and then to form an objective judgement of a theme, free from associative thinking. Casual interpretation of a book through its subject matter results in designs which do nothing to help the viewer's understanding of the book, and are the result of a similarly casual approach to the bookbinding. The mind will (naturally and economically) operate at the lowest level of intensity consistent with the demands made upon it. The easy way out has no place in creative bookbinding.

7 The 'one-board' frame is for assessing an individual composition.

position of the larger shapes on two or three cover skins, with any shapes which were to occur near the edges of the boards co-ordinated on the relevant pieces of loose covering leather. Each dimension on the sketch was increased by three times and the prepared onlays positioned, either first on another card frame of the exact size of the cover, or directly on the cover leather. Unless allowances are made for hygroscopic movement due to pasting or physical stretching when paring later before covering, the relationships between the adjacent edge onlays will be altered and continuity will be lost. Many minor adjustments to these shapes which lie at the edges of the boards are left until after the main paring of the covers, because it is not possible with such a flexible leather as goatskin to know the exact amount of movement. One can of course apply onlays after binding and covering of the book, but with untooled onlays these are vulnerable unless 'sunk' as shown in Figs. 29 or 33.

In *The Lord of the Rings* book-wall many different colour effects are used to create the appropriate intensity of colour not usually possible in leathers, and a brief digression at this point will explain some of these effects.

## Colour in bookbinding

In bookbinding with leathers one is at the mercy of the tanner for the range of colours. These are limited because the tanner caters mainly for the large (trade) buyer, but it is the individual hand-binder who is likely to require other than the stock range of colours. It is too expensive for the small binder to have leathers specially dyed because the manufacturer requires a large minimum quantity order to make this economic for him. However, it is possible by the clever juxtaposition of even a limited range of colours to achieve the effects one seeks. For example, colours may be changed in intensity by placing the opposite colours, or complementaries, adjacent to them (Fig. 75). I frequently edge an area of colour with either a complementary or a split complementary to make it appear more brilliant, or to soften the edge of an area.[8]

The retinal after-image of two adjacent complementary colours intensifies the original (Chevreul's law of simultaneous contrast), without apparently changing the hues, but when adjacent or simultaneously contrasting colours (or values) are not complementary their hues are changed. If violet and red are placed side by side the yellow after-image of the violet makes the red appear more orange and the green after-effect of the red turns the violet bluer. Where two hues, of even a dull *chroma* but of the same value (or tone) are placed in contact along one edge there is a retinal conflict as the eye tries to define the boundary between them, and a glow of colour results; the more brilliant the pairs the more conflict and the greater the glow (see Plate 70B). This effect is created by the nature of colour and the nature of the eye because the retinal image of any colour is its complement; a fact exploited by Op Art for its own sake.

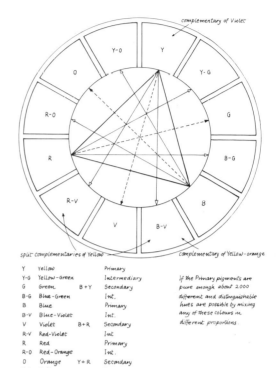

| | | | |
|---|---|---|---|
| Y | Yellow | | Primary |
| Y-G | Yellow-Green | | Intermediary |
| G | Green | B+Y | Secondary |
| B-G | Blue-Green | | Int. |
| B | Blue | | Primary |
| B-V | Blue-Violet | | Int. |
| V | Violet | B+R | Secondary |
| R-V | Red-Violet | | Int. |
| R | Red | | Primary |
| R-O | Red-Orange | | Int. |
| O | Orange | Y+R | Secondary |
| Y-O | Yellow-Orange | | Int. |

If the Primary pigments are pure enough about 2000 different and distinguishable hues are possible by mixing any of these colours in different proportions.

*Fig. 75*

8 The colour circle may be made up with a rotating inner disc.

119

Colour is also modified by the surface quality of objects. Leather, velvet and perspex, or even two leathers (i.e. calf and goatskin) of the same colour will appear different according to the way the surface modifies the light. Lustre, iridescence and luminosity will also affect the style and quality of the colour (see Plate 70A). But the use of colour effect is one of relationships, because any colour in the field of vision affects the perception of any other. Colours are chiefly affected by the colour of the field on which they are displayed as well as by the lighting in which they are viewed, and this is important when leathers are selected for onlay/inlay work.

Other visual properties of colour are used in *The Lord of the Rings* bookbindings. Coloured shapes can change the focal length of the eye, so that warm colours appear nearer than cool colours; pure colours, white and black appear nearer than 'atmospheric' colours. The visual image of a pale colour will appear to expand, a dark colour to contract in area. A dominant tint or colour will pull many discordant colours into harmony. Colour also has 'taste', 'smell' and 'sound' overtones. Colour may be used to give an illusion of movement. (Colour in actual movement as in TV, film, kinetics, is yet another dynamic.)

In bookbinding colour has nearly always been neutralized in its dynamic effects by the habitual use of decorative gold lines between areas, and this is a result of small modifications (the craftsman's 'rule of thumb') to tradition rather than a re-thinking of the whole problem, which is required.[9]

9 An indispensable introduction to the subject is Faber Birren's *Principles of Colour* (6), which is a review of past traditions and modern theories of colour.

59    Philip Smith
J. R. R. Tolkien *The Lord of the Rings* Back of book-wall
(Plate 43).

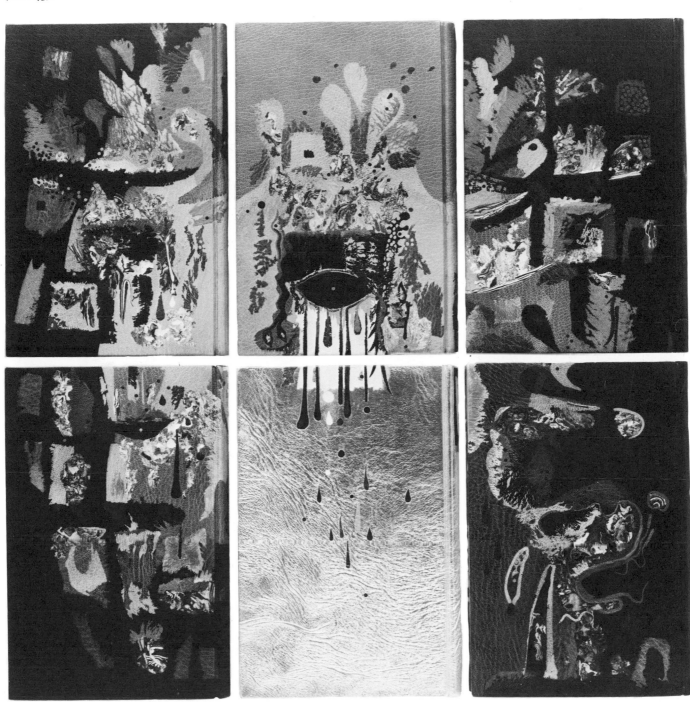

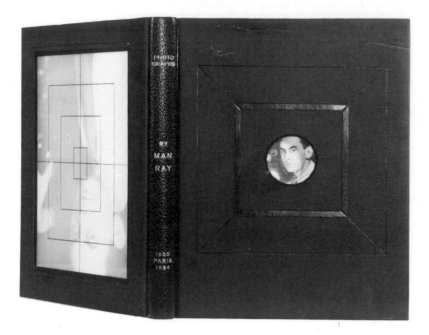

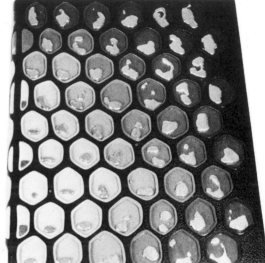

60   Henri Mercher
Man Ray *Photographs*
Black morocco spine. Black linen-covered boards. Inlaid lens over a self-portrait
of Man Ray which slides in and out with the opening and closing of the boards.
Back board inset with grained plexiglas (perspex) panel over reversed photograph
340 × 250mm (13⅜ × 10in) 1971

61   Henri Mercher
*Buffon* illustrated by Picasso (450 hours of work)
Black morocco. 133 novel mercury-filled, painted plastic capsules, inset in the
covers and spine. The containers are of various shades of grey towards very
dark green
370 × 270mm (14½ × 10¾in) 1972

61

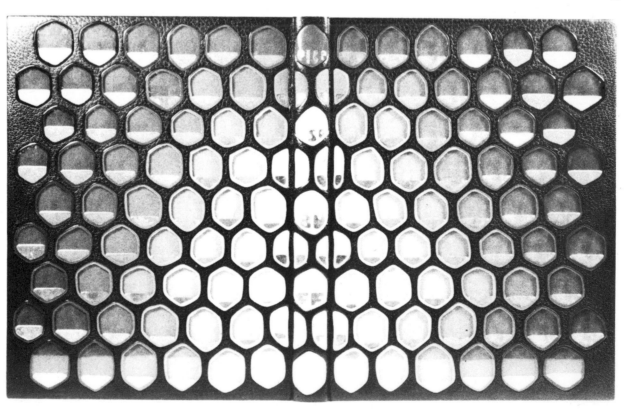

122

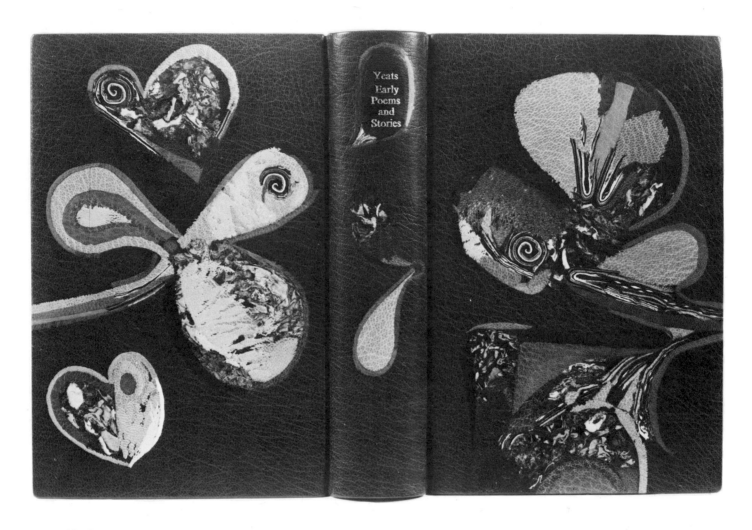

62   Philip Smith
W. B. Yeats *Early Poems and Stories* (See Plate 90 for colours)
190 × 134 × 40mm (7¼ × 5¼ × 1½in) 1970
Private collection

63   Philip Smith
J. W. Abert. Ed. John Galvin *Through the
Country of the Comanche Indians in the Fall of
the Year 1845* Howell Books (1970).
Scarf-joined bright-orange Cape goatskin,
black and tan 'Oasis'. Multicoloured feathered
onlays and maril. Brown Japanese paper ends
and doublures
$345 \times 260 \times 20$mm ($13\frac{1}{2} \times 10\frac{1}{4} \times \frac{3}{4}$in) 1970–71
Private collection

64   Philip Smith
J. W. Abert. ed. John Galvin *Western America
in 1846–47*
Black and ochre 'Oasis' and bright-orange
Cape goatskin onlaid to show through the
heavy grain texture. Sectioned onlays and
maril. Double book-box with hand-painted
sides
$345 \times 260 \times 20$mm ($13\frac{1}{2} \times 10\frac{1}{4} \times \frac{3}{4}$in) 1970–71
Private collection

65   Compiled by John Galvin *The Etchings
of Edward Borein* Howell Books. S.F.
California.
Figured natural Sudanese cowhide. Multiple
sectioned onlays on black, brown and purple
'Oasis'. Doublures onlaid with scenes depicting
buffalo and Red Indian on horseback
$305 \times 228 \times 35$mm ($12 \times 9 \times 1\frac{3}{8}$in) 1972
Private collection

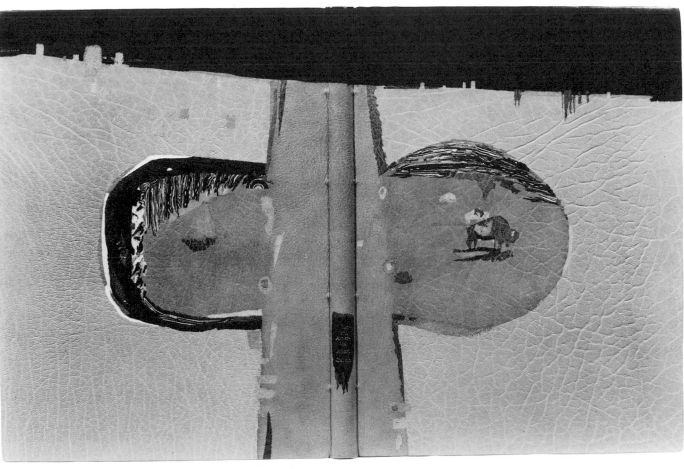

64

65

# 19 Case history of *The Pilgrim's Progress* binding

Description of binding procedure[1], with shaped boards attached by the tongue and slot method.

*The Pilgrim's Progress* by John Bunyan. A limited edition published by the Cresset Press in 1928 with black and white illustrations by Blair Hughes-Stanton and Gertrude Hermes. No. 168. (See Plates 46, 47, 66–68).

The book was received in two volumes, bound on five tapes with stained black sheep's parchment covers, hollow back and five shallow raised bands, and french grooves. The paper was foxed, with damp and light stains round the heavy deckle edges. Owing to the conditions of the commission it was decided to re-bind as one book.

The first steps before taking down (or 'pulling') are an examination for peculiarities (missing leaves, plates, etc.) to be discussed with the client, and a numbering of all unidentified prelims, etc., lightly in pencil.

The endpapers were untipped from the book-block and the pastedowns soaked off the heavy greyboards. By cutting all the thread loops inside the sections these were pulled free of the back linings and the tapes and the books taken down. (The covers and all evidence of the original binding were returned to the client.)

A 2 per cent solution of Chloramine-T bleach was made up in photographic trays and each folio (or bifolium) was immersed and piled up in the solution. When the last leaves had been immersed the wet pile (supported on wet-strength paper) was turned over and the bifolia removed one at a time and placed in a bath of running water to wash out any residue of bleach.[2] A final immersion in a tray of water containing a little Topane (orthophenylphenol) deposited a buffer in the paper against mould formation. The book was then blotted off (on Photoprinto paper) and hung up with a 'peel' on lines to dry (Fig. 76, Plate 98).

Whilst air-drying, a set of hand-painted designs for the first flyleaves and the board linings ('doublures' if of leather) was prepared. Sheets of very strong tub-sized Goatskin Parchment machine-made paper were immersed in a tray of water, blotted, and sprinkled with waterproof inks to a controlled configuration (using artists' sable paint brushes.) When almost dry the inked paper was again immersed and surplus ink washed off, the paper blotted lightly, and other colours dropped on to the damp surface. This procedure may be continued until the required effect is achieved (Plates 33A, 34E), when the papers are air-dried, pressed and allowed to remain flat under weighted boards.

The book was then removed from the lines, gathered and collated. Enough moisture was retained to assist flattening of the leaves without losing the type imprint. The book was then interleaved between signatures (or sections or 'quires') with Photoprinto, stacked between formica-surfaced pressing-boards and pressed with medium pressure.

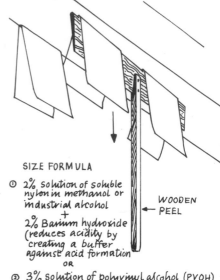

SIZE FORMULA

① 2% solution of soluble nylon in methanol or industrial alcohol
+
2% Barium hydroxide (reduces acidity by creating a buffer against acid formation
OR
② 3% solution of polyvinyl alcohol (PVOH) in water + deacidifier

WOODEN PEEL

*Fig. 76*

[1] The descriptive detailing of techniques varies; those which are special, or which I feel are of particular importance, or which are not generally available in other references, are given more elaborate treatment; others are more generally stated, but by cross-reference to sketches, photographs and the principles stated elsewhere in the book the intelligent reader will find himself informed on most particulars.

[2] Washing in clean water is usually sufficient to eliminate acidity in paper, but buffering against future acid formation is an added precaution. The de-acidifying agent Magnesium bi-carbonate ($Mg(CO_3)_2$) can be easily made in a domestic syphon passing the $CO_2$ through the solution of Magnesium carbonate ($MgCO_3$) and water under pressure (when the $MgCO_3$ will dissolve).

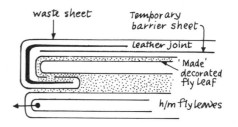

waste sheet
Temporary barrier sheet
leather joint
'Made' decorated fly leaf
h/m flyleaves

'Pilgrim's Progress' End sections

*Fig. 77a*

*Fig. 77b*

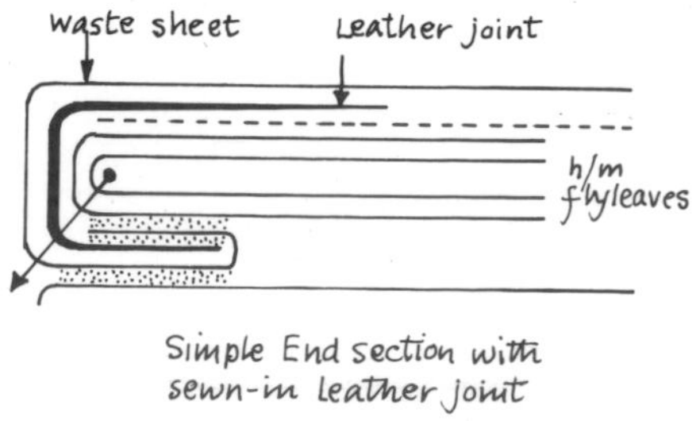

waste sheet    leather joint

h/m flyleaves

Simple End section with sewn-in leather joint

## Endpaper make-up

Endpaper sections[3] were made up as in Fig. 77a using PVA adhesive. The hand-painted paper was laminated ('made') to a darker oatmeal hand-made paper folio, the other leaf of which was 'made' to a lighter oatmeal paper (gluing the paper lying nearest the book-block with PVA). The leather joint and waste sheet were attached to the upper laminar leaving a flexible hollow (or gusset) at the back edge to ease the opening of the boards. The book-block was pressed overnight, then the Photoprinto was removed, the book re-stacked, and returned to the standing press under a greater pressure. Meanwhile a copy of the book was being read, notes taken and the design rough prepared (see Section 18).

## Preparation for sewing

The paper lost a little of its stiffness (size) during washing and was looking more like its 'original condition' and colour.[4] The bulk and type of paper was such that I decided to use alternate tape and semi-recessed cords for sewing supports; the former to facilitate flexibility and the latter to reduce torque. As many as possible of the old sewing stations and holes should be used when setting up for sewing. The two volumes were collated to be bound as one book and a thick collation line was drawn diagonally across the backbone (or spine) of the book between two of the sewing stations.

The head of the book with the old gilding was lightly trimmed using a plough and lying press. Very uneven deckles on the other edges were trimmed individually with a knife and straight-edge (steel) before sending the book to Mr E. Ham of Bath for gilding. He is the best gilder I know for deckle gilding, a difficult technique. By this method the whole of the original margins is preserved, while by scraping and gilding, they are afforded some protection against dust and light.[5]

Gilding 'solid' and in the round (instead of gilding before sewing, or 'rough') is more of an enclosure and is said to make the paper almost fire-proof when the book is shut, but it does look more like a block of metal than of paper. It is however difficult to get hand-made papers to lie tightly against each other, so this effect cannot be achieved. I prefer the 'natural' look of gilding before sewing, which relates better to my present cover treatment. Edge treatment, and end-band style, must not be neglected when overall unity of design is considered.

After the 'rough' gilding the book was prepared for sewing on three semi-recessed (sawn-in) cords and two tapes. The book-block, with the endpaper sections removed (or slipped down 5mm or $\frac{3}{16}$ in from the spine) was placed between millboards and the positions of the kettel-stitch kerfs, tapes and cords were marked, the kettel-kerfs and recesses for the cords being sawn in. It was necessary to make one new kettel-kerf station and two new ones for the tapes (drawn in

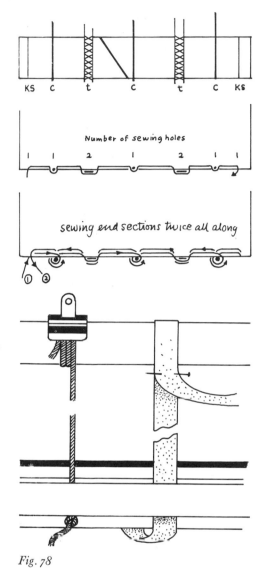

*Fig. 78*

3 Figs 40-55 give the profiles of several different endpaper assemblies used for different book-blocks; Fig 55a shows a standard procedure in making.

4 If the paper requires re-sizing two formulas now in use are: (a) 3 per cent solution of PVOH in water (polyvinyl alcohol – also useful in a stiffer solution as a release layer before gluing the backbone) or: (b) 2 per cent solution of soluble nylon in methanol (or industrial white spirit). Add 2 per cent barium hydroxide which reduces acidity by creating a buffer of barium carbonate against further acid formation. (See Appendix IV.)

5 French chalk is dusted between the edges of the leaves to facilitate leaf separation after gilding; it is beneficial if some is left in the book against possible acid formation.

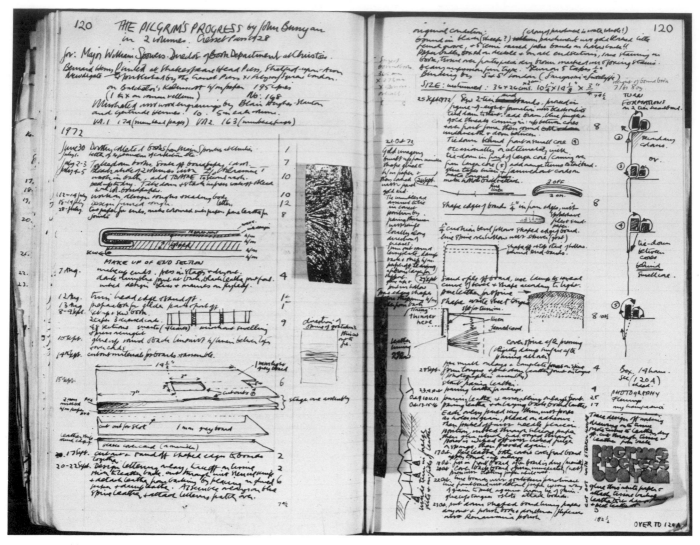

66   Philip Smith
*The Pilgrim's Progress*
Work sheets in Record Book

67   Philip Smith
Definitive client's sketch, half-scale

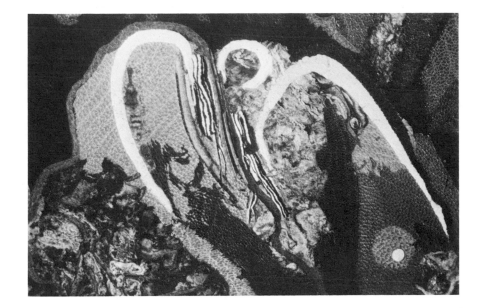

68A  Philip Smith
John Bunyan *The Pilgrim's Progress*
Feathered onlays and maril. Tongue and slot
board attachment. Blue 'Oasis' spine. Hand-
painted flyleaves and doublures. Edges gilt on
the deckle

68B  Philip Smith
Detail from front board

68A

across the backbone with pencil and carpenter's set-square). The book was removed from the lying press (convenient for holding the backbone secure and level during marking and sawing-in) and the endpapers' sewing holes were pricked through the lower opening of the fly-leaves (sawing these in would leave unsightly cuts and thread showing at the first opening in the book). I usually sew through the leather joint fold (see Figs. 77B, 50) but did not do so on this occasion.

*Sewing*

I placed the book-block, spine away and head to the left, behind the sewing frame, which for this book was set up as Fig. 78. (The advantages of a single-post sewing frame are that the arm working 'blind' inside the sections is unhindered, and in this model the first section to be sewn may be placed right to the edge of the press bed so that the needle pierces the first section at a 45° angle, without obstructions or the need to pack the book up on a pressing board (Plate 69).) A knot was tied in the end of each cord and the free end inserted below the grip bar, then passed up around the top sliding bar and given two or three turns about this bar before being held in place with a spring clip (Fig. 78).

So as to obviate the need to pass the bulky tape roll between the bed and lower grip bar a good length of tape was unrolled and the end inserted from below upwards from the left sewing station, passed up and around the bar, where it was pinned below. The tape was then taken, *without cutting*, round the bar to the next tape station, pinned, and the free end dropped and inserted between the grip-bar and the front edge of the platform. It is then taken along below the platform, between the grip-bar and bed and up again at the other stations, if required. The cords and tapes were then positioned to lie between the screws of the grip-bar, and the grip-bar tightened. Tension could have been increased by moving the sliding bar up the post.

It is immaterial at which end one begins sewing, the main thing being to check the signatures and the pagination before sewing each section and to align the head each time. With this quarto-sized book each endpaper section was sewn all-along and returned (i.e. twice along), passing the thread around the 8-cord supports and over the tapes. The free end of the 25/3 linen thread was picked up (as a sewing support) on each kettel-stitch at that end of the sections (Fig. 79). To prevent excessive initial wear on the thread it is advisable to use several short lengths – enough for about three sections – rather than a few long ones. Sewing may take a little longer due to frequent joining, but this is preferable to worn thread.

Every book-sewer will know that the sewing thread tends to unravel due to friction against the paper as it is pulled through the holes, and tends to knot. The free passage of the thread may be made, with less wear and friction on the thread, if the left thumb (inside the section) is used as a diversion point around which the thread may run to the next sewing station (Fig. 80). For recessed cords and tape slips it is

*Fig. 79*

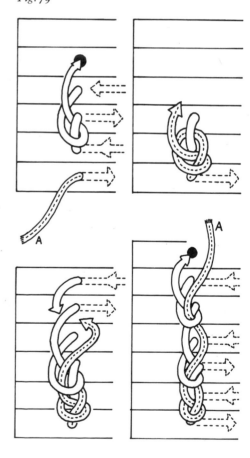

*Taking end of thread up to re-inforce kettle-stitch knots. (Kettle-kerf shown as holes)*

only necessary to pull the thread at the kettel stitches, remembering to pull only parallel with the section folds, never at right angles, or the thread will slit the sections. Do not pull the kettel-stitch knot too tightly because the sharp bend is a weak point (lessened where the 'waste' end of the thread from the first entry is looped around). Tension may be held while the kettel-stitch is made by placing a clamping finger on the back-fold there. The knot should be pulled only finger-tight. In this way the waxed linen thread, which has only slight elasticity, is allowed to settle to its natural tension. Terylene thread has several times the breaking strength of linen thread, but its elasticity is its main disadvantage.

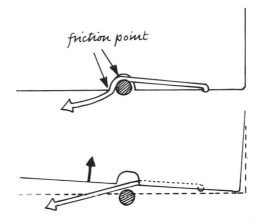

In sewing, to prevent the thread from knotting due to friction, nudge the section slightly away from the support to allow a space for the thread to pass friction-free (Fig. 80). When the thread is fully through the hole the section is brought back into line. To prevent accidental tearing should a knot develop, I pass the needle beyond the recessed cord (as in sewing around a raised cord) and out on the 'wrong' side, pull the thread through and then slip the needle and thread back to the 'right' side to pass in front of the cord (that is, the side nearest the operator) (Fig. 80). The needle should not be so sharp as to cut the paper when feeling for an inside sewing hole or to easily pierce the thread accidentally when passing into the section from the outside. (Fig. 81 shows how the needle pierces the thread when locking the needle to it.) I find that a strong light behind the sewing frame enables the needle end to be silhouetted through most unfilled papers and this speeds the sewing process.

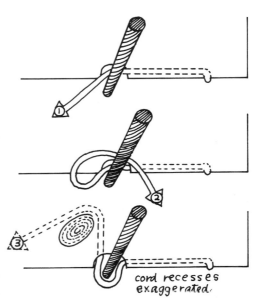

cord recesses
exaggerated.

*Fig. 80*

Check from time to time that slack loops have not formed inside the sections. A link-stitch is used across the back of the tapes (the herringbone pattern on double cords is caused by catching up in like manner) to connect sections and to even up the tension in the sewing (Fig. 84). I always make joins in new lengths of thread on the outside of the sections in front of the sewing supports (Fig. 83). The cut ends may then be trapped by subsequent loops across the supports, and the join is further strengthened by the gluing of spine and linings. It is also less unsightly than having knots inside the sections (Fig. 89). The same tension should be kept throughout the book, so that no over-tight or sloppy links between the sections will adversely affect the shape of the book during rounding and backing.

*Fig. 81*

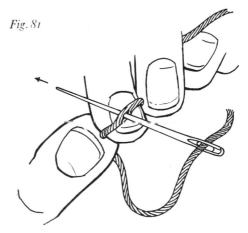

Locking needle on thread without knot.

Sewing is a most important operation as it is the foundation of the binding. A heavy band-stick may be used to consolidate the book block after every three to four sections as it is built up (Fig. 85). The examination of old books in libraries reveals that too little swelling was left at the spine, causing the book to gape (Fig. 86). This is especially true of those printed on hand-made paper, with its tendency to cockle in every direction due to its felted nature, and to the type imprint originally put into a damp substance. When an old book is taken down it is often necessary to repair the back folds of some sections, and with the increase in swelling resulting from the accumulated thickness of paper, one is tempted to use a thinner thread to compensate. This may be a bad decision. I think it is better to have a little surplus swelling in the spine of the book, so long as the backing shoulder does not project above the board (Fig. 87).

When the last endpaper section is sewn twice 'all-along', run the needle in a spiral down the kettel-stitches for reinforcement. On books with an even number of sections it is necessary to thread the needle on to an extra short length to do this. Cut the cords above the book (about 50mm or 2in from the upper section) and release the grip-bar (or other support attachment). Continuous tapes may be unpinned and the tape pulled gently through to the end leaving an extension of about 40mm (1½in) on each side of the book-block, and cut off. Draw through to the next station and do the same. No tape is wasted.

Although the (original) two volumes of *The Pilgrim's Progress* had undergone wet processing there was still a 'memory' in the paper fibres of the former backing of the sections and a tendency for them to return. This had to be accounted for in the preparation for backing. I normally force the old backing angle out of the paper by bending the section over the edge of the bench with the thumb.

The single book now assembled was put between thin millboards, knocked up square to head and spine, and lowered between the cheeks of the lying press, projecting above them by about 80mm (3in). A bone folder was rubbed over all the sewing holes to close them against subsequent entry of adhesive, and the swelling reduced between the backing hammer and knocking down iron. This process sinks the sewing thread into the softish paper substance and removes air by compacting the folds. The book was then removed from the lying press and accurately squared up. The endpaper section was turned back and a fence of waste paper, as in Fig. 55A, was positioned about 5mm (³⁄₁₆in) from the back fold of the last (or end) sections of the book-block and the exposed strip glued, the fence removed and the endpaper-section closed on to the book-block. Make sure that neither endpaper-section projects beyond the spine of the book-block, and is carefully aligned with the head.

### Rounding and backing

The extended sewing supports were then temporarily covered with the millboards (or other waste card) and a light coat of PVA (or PVOH adhesive which would be water soluble at a later date)[5] brushed along the spine, and rubbed between the sections with the thumb. (Be sure to brush out from the centre towards head and tail (Fig. 88).) There were forty-eight sections in this book, bulking it to 50mm (2in). While the adhesive was wet the book was again given its final accurate squaring up and the backbone left to become almost dry under a weight. The backbone was then rounded (*18, 52, 58*). The flat of a backing board is very suitable for this operation.

Many authorities consider that the best shape of the rounded back

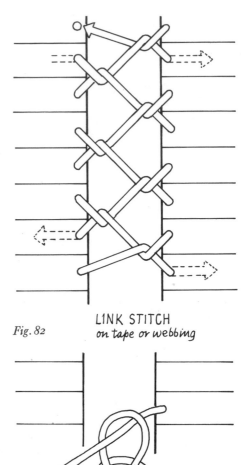

Fig. 82    LINK STITCH
on tape or webbing

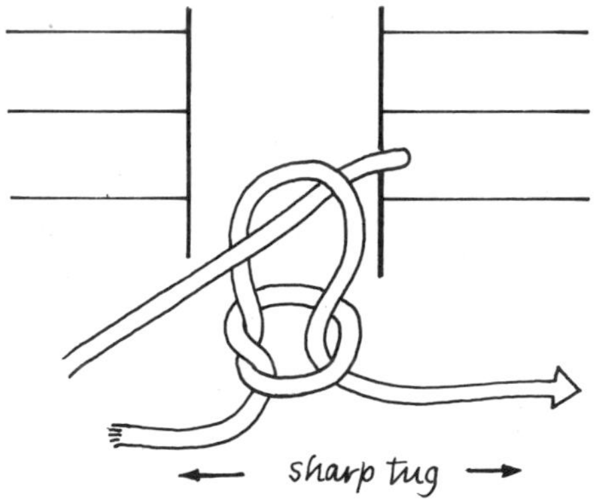

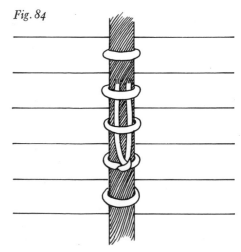

Fig. 83    WEAVER'S KNOT
← sharp tug →

Fig. 84

Join on new thread at back of sewing supports

of the average sized book is one-third of a circle. It is this shape
in which the sections seem to lock best when backed over. I noticed
when backing the book shown in Plate 64 that the angles in the bend
of the paper caused the gold edge at that point to change 'colour',
creating two pronounced lines meeting at an angle (DAE in Fig. 89).
This led me to investigate the geometry of this apparently preferred
shape, and this is shown in Fig. 89. If the line BC through the
shoulder line is taken as the base of an equilateral triangle and a circle
is drawn through the apices, the arc BAC (120° angle) is exactly
one-third of the circumference of the circle. Other interesting
relationships could be noted. A 3° angle BAD and EAC may give the
proportionate thickness of the board or the height of the backing
shoulder. AX=OX; MO=MX with M the centre of a circle the
diameter of which is equal to the thickness of the book. Although it
may be the optical (or aesthetic) effect of the backing shape which
has been considered, this investigation seemed to offer some
geometrical 'proof' of the correctness of one-third of a circle on
books of this size. It must be noted, however, that this formula does
not always hold true for very thin books (perhaps with thick sections)
or for very thick books. The former would probably require a
rounder and the latter a flatter backbone. The circumstances of each
case must be considered on merit.

With much opening, the round seems to flatten a little and the leaves
of the book tend to 'creep' towards the foredge leaving the 'squares'
of the boards narrower there. When judging the foredge squares
I allow a little leeway for 'creep', so that on a new, unopened, book
the foredge squares are a little wider than the head and tail squares.
Nothing looks so disagreeable as bad squares on a bookbinding, and
yet perfect squares are one of the most difficult objectives to achieve,
with the dimensionally unstable materials used by the bookbinder
and the printer.

The backing boards may be tipped to the waste sheet by two spots
of PVA near the fold, and placed a distance equal to the caliper of the
proposed board from the back edge. Screw up tightly in the press
(Fig. 90), and glue the backbone with a thicker application of PVA.
When backing one may stand and work either from the side or the
end of the press, with the handle of the hammer parallel to the
backbone. At the 'tack' stage begin to work the sections over
commencing each side along the lines (a), then (b), then (c) and
finally, using first the heel of the hammer, then the face, along the
lines between (c) and (d). I always straighten and sharpen the edge of
the shoulder by sliding the corner of the hammer face along lines (d)
before applying paste to set the shape and applying the linen lining.
All blows of the hammer should be *glancing* ones in the direction of
the curved arrow (Fig. 90). It is the slight 'tack' of the adhesive
between the hammer face and the backbone which helps to ease the
sections over.

The book was backed as described, and the spine glued again and
lined with fine lawn (or handkerchief linen), allowing for 50mm (2in)
overlap on to the waste sheets (Fig. 90). The linen may be used as

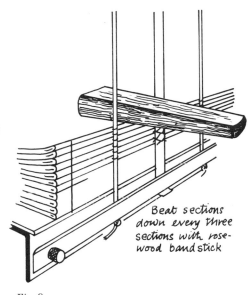

Beat sections
down every three
sections with rose-
wood band stick

*Fig. 85*

Not enough swelling in spine

*Fig. 86*

*Fig. 87*

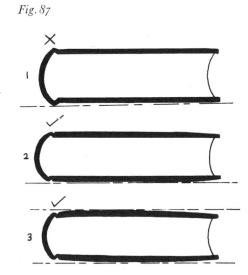

'in-fill' between the sewing supports (which are left outside the backing boards). After backing and lining leave the book in the lying press to set for several hours.

The design of the cover imagery and all surface features had been completed so that the structure of the boards was known before this stage was reached. The concept for this book included shaped or profiled boards. For various practical reasons, such as strength, the availability of only smallish skins and colour changes across the image, the tongue-and-slot method of board attachment was selected.

Although the imagery (Plate 68) flows across the spine linking both boards, the 'composition' must work for each board separately, so that the image of each board seen by itself should appear complete (Plates 46, 47).[6] This is another special requirement of bookbinding design and a good designer will see that it is met. The imagery is a door into the contents just as, physically, the cover of the codex form of book is hinged like a door. The line formed by the joint (hinge) is often thought of as a break in the continuity of design across both covers, but as it is part of the natural structure and function of the object it can be accepted. The two parts of the binding for *The Pilgrim's Progress* are represented by two separate but linked images. The dreaming figure of the author, Bunyan, stretched out in his prison cell at the foot of the spine, extends on to both boards.

### Preparation of boards

When the backing is set the book may be put between pressing boards up to the shoulder and consolidated in the nipping press. During this time the boards may be made up. The boards for this book were assembled allowing for a slot in the back edge (Fig. 91). The recesses and edge profiling were cut out of the upper laminar of 1mm ($\frac{1}{25}$in) board where recesses were not required for the whole board laminate. When all the boards had been glued together with PVA, including one layer of hand-made paper between the heavier boards to increase stability, both boards were clamped together with inner surfaces adjacent to each other. The profiling was cut with a sharp knife and then filed and sanded true, on both together. The outer edges of the boards were bevelled to about half the thickness of the board and commencing 1cm ($\frac{3}{8}$in) from the outer edge; this rounded 'cushioning' followed the profiling. Holding the board surfaces vertical below a light source, and making small movements to catch the shadow, is a good method revealing the trueness or otherwise of the cushioning. A spokeshave was used for bevelling the edges, followed by the sandpaper block to complete the cushioning. The hinge corners of the boards were minimally 'back-cornered' (see Fig. 1).

### Endbanding

The two-tier endbands were next considered and silks selected to

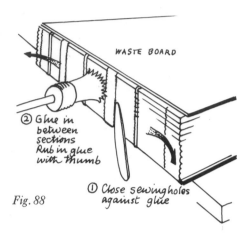

WASTE BOARD

② Glue in between sections
Rub in glue with thumb

① Close sewing holes against glue

*Fig. 88*

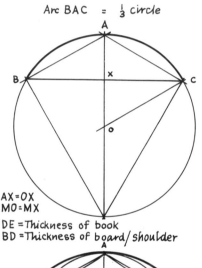

Arc BAC = $\frac{1}{3}$ circle

AX = OX
MO = MX

DE = Thickness of book
BD = Thickness of board/shoulder

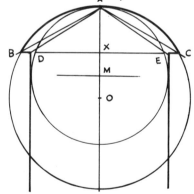

*Fig. 89*

6 The whole meaning of a design in expressive bookbinding cannot, of course, be experienced when the book is displayed flat. This factor is almost always overlooked by librarians and others displaying this type of design.

'pick up' colours used in the design of the covers and doublures (the term doublures is used here, although strictly speaking this term is used for leather board linings). The cores around which the silks were worked are made from a strong laminate of morocco and vellum. The formation of the endbands is shown in the sketch (Fig. 92) and in Plate 34A. Two main colours were used for the tie-downs and short lengths (waste off-cuts) were turned round the cores and glued down on the backbone. There should be a tie-down about every five or six turns. The endband silks are sewn through the lawn lining, which means that the tie-downs do not necessarily have to penetrate evenly or below the kettel-stitches.

*Spine strip for tongue-and-slot attachment*

The leather for the spine strip was onlaid with the titling and other linking features separately from the covers. The titling was designed, using strong geometrical letter forms which could conveniently be cut out as one piece from thinly pared morocco, to read as part of the structure of the overall image linking both boards. A piece of gilder's interleaving tissue was pasted and the piece of black morocco pressed to it. When dry the drawing for the lettering was transferred in reverse to it, and cut with a stencil knife. The tissue backing was removed by first dampening the leather and placing the tissue-side down on a glued waste paper surface. The paste on the tissue was softened and the leather peeled off easily without distortion, leaving the tissue stuck to the waste paper. The titling was glued and laid in position on the blue spine-covering leather over other onlays forming part of the imagery. This spine strip was then pared, dampened slightly on the grain side and pressed. (All pressing of damp laminates is done with non-stick barrier-papers – i.e. silicone release-paper.)

The hollow back (two on, three off) was made up of best Kraft paper (which is relatively acid-free) with a lawn reinforcement for strength (Fig. 93). After the hollow back was glued over the lawn on the spine a further lining of leather was glued over the hollow. By this means any make-ready for the covering may be made, for example, any compensations for the head and tail turn-ins (Fig. 94). A medium-grade sandpaper block was used and the backbone left completely smooth. The spine-strip was given final attention by paring and sanding to a feather edge at head and tail (Fig. 95), and both this and the leather lining over the hollow back were pasted before covering.

A larger proportion of time and effort in bookbinding is spent in 'make-ready' operations (similar in meaning to the same term used by the printer), which help to level up surfaces or fill in cavities. If the spine leather is to be put on without any bulge showing where the leather is doubled at the turn-in, it is sounder to take material away on the spine lining, where it is 'non-functional', rather than where strength is required at the hinges and edges. Continual thought is given to the problem of priority between wear-strength and crisp appearance.

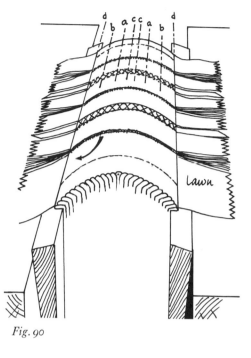

*Fig. 90*

*Fig. 91*

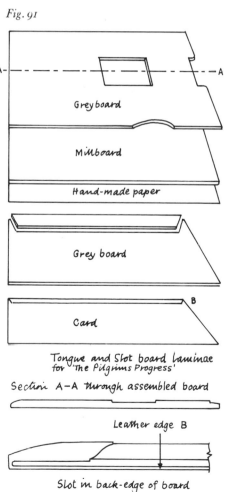

Tongue and Slot board laminae for 'The Pilgrims Progress'

Section A–A through assembled board

Leather edge B

Slot in back-edge of board

## Boards

The corners of boards are very vulnerable points and will be much
more resistant to wear and knocking if they are rounded off; but
rounded corners do not look so precise as sharp, square ones. Plastics
have an advantage in this respect, as there is greater molecular and
fibrous adhesion in them than in millboard, which tends to spread
open on impact. However, a sharp metal or acrylic reinforcement
at the corners is likely to cut through the leather corner on impact,
if it is used under the covering material. A good solution would be
to cover a board containing or wholly made with acrylic or other
'hard' substance, leaving the corners exposed. As with vellum tips,
the covering material could be made to 'fair' off into the corner,
which could also be rebated to accommodate it (Fig. 96 and Plate
96). Bindings can be designed making a feature of blunted or
rounded, or even angled, corners. There is no 'rule' stating that
corners or even whole bindings must not be other than the
conventional rectangular ones. There are no non-functional areas
on the binding for *The Pilgrim's Progress* which interfere with the
proper requirements of a book *per se*.

## The tongue

The board make-up for this binding is shown in Fig. 91, including
the slot structure. The negative board cut-out of the slot is retained
in position in the slot until the board has to be covered. The tongue
make-up on the book-block consists of the outer spine leather, the
waste sheet to which are glued the fanned-out cords, the tape slips
and the lawn lining projections (Fig. 94). The leather joint was
pasted and glued with PVA before being put down against the inside
surface of the waste sheet. It was pared head and tail so that it
feathers into the turn-in from the spine covering (Fig. 35). After it
was dry the laminated tongue was trimmed off using the negative
board cut-out as a template (Plate 34B). The total thickness of the
tongue should be designed to equal the accommodating slot in the
board (Fig. 97).

## Work on detached boards

The leather for the board covering was cut to size and the images
were assembled by selecting onlay pieces from a large collection of
previously cut and pared leather and maril. Each selected piece was
carefully shaped to reproduce the effect of the original image, recalled
by the sketch (Plate 67). Complex pieces, such as the 'grid arch'
(left, back cover), were backed with gilders' tissue and cut-out and
treated as explained for the title lettering.

In a design which relies on allusion, ambiguities and spontaneously
shaped fragments of colour, the use of precise geometrical forms

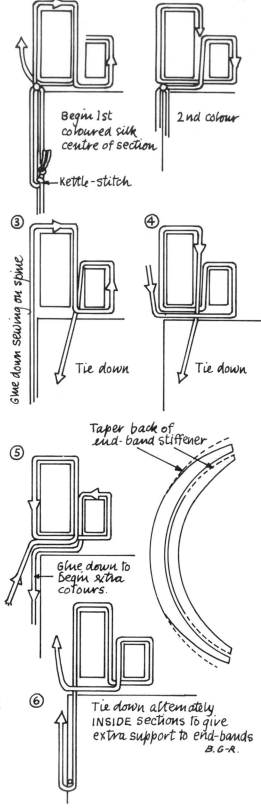

Fig. 92

136

would be out of place.[7] There is a fine distinction between incompetent craftsmanship and this spontaneous working which comes from a previous training and work in the traditional methods, and linked to a thorough background of designing. The way of developing images directly from the materials is outside the scope of the non-executant designer, or even in studios where there is a division of labour between specialists in the various areas involved in bookbinding (usually a designer and a team of artisan craftsmen), which is what happens, for example, in the Paris school.

## Further use of potentials in the materials

Various properties of the materials were exploited in the interpretation of details in the image. Some of the shaded white areas were made from white alum-tawed pigskin, the surface layer of which is translucent. Where it was required to show the 'shadow' or colour of the underlying leather through the white pigskin to a defined configuration, the pigskin was pared from the epidermal or grain layer and again pared extremely thin with the knife in the areas where the 'shading' is required. The piece was then pasted, put on to the black skin and then rubbed down through siliconed paper (or transparent acetate) with considerable pressure. The damp pigskin becomes transparent but dries translucent, leaving shaded white areas. The placing of onlays on the skin before covering presents problems of distortion and positioning. The likely dimensional changes in size with paring (which stretches) and with pasting (which swells the fibres) and with boarding (which reduces the area) must be assessed, otherwise fragments of the image intended on the face of the board may end up on the edges or inside the board! Allowance must also be made for the give and take of working the leather at the corners and, in this binding, on the shaped edges.

The leather with the onlays in place was damped, pressed, dried and then pared all over to make-ready. The thickness of onlays on the grain side is removed from the flesh side; after pasting and covering this results in 'sunk' onlays (Fig. 33). Anthony Cains tells me that the adoption of this technique proved useful when mounting fragments of old leather covers on to new leather when restoring, for it leaves no vulnerable protrusions. Onlays near the edges of the leather (which stretches most under a spokeshave) must be re-set with glue before pasting for covering.

## Covering of the boards

The edge of the skin nearest the hinge was pared steeply to a feather edge for tucking into the slot, and the corners were shaped as in Fig. 98 (see also Figs. 56, 57). The grain side of the skin was dampened slightly and the flesh side given several applications of paste. The board was placed in position on the pasted side (checking for position of edge onlays), this turned over and the leather rubbed down all over through a release-paper. The board-negatives from

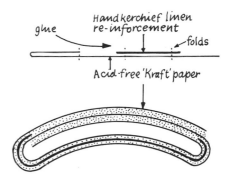

Hollow-back made off the book re-inforced when no turn-in is inserted - but is turned in on to itself on the outside of the back-linings.

*Fig. 93*

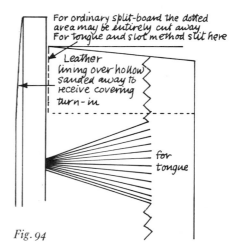

*Fig. 94*

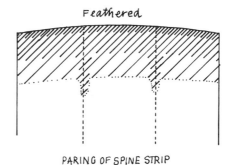

PARING OF SPINE STRIP

*Fig. 95*

7 'Too explicit a line or image deprives the viewer's mind of imagining that it creates.' (adapted from 29, p. 339)

69   Single-post sewing frame of non-corroding metals designed by the author.
Above left: setting up for cords. Above right: setting for tapes. Lower left: frame
converted as a ploughing jig. Lower right: sewing on tapes
Parts: 1 Sliding bar. 3 Pillar. 6 Grip-bar. 7 Grip adjusting bolts. 8 Rubber strip.
9 Base. 11 Sliding angle. 12 Finger nut. 14 Fixed guide bolts

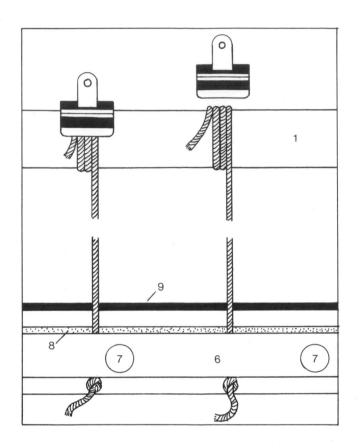

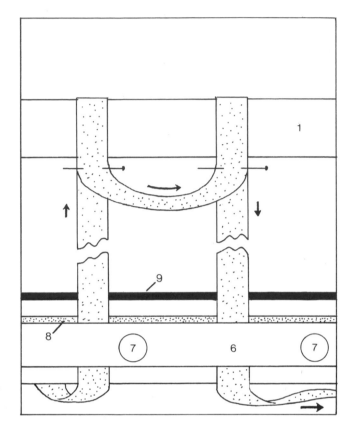

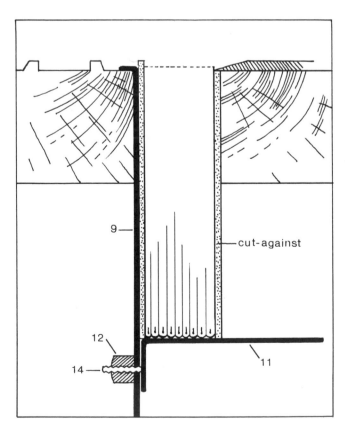

70　Philip Smith
Sliding and revolving panels – variable boards in notational sketches.
Lower left: R. B. Stacy-Judd *Atlantis – Mother of Empires*
Dark blue and bright green 'Oasis' with feathered onlays and maril. Moving
panel, lower centre, changes to gold/black/white
305 × 242mm (12 × 9½in) 1971
Collection: Alan Jay Lerner

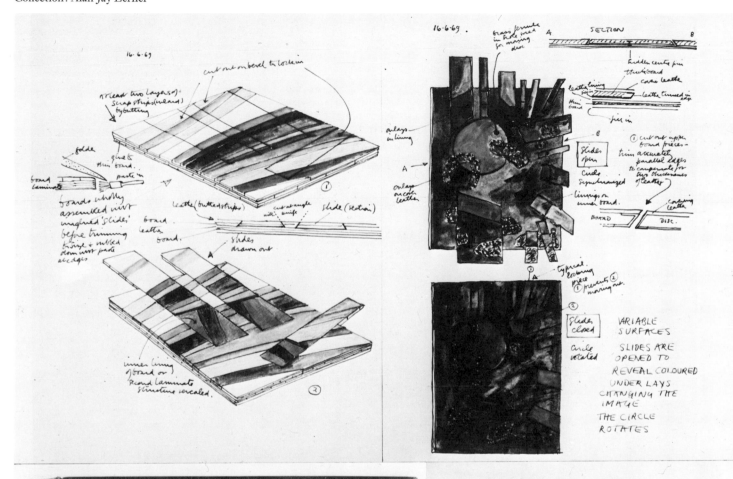

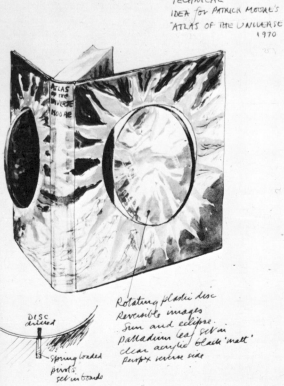

any recesses or cut-outs (slightly reduced on the edges by sand-papering to compensate for the thickness of the leather) were pressed into position (a nip in the press sharpens the recess edges). The leather corners were mitred off and shaped, then the hinge edge was turned into the slot, the edges of which would be completely sealed with leather with the board liner with the leather edging glued in place. The leather was worked into the board profiling, with the turn-in notched as in Fig. 99. The board was turned over (on a foam-plastic sheet) and immediately filled in with thin card to level up. As usual the in-fill card and the turn-ins were cut through simultaneously, the pieces of waste leather removed and the in-fill glued down with PVA and paste mix (Fig. 24).

Any small adjustments to the image were made at that stage by application of more onlay fragments to the soft, damp cover. (These are easily recessed by local pressure with the bone folder.) When almost dry the covered board was pressed, with a foam-plastic sheet on the grain side, and allowed to 'mature' dry for several hours. (My bindery is usually about 17°C (63°F) 63 per cent R.H.) The drying may be assisted with a fan-heater.

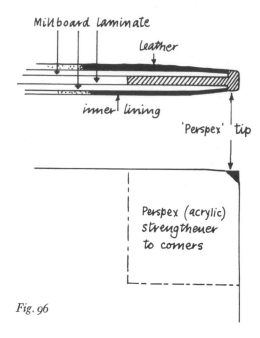

Fig. 96

### Lining the boards

The in-fill card is the first liner and the following day the boards were re-lined with Goatskin Parchment paper, which has a strong 'pull'. Pull may be controlled by the amount of liquid in the adhesive, or by damping and air-drying after the liner has been put down and dried out. (See 36, pp. 224–8 for a good account of the effects of wet adhesives on paper and board.)

I usually observe the behaviour of the boards over several days in different temperatures/humidities, and line accordingly. Boards look better pulling towards the book than warping away, but they should be flat under all normal conditions. I estimate that if the boards are flat after the penultimate lining, the doublures will prevent the boards warping outwards. If the board is level after filling in, I feather the edges of subsequent linings along the straight edge of a paring-stone, using sandpaper. On this book the in-fill card followed the profiling of the foredge, and the doublures (hand-painted Goatskin Parchment), were carefully cut to follow the edges of the boards – allowing for swell in gluing (Fig. 99.)

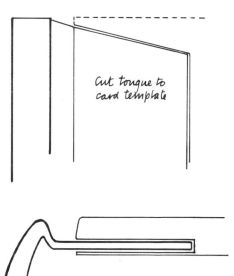

Fig. 97

Before the doublures were finally put down the gold kid in the recesses was worked in the following manner. The gold-surfaced kid was pared for puckering to allow for 'movements' in the design by judiciously paring thinner in places, to allow creases to form where needed. Pieces of thin manilla card were cut to shape (trumpets and architectural shapes on the front board, and trumpets and a 'sun-burst' on the back board) and pasted to a piece of thin hand-made mending paper. The gold kid was pasted and puckered over the manilla shapes and on the paper, left until dry and then all but a fibrous stabilizing layer of the paper peeled off the back. The gold areas were trimmed to shape and glued to fit in the recesses. (The covers could then be pressed without injury to the puckered kid.)

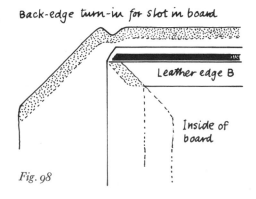

Fig. 98

## Attachment of the covered boards

The boards were prepared for attachment to the tongue of the spine leather. First the slot cut-out negative was removed from the cover with tweezers; the tongue extending from the spine was glued each side and a little adhesive introduced to the slot of the board with a paint brush (or by transfer from a slip of oilboard). The boards were then pushed on to the tongues, adjusted for squares and the book pressed, first through foam-plastic pads, then with formica (plastics) surfaced boards – with 'tins' (non-ferrous metal sheets) inside the boards. The board-lining doublures were glued and set in position and the book pressed again. During the maturing process the book was alternately pressed for a period, then left to stand, boards agape, for a period.

During all the operations the book-block had (after the endbanding stage) been capped-up with a silicone-paper wrapper as a barrier against damp from the boards and to protect the gold edges. A sheet of Photoprinto (blotting paper) had been kept between the leather joint and the first fly-leaf to prevent set-off of colour and pressure marks from the joint. These barriers were finally removed after the leather and the hand-painted papers had been treated with micro-crystalline wax polish.

## Book-box

A book-box (Fig. 100) was made at a convenient stage (i.e. when the book is dry after covering and lining) and finally a binder's note was tipped to a guard provided in the last section, reporting the past history of the book and the use of any adhesives, chemicals, etc.

Another style of book-box is described in Fig. 101.

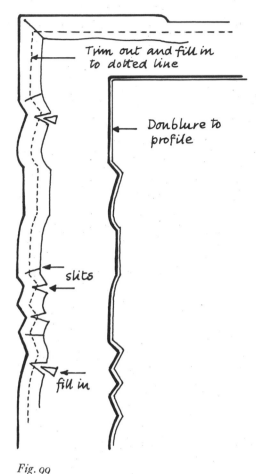

Trim out and fill in to dotted line

Doublure to profile

slits

fill in

Fig. 99

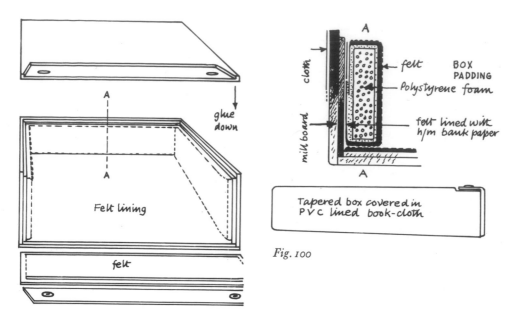

glue
down

cloth

mill board

A

A

felt

BOX PADDING

Polystyrene foam

felt lined with h/m bank paper

Felt lining

felt

Press-studs

Tapered box covered in PVC lined book-cloth

*Fig. 100*

*Fig. 101*

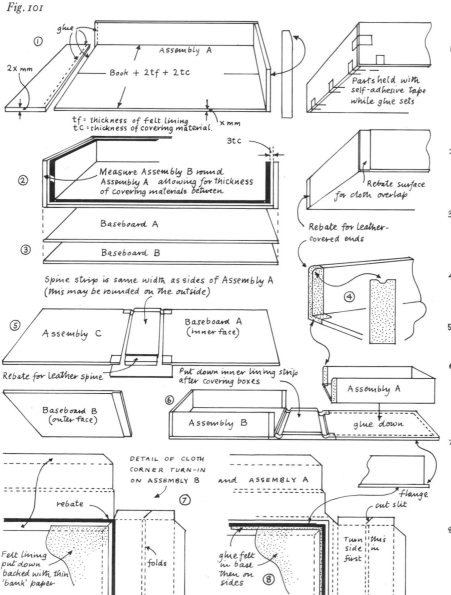

① glue

2x mm

Assembly A

Book + 2tf + 2tc

tf = thickness of felt lining
tc = thickness of covering material.

x mm

② Measure Assembly B round Assembly A allowing for thickness of covering materials between

3tc

③ Baseboard A

Baseboard B

Spine strip is same width as sides of Assembly A (this may be rounded on the outside)

⑤ Assembly C

Baseboard A (inner face)

Rebate for leather spine

Put down inner lining strip after covering boxes

Baseboard B (outer face)

⑥ Assembly B

Parts held with self-adhesive tape while glue sets

Rebate surface for cloth overlap

Rebate for leather-covered ends

④

Assembly A

glue down

DETAIL OF CLOTH CORNER TURN-IN ON ASSEMBLY B

rebate

⑦

Felt lining put down backed with thin 'bank' paper

folds

and ASSEMBLY A

flange

cut slit

Turn this side in first

glue felt in base then on sides

⑧

## DROP-BACK BOOK-BOX

1. Place bound book on millboard and cut to size; allow for thickness of total lining and covering material clearance all round, including thickness of book, when cutting sides. Glue edges and assemble A.

2. Place Assembly A on millboard and cut to size allowing three thicknesses of cloth (covering) clearance between.

3. Cut two baseboards A and B and spine strip (2x mm) Cut leather for spine. Make all surface rebates to receive leather flush.

4. Cut four thinly pared pieces of leather and cover open ends of both Assemblies A and B.

5. Make "case" Assembly C from Baseboards and spine strip.

6. Glue bases of both Assemblies A and B and fit to Assembly C. Sandpaper all edges and make rebates to accommodate overlaps of covering cloth.

7. Cut out book-cloth (or buckram etc.) with corner profiles. Cover both box Assemblies; cover the inside of the spine strip and hinges with cloth (or leather) lining.

8. Line inside of Assembly A base and sides. Also base of Assembly B (lid) with felt. Title and decorate box as required.

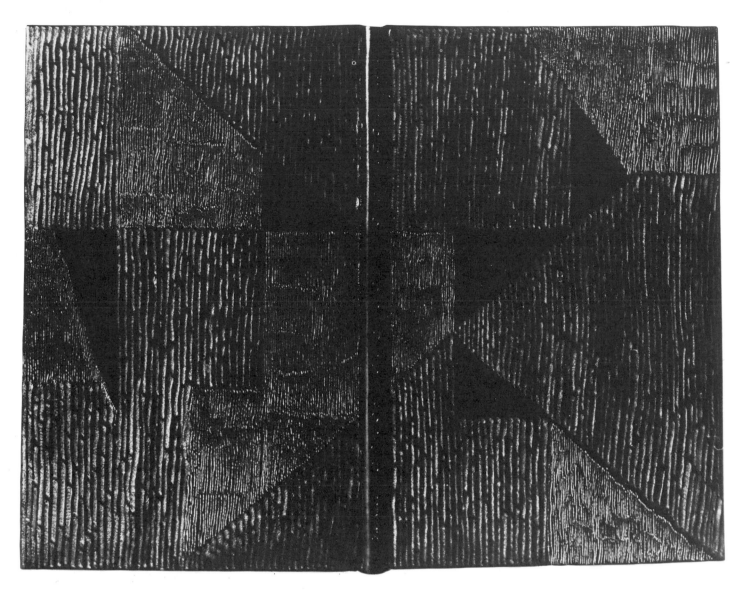

71    Monique Mathieu
Poems by André Frenaud *Pour l'Office des Morts* illustrated by Raoul Ubac.
Ed. Pab à Alès.
Black calf scribed with a hot tool. Blind lettering. Large quarto. 1965

72   Monique Mathieu
André Suares *Passion* illustrated by G. Roualt
Natural veined calf. Calf onlays in relief. Large Quarto (section 23) 1967

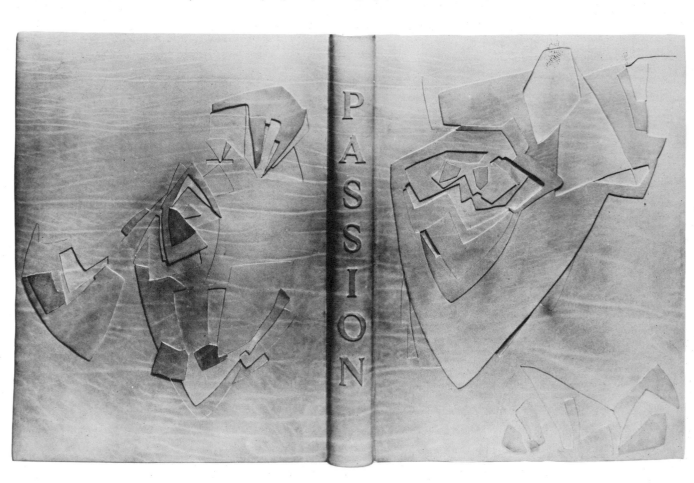

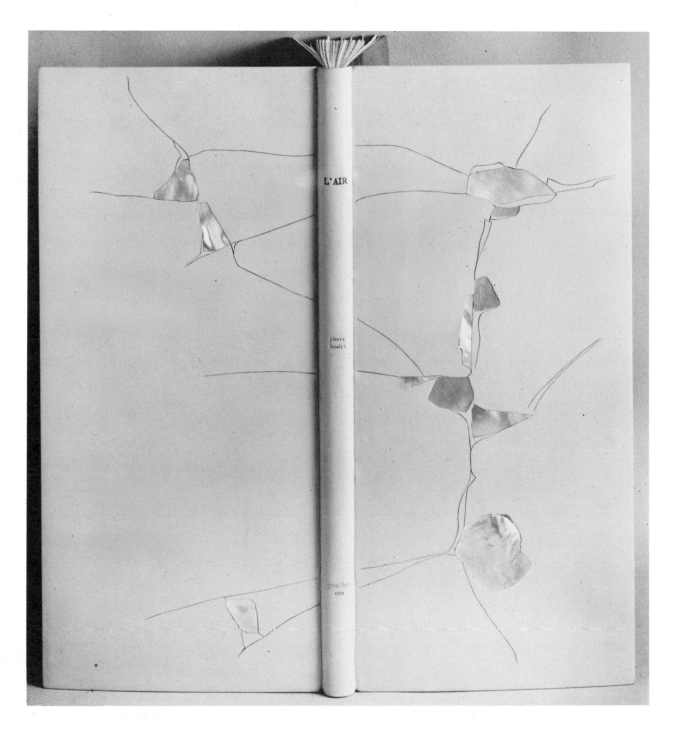

73   Monique Mathieu
Poem by Pierre Lecuire *L'Air* illustrated by Genevieve Asse.
Ivory box calf. Tinted incised lines. Fragments of mother–of–pearl inlaid. 1967

74

74　Gotthilf Kurz
Homer *Odyssee* Bremer Presse. No date
Dark-red morocco. Blind tooling
345 × 220 × 40mm (13½ × 8⅝ × 1½in)

75　Gotthilf Kurz
Platon *Das Gastmahe* Ars Librorum, Frankfurt.
Blue 'Oasis' morocco. Blind tooling
420 × 320 × 40mm (16½ × 12½ × 1½in) No date

75

76  Gotthilf Kurz
Homer *Odyssey* Bremer Press
Natural native niger morocco. Hand-cut plastic block stamped in blind.
Tooled title
345 × 230mm (13½ × 9in)

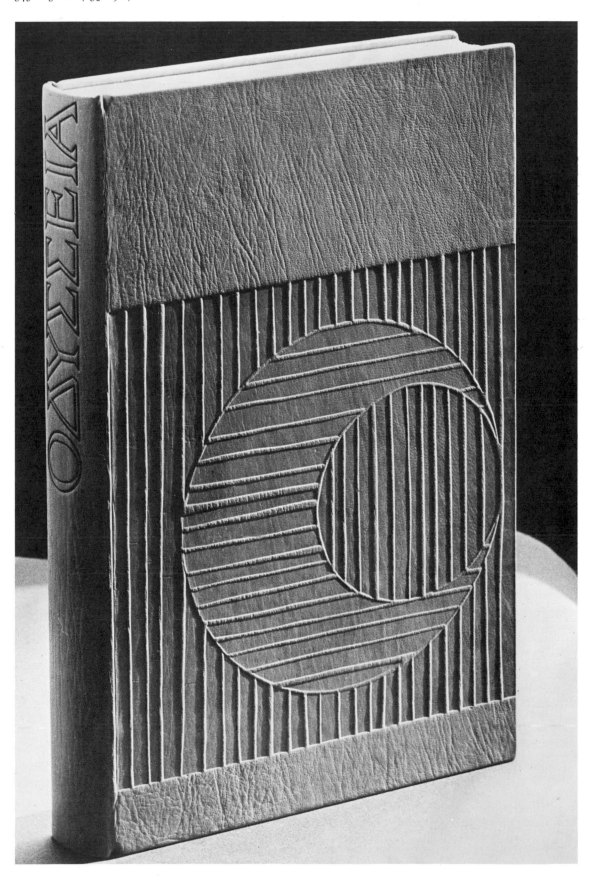

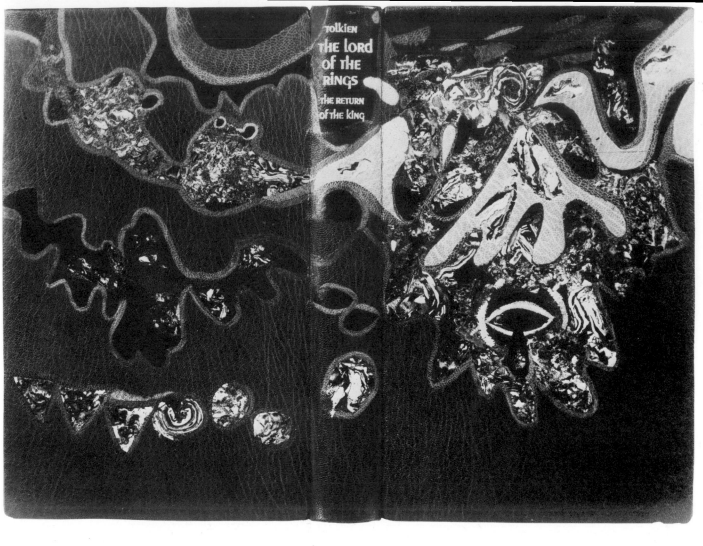

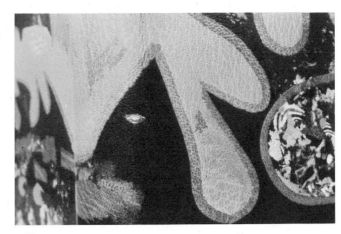

79A    79B

79C    79D

79E

77    Philip Smith
*The Lord of the Rings*
Vol 3. Set 5 of book-wall (Plates 44, 45)

78    Philip Smith
*The Lord of the Rings.*
Vol 3. Set 4. (See Plates 40, 41 for colours)

79A    Philip Smith
*The Lord of the Rings*
Detail. Vol 1. Set 4. back cover

79B    Philip Smith
Detail. Vol 1. Set 4. spine

79C    Philip Smith
Detail. Vol 1. Set 7. front cover

79D    Philip Smith
Detail. Vol 2. Set 6. back cover

79E    Philip Smith
Detail. Vol 1. Set 1. back cover.

80A

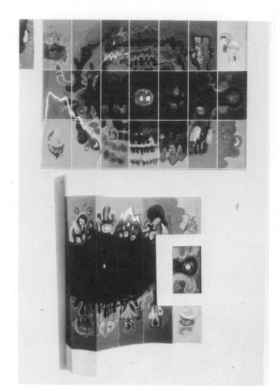

80B

80C

80D

80A   Philip Smith
*The Lord of the Rings*
Original sketches folded together. Back and
front cover designs. Vol. 1. Set 4. Isolated in
card frame

80B   Philip Smith
Colour sketches for *The Lord of the Rings*
book-wall

80C   Philip Smith
Onlay work with mounted needles (Fig. 31)

80D   Philip Smith
Book-wall volumes at different stages of
binding

80E   Philip Smith
Some of the spines

80E

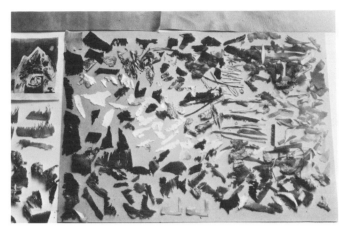

81A        81B

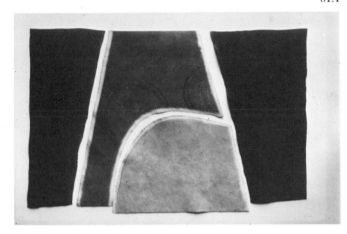

81C

81D

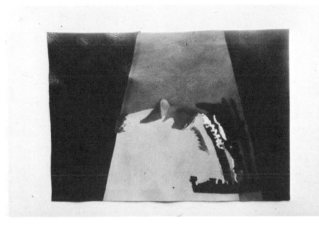

81A   Philip Smith
*The Lord of the Rings*
Title piece onlay of No 4 Plate 82. The small book-wall

81B   Philip Smith
Feathered onlay fragments for No 2 Plate 43

81C   Philip Smith
Leather scarfed for joining, No 3

81D   Philip Smith
Leather joined and onlays begun, No 3

81E   Philip Smith
Checking link-up of No 3 and No 6

81F   Philip Smith
Detail of 'snuffed 'onlay, No 3. back

81G   Philip Smith
Detail of 'netted' onlay, No 2. back

81E        81F                              81G

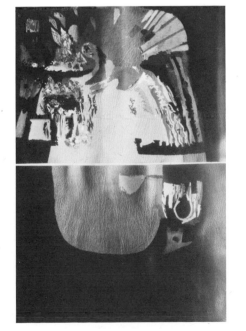

83A

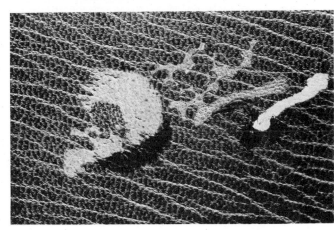

83B

83C

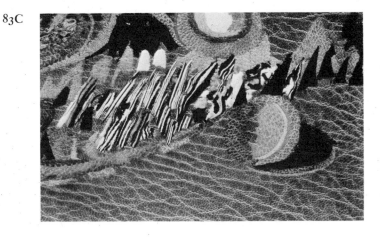

82    Philip Smith
J. R. R. Tolkien *Lord of the Rings*
Deluxe India-paper edition (From book-wall plate 43)
Black and grey 'Oasis', puckered silver kid onlays,
feathered onlays and maril. Palladium edges and title
230 × 150 × 28mm (9 × 6 × 1⅛in) 1970-71

83A    Philip Smith
*The Swiss Watch* (Plate 13) Detail of movements and grain

83B    Philip Smith
*The Waste Land* (Plate 41)
Detail of boarded grain resembling wind-blown sand

83C    Philip Smith
*The Waste Land*. Detail from front cover

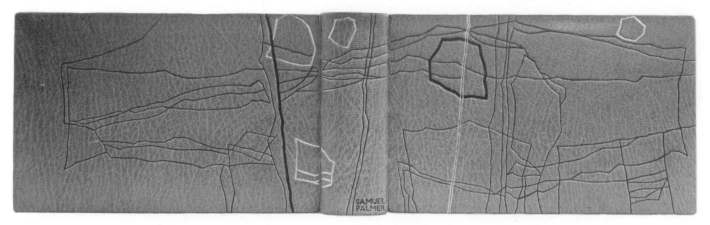

84

84 Ivor Robinson
Martin Butlin *Samuel Palmer's Sketch Book – 1824* Trianon Press
Natural 'Oasis' goatskin. Tooled in blind and gold
$123 \times 167 \times 40$mm ($4\frac{7}{8} \times 6\frac{1}{2} \times 1\frac{1}{2}$in) 1969
Private collection

85 Ivor Robinson
Marc Chagall *Dessins pour la Bible*
Black Cape goatskin. Onlaid black calf and yellow goatskin. Gold tooling
$360 \times 257 \times 36$mm ($14\frac{1}{8} \times 10 \times 1\frac{3}{8}$in) 1970
Private collection

86 Ivor Robinson
N. M. Penzer *The Most Noble and Famous Travels of Marco Polo*
Argonaut Press.
Black 'Oasis'. Onlaid black and white calf. Gold tooling
$261 \times 190 \times 63$mm ($10\frac{1}{4} \times 7\frac{1}{2} \times 2\frac{1}{2}$in) 1971
Private collection

87 Ivor Robinson
*The Eclogues of Vergil*
Brown 'Oasis'. Onlaid black and white calf and natural 'Oasis'. Gold tooling
$337 \times 249 \times 33$mm ($13\frac{1}{4} \times 9\frac{3}{4} \times 1\frac{1}{4}$in) 1972

85

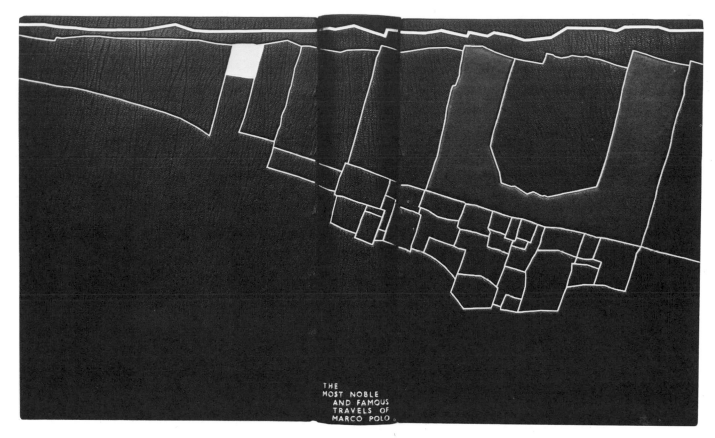

THE
MOST NOBLE
AND FAMOUS
TRAVELS OF
MARCO POLO.

86

87

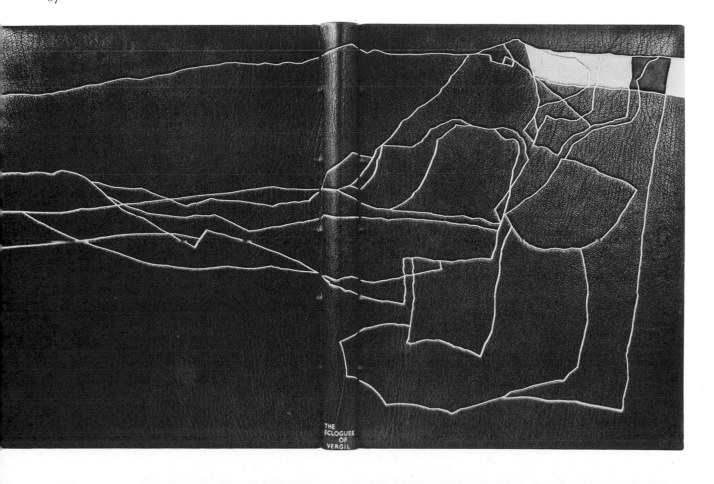

THE
ECLOGUES
OF
VERGIL

88   Santiago Brugalla
François Villon *Le Testament*
Clip-book of more than fifty development sketches for the binding

89   Santiago Brugalla
François Villon *Le Testament* illustrated by Maurice l'Hoir
Red and grey morocco. Red, black, orange and grey onlays. Gold lines,
palladium pearls (dots)
380 × 280mm (15 × 11in) 1966

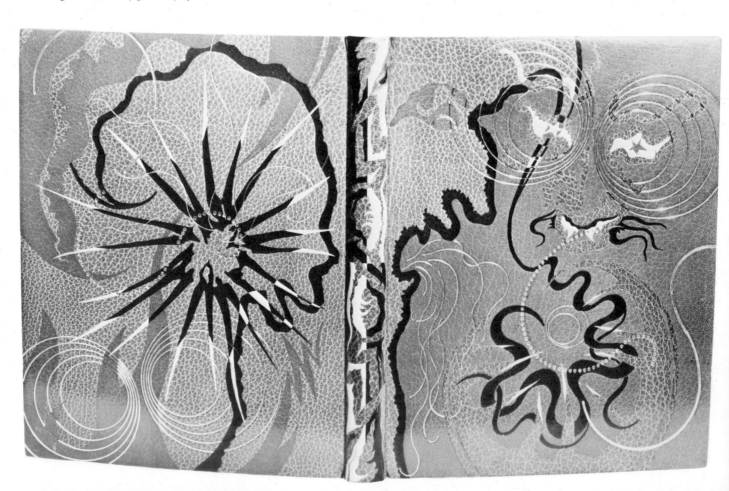

90　Philip Smith
W. B. Yeats. Above left: *Early Poems and Stories* Above right: *Poems 1899–1905*
Lower left: *The Cutting of an Agate* Lower right: *Ideas of Good and Evil*
Oasis morocco. Book-box with four compartments
Each book 190 × 134 × (24–40)mm (7½ × 5¼ × (1–1½)in) 1969–70

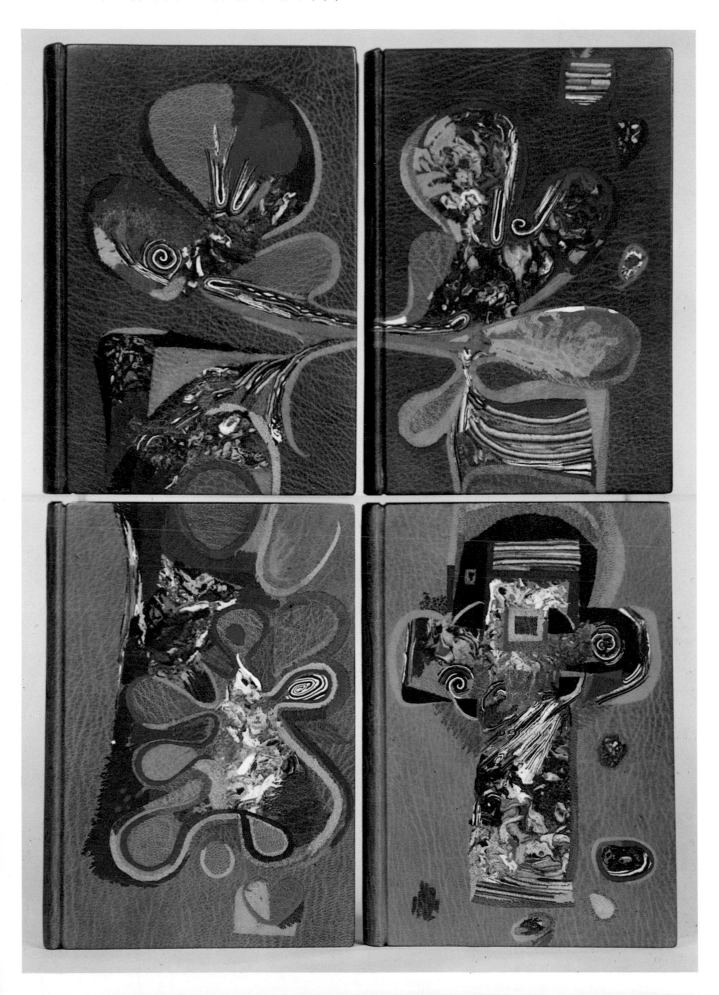

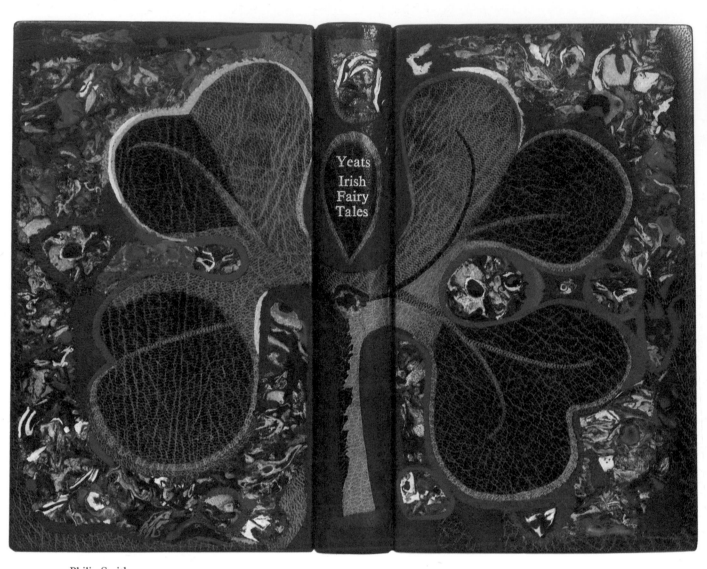

91   Philip Smith
Ed W. B. Yeats *Irish Fairy Tales*
Green and Purple 'Oasis', scarf-joined. Feathered onlays and maril
160 × 100 × 19mm (6¼ × 4 × ¾in) 1969
Private collection

92   Emilio Brugalla
Charles Baudelaire *Les Fleurs du Mal* illustrated by Henri Matisse
Grey morocco, modelled and tooled in blind

93   Santiago Brugalla
Rafael Alberti *Los Ojos de Picasso*
Black, grey, orange, red, mauve, blue and green moroccos. Some raised and
inset work. Gold tooling
460 × 350mm (18 × 13¾in) 1967

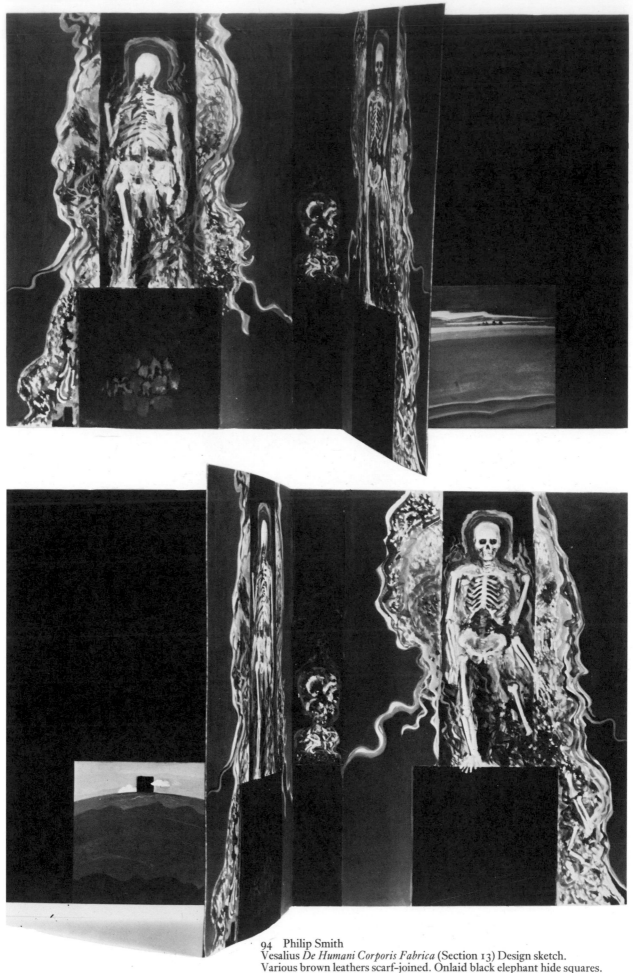

94    Philip Smith
Vesalius *De Humani Corporis Fabrica* (Section 13) Design sketch.
Various brown leathers scarf-joined. Onlaid black elephant hide squares.
Skeleton modelled in low relief and onlaid, in recessed maroon leather panel.
Black leather flyleaves with onlaid leather 'landscapes'. 1974

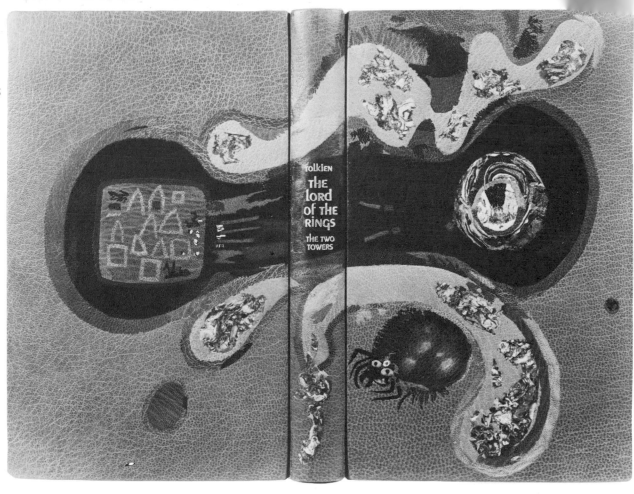

95  Philip Smith
J. R. R. Tolkien *Lord of the Rings* Volume 2, set 7.
In the book-wall (Plate 45)
230 × 150 × 33mm (9 × 6 × 1¼in) 1969

96  Philip Smith
J. R. R. Tolkien *The Lord of the Rings*
Blue and black 'Oasis'. Onlays of black elephant hide, puckered silver kid,
maril and feathered onlays. Corners reinforced with blue and black plexiglas
(perspex). Agate inset through board. Palladium and gold edges.
230 × 150 × 30mm (9¼ × 6 × 1⅛in) 1973
Crafts Advisory Committee presentation to HRH The Duke of Edinburgh

96

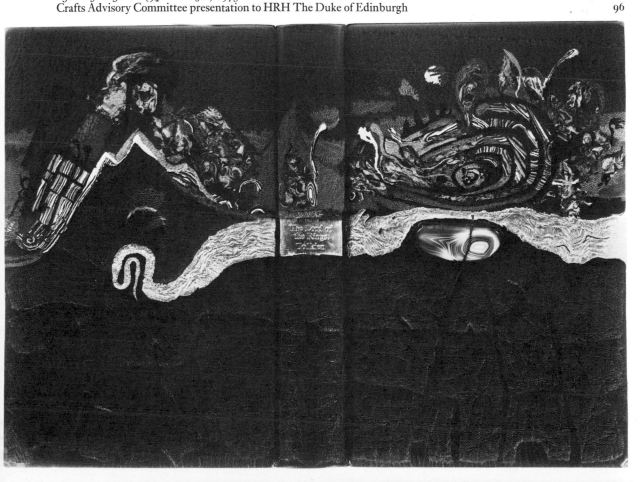

## 20 Conservation versus creation?

At the present time there is a good deal of conflict and misunderstanding between the conservator (of library materials) and the creative bookbinders; the latter being thought in general to care too little about the structural and chemical well-being of the books they are 'over-packaging'. But there are two sides to every coin! Today specialists are emerging in all fields. The 1966 flood in Florence can now be seen to have been beneficial to all sides in bookbinding, giving a great impetus to conservators and to structural bookbinders especially. Research into sounder methods in the conservation of library materials develops apace, as also does research into non-destructive methods of binding; notably under Peter Waters and Chris Clarkson (who has a special interest in un-glued and limp vellum bindings) at the Library of Congress in Washington, and Anthony Cains in Dublin. Greater financial resources are being poured into the work all over the world, but methods recommended yesterday for, say, bleaching, fumigation or de-acidification are obsolete and even condemned today (Section 21).

The methods of the conservator are aimed at decreasing the rate of change and decay in materials. The conservator tries to prevent forms going out of existence; to put materials into their original functional condition; and to build in safeguards against the active agents of deterioration in the environment; in short, to prevent the shrinkage of our heritage.

The creative artist (as bookbinder) on the other hand tries to bring immaterial forms into existence; to increase our cultural heritage. Where the artist may work alone, perhaps advisably, the conservator, with less autonomy, must work as a member of a team, or at least in consultation with a network of research; a picture well drawn by Anthony Cains in his article.

### The future of the book

The book made entirely from plastics materials will fill a larger proportion of industrial book production, mainly because the manufacture of paper removes too great a bulk of vegetable resources which cannot be replaced as fast as it is consumed, and these resources can be re-cycled only at considerable loss of quality. Thermoplastics on the other hand can be melted down, ink and print preparation materials may be separated out and the plastics re-used with negligible loss of quality. There is in any case no such thing as waste material; with the right installations for recovery and re-cycling no resources need be wasted.

Conservators will continue to protect and prolong the life of existing books, and fine binding as an art will continue indefinitely so long as there are artists capable of working this medium. Miniaturization in computers and electronic storage systems will take over the role of reference libraries. Central exchanges will transmit news and other information to tape convertors in the home. Already it is possible to record the whole of the Bible, or Shakespeare or Beethoven's musical compositions on a 40mm ($1\frac{1}{2}$in) plastics square. The projection system is at present bulky but eventually will be reduced to pocket size. The whole British Library could be contained in an average sized filing cabinet, and audio-visual aids of all kinds could replace the reading book, as we know it.

97   Bryan Maggs
John Gay *Trivia*
Dark-blue 'Oasis'. Gold tooling
$285 \times 195 \times 20$mm ($11\frac{1}{4} \times 7\frac{3}{4} \times \frac{3}{4}$in) 1969
Collection: British Museum

## 21 New attitudes to conservation

by Anthony Cains

In the field of conservation one must be thoroughly honest. This means that one must work in terms of function and not effect; that one records and makes known the processes to which one subjects the work and that the materials used are, to the best of one's knowledge, also honest – seen and unseen! It precludes a 'double standard' in workmanship – quality of execution and methods.

The term 'restoration' has unpleasant implications and one is obliged to use it in combination with the word 'conservation'. In practical terms they imply the following:
Conservation means good storage and maintenance, that is, library and archive hygiene, careful handling and display and in the hands of the restorer/conservator such operations as cleaning, fumigation, de-acidification, buffering, sizing and the manufacture of dust-proof containers (*44, 21, 33*). Restoration in the traditional sense is performing skilfully such operations as the removal of stains and disfigurements, infilling of lost original material and the replacing of irreparably damaged binding components with new material, for example, when re-sewing, but controlled by the ethics and standards of modern conservation in general. This manifests itself in a completely honest approach in terms of methods and materials.

Simply, the new material should be distinguished from the original – by this I do not imply a screaming contrast but warn against any attempt to perfect the subject or produce when binding, a sterile facsimile. The restorer's responsibility is to stabilize and protect the subject; no more and no less. (Cf. *39*, Preface p. xviii.)

### On receipt of the book

This may sound obvious, but nevertheless check the collation and pencil collate any unidentified leaves, plates, etc., and if the book appears incomplete, refer the fact to the client before pulling the book. Keep a well documented record of the book as received – noting its condition with as much detail as time allows. Note the condition of the paper and the image and the condition and construction of the binding. This can be done to an extent depending on the value and interest of the volume, and its binding, and at various levels depending, above all, on the interests of the observer and his knowledge and ability. Once the binder makes the effort to do this, the rewards will be great – his knowledge and skill will be vastly improved. Much benefit is to be derived from the study of book construction and design. Take notes on the materials used and how well they have endured (*22, 53*). Make careful drawings of clasp forms, corner cutting, lacing-in – board attachment methods, etc. Analyse the sewing method, the endbanding method (*48, 38, 46, 43, 29, 54, 60, 40* etc.).

### Dry cleaning

Before beginning the wet processing the subject must be dry cleaned but great care must be taken to avoid abrading the surface or removing the image. The powdered rubber 'breadcrumbs' of 'Draft clean' will be found most useful for removing general surface grime and the powered eraser for fine detail. Professor Wächter refers to their value in the restoration of flood damaged material (61). Various grades of rubber are available, suitable for use on paper and skin (1).

## Image fixing

It is often necessary to fix poorly adhering pigment before proceeding with the restoration of the subject. We have found gelatine and gelatine hardened with a little formaldehyde particularly useful when dealing with tempera (61), when the leaves require wet processing. Alcoholic solutions such as soluble nylon or Paraloid B72 dissolved in xylene can be used but it is advisable to immerse the whole subject in the solvent of the fixative resin before application, thereby removing impurities soluble in that solvent. This avoids the danger of creating an ugly 'halo' stain around the fixed image area. In all cases, attention should be paid to the extent to which the fixative and solvent alters or affects the colour and its components, for example, the gamboge component of Hooker's Green is soluble in alcohol.

## Washing

Washing is undoubtedly the most beneficial wet process and the safest. It removes impurities and de-acidifies most papers providing the paper can be wetted. Some difficulty will be experienced with papers that have been sized with rosin and alum, starch, or gelatine hardened with alum. This can be overcome by first immersing the subject in Ethanol and then in the washing water, or by adding a trace of non-ionic wetting agent to the solution (25b). Most printed books can be washed provided that any unstable image or colour is fixed previously. If the paper is badly degraded, through the action of mould for example, then handling will be difficult, but given the correct mechanical support and processing technique, washing is possible. Supports can be metal, plastic, fabric or paper either rigid or flexible. The rigid types would be used for the more fragile material, but are expensive to produce. A very good frame is one made of stainless steel mesh drummed into a flat frame. Two frames make up a support, sandwiching the subject, and lock together, but of course they will have to be made by professional metal workers. This type is used by the Patologia del Libro in Rome. The restorer can make his own from readily available materials such as perspex (plexiglas) or wood for the frame, on to which is fixed a nylon mesh. Flexible supports can be of 'wet strength' paper, that is a paper sized with a cross linked synthetic resin terylene or nylon fabric, nylon mesh as used in silk screen printing (the coarser grades), PVC perforated sheeting, etc.

Wetting agents should not be used unless absolutely essential, since their long term effects on the cellulose are not known. If one must be used a lengthy rinse in running water must follow. The cellulose derivatives have good cleaning power and are to be recommended, since at low concentrations (about 0·2 per cent) they have a certain detergent action (25b) through their ability to hold dirt particles in suspension.

## Bleaching

Bleaching is without doubt the most potentially damaging of all restoration processes. The restorer should read all that is available in conservation literature and keep up with developments in new materials and methods (45, 25). The decision on whether to bleach or not and which method to employ must be taken on the dry subject, and only after a thorough washing in hot or cold water and treatment with organic solvents for specific stains such as mineral oil stains. It is most important to consider the subject matter, for example in archive work many stains and imperfections are considered important parts of the document as it has survived to the present day. But any foreign matter the continued presence of which would degrade the paper must be removed or neutralized.

The most common cause of staining and discoloration is the presence of traces of iron and copper incorporated in the paper during its manufacture or subsequently as a component of the image pigment. Bleaching is not the answer in this case – possibly the use of a sequestering agent is (31a). When considering a printed book – one that is likely to be placed on permanent display for the beauty of its typography or illustrations – then efforts can be made as thought necessary to remove severe disfigurements. But if the treatment required for this purpose is too drastic – for example the use of oxalic acid to remove iron stains – and will degrade the paper too much, then the stains are better left well alone.

## Bleaching agents

In the restoration department of the Biblioteca Nazionale Centrale in Florence (5, 11) the agents employed in order of frequency are sodium hypochlorite and ethereal-hydrogen peroxide. Permanganate and chloromine-T are used hardly at all. During 1972, it was hoped to get into operation a chlorine dioxide bleaching chamber (23). For all bleaching procedures, the best ones are those where the bleaching action is under constant view, which do not require lengthy treatment, and where the bleaching action can, if required, be stopped immediately. Permanganate bleaching is very popular in Germany (3), and is effective for the removal of mould stains – but the bleaching action cannot be seen to be happening and the material itself is known to be the most cellulose degrading of all oxidants (25).

Chloramine-T should only be used for bleaching slightly discoloured material. It is a total fallacy to think that because it has the reputation of being a mild bleach, it can be used for long periods – and even at high solution temperature – without danger. Ethereal hydrogen peroxide can be very useful for certain stains but great care must be taken when using it (*45*).

Commercial hydrogen peroxide is stabilized with acid, and in its acid condition is extremely degrading to cellulose.[1] Therefore it is not advisable ever to have the two layers present in the same container. After preparation of the ethereal extract the lower aqueous *acid* layer must be removed. Use of a separating funnel makes the entire procedure easily done.

The use of hypochlorite has been frowned upon, yet when properly employed it can be extremely useful. Before using it all paper should have been thoroughly washed in clean tap water, then after bleaching an anti-chlor should be used followed by extensive rinsing. The most important safety factor is making sure that the pH of the working solution is kept as close to pH 10 as possible, and never lower than pH 9 (*25, 51*). For this control a pH meter should be used – the colour of ordinary pH indicators is affected by the bleach solution. In Florence we felt that a rapid (1–2 min.) treatment with a high concentration of the reagent, followed by use of an anti-chlor and extensive washing, was safer than a more prolonged exposure at a lower concentration.

No bleaching solution should ever be used unless followed by thorough washing, and the necessary corollary to this is that anything which cannot be washed cannot be bleached. And this stricture applies also to the use of Chloramine-T (*25, 61*).

## Sizing

The value of sizing in restoration is principally to give the paper better resistance to handling. By partly sealing the paper surface, particularly when this is porous after wet processing, sizing helps prevent the penetration of dust and grime. The traditional gelatine size is being steadily replaced by more biostatic sizing media (in particular the cellulose derivatives) and starch sizings, used by many restorers to surface size rosin-alum and gelatine-alum papers, should also be discarded. Not only is it, like gelatine, more vulnerable to biological attack, but starch fluoresces strongly in ultra violet radiation, so making more difficult, or impossible, the optical examination of a manuscript treated in this way. Various different materials have been tried out over the past few years as possible replacements for gelatine, but undoubtedly the cellulose derivatives (not all are suitable) will have wide application in this field. They are extremely easy to use, and are available in many grades and types. Cellulose derivatives in solution can be used cold for sprayer application, or like gelatine size, can be used for immersion sizing. It is also possible to add buffering agents, such as magnesium bicarbonate to these solutions so that sizing and

1 The research into the preservation of textiles is often relevant to that of graphic art, particularly to cleaning, bleaching and reinforcing methods and materials: see the IIG 1964 Conference on *The Preservation of Textiles*. A prescription (derived from textile and paper research) was recommended by my colleague in Florence, Joe Nkrumah, and used successfully by Maighread McParland of the National Gallery of Ireland, and is as follows: 5 gms sodium hydroxide, 5 gms sodium carbonate, 20–25 gms sodium silicate, 5% hydrogen peroxide 25 vol, 1 litre water. Refer also to the IIG 1972 Lisbon Congress publication, *The Conversation of Paintings and the Graphic Arts*, A. Sharin and Prof D. Wächter, page 956. The method is recommended for bleaching paper containing mechanical wood fibre.

buffering can be carried out together. It would be possible to do a soft sizing on the paper while washing it. It should always be kept in mind that extremely dirty or acid papers need cleaning, washing and sizing in separate processes.

## De-acidification/buffering

The first of these processes removes free acid present in the paper while the second leaves behind compounds which will preferentially react with acids in the future and so, to a certain extent, protects the cellulose. Since in Florence our books were washed, we did not need to de-acidify and used just the Barrow one-shot (magnesium bicarbonate solution) treatment. It is very convenient to be able to size and buffer at the same time. As with bleaching methods, existing de-acidification and buffering methods are under review at the moment, so restorers are strongly urged to keep up with the literature.

The available methods all have their disadvantages – apart from the high alkalinity they can confer on the paper. The aqueous buffering solutions can affect ferro-gallate inks through their alkalinity reacting with the iron and changing the ink colour to a pale brown, and the solvent in non-aqueous solutions (2, 4, 57) can react with certain inks - for example, aniline blue-black in printing ink – causing it to run or feather. Yet on the whole they work well. The biggest problem in this field at the moment is the development of methods suitable for rapid and economical application to a wide range of library and archive materials. Langwell's vapour phase (31) de-acidification was a very sound idea but it is discredited by some. D. Smith (57) has devised a spray technique which is still in its development stage. But so far, no magic solution to this problem seems in sight.

## Mending

The approach to the physical strengthening of paper or skin is a good gauge of the attitude of the conservator/restorer to the preservation of library and archive material. Most restorers spend more time discussing this aspect of their work than the more important 'chemical' wellbeing of the subject – mainly because of our lack of understanding of the chemistry of paper and its image, and also because its results are much more 'visible' and 'tangible' than those of many other restorative processes. The repair methods in use at the present moment can be divided into several groups (11).

*Wet processing* where all components are humidified and assembled (referred to by Wardle as 'full repair', 66).

*Wet processing* where the components are dry, but an aqueous adhesive is used to join the components (infilling, subject) called 'mending' by Wardle. The mended subject may be slightly humidified and pressed to ensure a flat finish.

*Dry processing* where all the components are dry when assembled. Thermoplastic resins such as the methacrylate dispersions are applied to the reinforcing paper and dried prior to their use and then fixed in position with a heated spatula, followed by hot pressing to consolidate (*25a*).

*Solvent processing* where all components are dry and the assembled whole is 'set' by the application of a suitable organic solvent for the synthetic resin adhesive involved (*28*).

*Combination* of several of the above-mentioned 'groups' together, i.e. 'orthodox' with the heat-set paper-tissue method.

Under the first group comes liquid-fibre mending and reinforcement, used extensively on the Continent, mainly Germany and the East European countries. This is an important development of an old idea based on the working principle of the paper-mill laboratory sheet-forming apparatus (*59*).

The first two groups may be regarded as 'orthodox' or 'traditional' (except perhaps liquid-fibre mending) in that the methods are readily reversible, so the exponents maintain, because natural water-soluble adhesives and 'natural' materials are used, although it has been shown in the field of painting conservation at least that most natural adhesives have hastened the decay of the subject. The traditional restorers' resistance to 'synthetics', e.g. resins, fabrics, adhesives, etc., even those proved biostatic, reversible, permanent and durable, is gradually crumbling as confidence in each new material increases – the test of time that is constantly referred to. It is well to remember how difficult flour paste is to remove after ageing, particularly when it is well impregnated into the paper felt. Hence the interest in enzymes, which are expensive and difficult to control outside the well-equipped laboratory.

In the main, this resistance is our fear of the unknown and an inability to assess modern materials and to interpret the available literature. In the case of soluble nylon, for example, it is that its use is recommended without due regard to available international literature on its limitations. This is true of many other materials accepted for restoration purposes purely instinctively, empirically. Restorers must look world wide for guidance. The encrustation of paper documents, books, prints – with layers of backing paper or calico, or making board-like sandwiches from layered mould- or vat-made paper and flour paste, and so on – is totally repugnant, and destroys the original character of the subject. The use of gossamer-thin tissues of pure cellulose for reinforcing; long fibre papers of pure cellulose for infilling and reinforcing (backing); liquid fibre – pure cellulose techniques for infilling and the overlaying of thinned or weakened areas with a fibre reinforcement, is far more acceptable in our opinion.

## Edge trimming

The only time that this is permitted is:
a) when a leaf projects slightly from the book block and carries no image, but only with the permission of the client or custodian.
b) to remove minute fragments and edge fibrillations.

Each leaf must be considered individually and the very minimum removed. Do not use guillotine, plough, scraper or sand the book's edges of any early or otherwise valuable material. Although collectors will revolt – it is advisable to open uncut head and foredge folds on library volumes but consult the librarian before doing so. It is better for the binder to slit them open with a sharp knife than a reader with his pencil.

## Notes on conservation bookbinding

Bookbinding is the process of making the *protective* cover for the stabilized object. This includes sewing – the most important single operation of binding; boarding, and board attachment to the sewing supports; endbanding – that little understood but very important operation; spine lining, where the importance of good quality materials is neglected and the hollow back used too much – and its value over-estimated, also used as a means of obscuring poor construction.[2] From a study of early binding methods and materials, the first thing that is impressed on the mind is that the permanence of the book rests primarily on the permanence of the materials used, then upon its storage and use, and finally, its method of construction.

In other words it is useless doing fine, or any kind of work with poor materials and then sending the book back to a dirty or damp bookstack. This also applies to modern designed bindings – they are too expensive a production for ephemeral materials to be used. Materials must not be selected for use merely because they are the right colour. Lumps, bumps and raised decoration may be criticized because they may abrade if carelessly handled (Plates 1, 19). But the first question must be, as in all other aspects of restoration: is the material used satisfactory? Nothing does more to alter the original 'feel' and appearance of the book than pulling it and re-sewing. When re-sewing do not neglect to use the best materials available and the best sewing techniques. Our BNCF experience has shown that linen is undoubtedly more permanent than white tawed or tanned supports. Just as the recessed cord method does not answer all the sewing requirements, neither does the tape method. A book for rebinding should not be sewn in a particular way simply because of some concept of style: e.g. an early printed book bound in an 'incunabulam style' on double cords; but because of the size of the volume, its weight, its value and the need for a really good conservation-grade binding demand it; that is, the specification is made not only with reference to 'period' but mainly to the conservation/binding needs of the book.

2 The fine-binder will very often use a hollow-back with a 'decorative' spine. With a tight-back all tooling, onlays, etc will soon distort and disintegrate. A tight-back of leather is inherently weak in that it is this layer attached directly to the backbone which is exposed to the action of the atmosphere, and with its continuous flexing it is the first area of the covering to break down. The hollow creates an extra protective back *over* a lined 'tight-back', and would preferably be reinforced with linen or lawn (Fig 93). C.P.S.

The first gluing is always with a (permanently) water-soluble adhesive such as the cellulose derivatives. This layer acts as a 'release layer' in the event of the book being 'pulled'. The lining may be attached with paste or animal glue, but again, a more biostatic adhesive, such as an internally plasticized polyvinylacetate is to be preferred and always used as thinly as possible. Methycellulose may be added to the PVA to retard its drying and to dilute the mixture instead of water. When the spine folds are covered either with a zig-zag of folded paper or loose guards the 'release layer' is not so significant – PVA may be used directly without fear of the future consequences.

The only materials for covering that I have full confidence in are tawed goat and pig skins and full thickness sheep and goat vellum. In the vegetable tanned leathers I have less confidence, but Nigerian 'native' tanned natural 'A'-grade goatskin is the best of these, followed by 'native' dyed. English retans, although beautiful, should be regarded with suspicion although 'Oasis' is about the best in this group. Chrome tanned skins or combination tannages containing chrome are regarded as more durable than vegetable tanned skins. They do not tool well but in conservation work this is not considered important. Vegetable pre-tannage with chrome tannage for goatskins is used by at least one very important conservation centre in Germany (3, 4) and has been used successfully in the BNCF on an experimental basis. It is better to cover a book in a good linen or cotton buckram than a leather of uncertain durability, or to continue a bad binding specification merely because a change would break the 'continuity' of the bookstack – spoil the appearance!

## Limp vellum binding

A limp vellum binding with foredge yapp and ties or toggles; laced-through linen endbands on tawed core; sewing supports laced-through. This is a most important conservation binding method because of the known permanence of the materials used and because of the simplicity and easy 'reversibility' of the construction. Little or no adhesive is used, the joins being effected mechanically by lacing-through and 'locking' corners. It is largely true of leather structures that the adhesive is a 'jig', a tool to hold the bits together during assembly. Once assembled, they will not come apart even if the adhesive breaks down.

## Boxes

We must avoid the 'restoration' of any early binding construction of fine workmanship or rarity. Bibliophiles are, of course, interested in preserving the 'original' untouched condition and this includes even the humble paperback and publisher's wrapper. A well-made box is often the best solution. However, the 'original' condition must be such that the subject will not deteriorate further. Its condition should be stabilized. Even if the bookblock has to be treated for severe damage, the binding with all its components can be preserved by careful removal, that is, leaving the cover sewing supports, linings and endbands *in situ* and locked together and rebinding the book. The original cover and newly-bound book can then be preserved together in a box. Boxing is probably the simplest way of conserving library and archive material given a reasonable storage ambience. They should be made as carefully as possible and with good materials – office files just will not do! Boxes for loose documents, prints and drawings, books and manuscripts, bindings, malculatura, fragments, etc. Also cotton velvet bags – 'chemise covers' – for valuable bindings and bound manuscripts, portfolios, envelopes, slip cases, loose leaf covers, etc. But everything made well, accurately, and carefully from fine materials, e.g. linen buckram, rag board, permanent durable paper for lining, etc., made to last for the particular collection and its conservation needs. Even boxing regarded as 'temporary' should be well-constructed from best quality materials. There is never any guarantee that the conservation of the material will go beyond the boxing stage!

*Note:* For invaluable help in writing this short article I have to thank Margaret Hey, researcher, chemist and teacher. All errors are mine. Also Signora Barbara Guiffrida-Ruggeri who has always been unfailing in her help during the wonderful and happy years spent in Florence.

98   Roger Powell's bindery. The studio has excellent daylighting and ergonomic layout. Note the nipping press adapted with heated laminating unit, storage space, drying lines and peels

99   Roger Powell's bindery. Note the tooling turn-table at left edge. Dark room and laboratory are off the main studio

## 22 Case history of repair and rebinding of an eighth-century vellum manuscript

by Roger Powell

Douglas Cockerell used to say that when a craftsman died much of his accumulated knowledge and expertise died with him. And now that the traditional apprenticeship system in many crafts is virtually gone for ever, the statement is certainly as valid as when Cockerell was speaking. This inevitable loss has been aggravated by some top-ranking craftsmen who have deliberately withheld their knowledge until it was too late through fears that apprentices would steal a declining market. But a change may be on the way.

With the growing realization of the importance of, and interest in, conservation it is increasingly becoming the practice to record and publish what is done in the course of operations for the repair and conservation of valuable artefacts in all fields. Among others, this is especially called for when dealing with books because the process of rebinding, if and when it becomes necessary, affords the opportunity for seeing what went before – not only the successes or failures of the binder who last dealt with it, but often what happened at the hands of his predecessors. The recorded details of both the old work and the new, apart from mere historical interest, may be of great value to the next binder when repair, rebinding, or both, again becomes necessary; no binding lasts for ever. Or these same details may serve as warning or guide-line to binders facing similar problems. One may even hope that they may act as enlightenment for librarians! So what follows is an attempt to explain what happens in one bindery in relation to a specific book, and to explain it in some detail.

The book in question is an eighth-century copy of the Gospels. It was incomplete and severely damaged by moulds, rough handling and bookbinders. It is known to have been rebound about 1707, and on this occasion the edges were cut severely. It was again rebound in 1862, and this time the binder cut it into single leaves throughout. At a period in the seventeenth and eighteenth centuries it was common practice to cut away much of the margins of paper-leaved books, and to pulp them to make boards; there was a duty on millboard.

The eighteenth-century binder may well have done his severe edge-trimming as a matter of habit when binding paper-leaved books – the off-cuts would have been useless for pulping. But the heavy cutting may not have been such wanton mutilation as might be supposed; there is ample evidence of great damage to the vellum by moulds particularly at beginning and end, and in the margins. Much of what was cut away may have been virtually beyond repair. Cutting the book into single leaves was undoubtedly the work of the nineteenth-century binder; a few corners turned in when he ploughed the edges before edge-gilding show that he made a very light cut indeed. But the practice was prevalent at the time with binders who were after all concerned almost entirely with binding paper-leaved books for which overcasting is sometimes tolerable. They failed to recognize the different needs of paper and vellum, often with disastrous results. All that can be said in this instance is that after sawing-in for the six cords on which he sewed, he made an exceptionally neat job of overcasting, and kept his 'sections' to only two or three leaves.

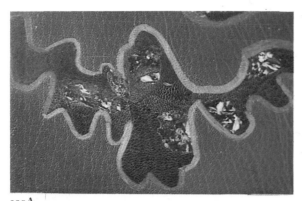

100A

100B

100C

100D

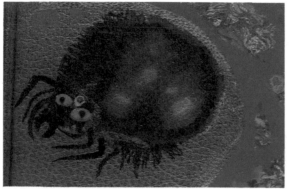

100E

100F

100G

100A  Philip Smith
*The Lord of the Rings* Detail. Vol 3. Set 5, back cover

100B  Philip Smith
*The Lord of the Rings* Detail. Vol 2. Set 3, back cover

100C  Philip Smith
*The Lord of the Rings* Detail. Vol 2. Set 7, front cover

100D  Philip Smith
*The Lord of the Rings* Detail. Vol 3. Set 4, front cover

100E  Philip Smith
*The Waste Land* (Plate 24) Detail. Front cover

100F  Philip Smith
*The Lord of the Rings* Detail. Vol 1. Set 1, back cover

100G  Philip Smith
*The Lord of the Rings* Detail. Vol 2. Set 6, back cover

101   Santiago Brugalla
*Les Sept Pêches Capitaux*
Morocco. Gold lines and palladium dots, with punched and inset leather buttons
250 × 180mm (10 × 7¼in) 1970

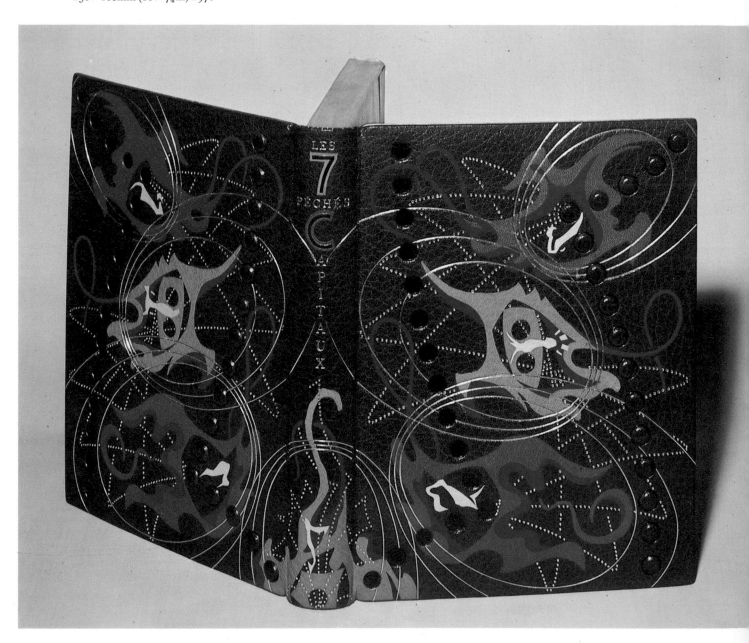

Because the repair and rebinding of an outstanding manuscript, and of such an early date, is a rare event, the opportunity was taken to find out as much as possible about it while the leaves were separated. As part of the research every page was photographed in black and white, together with selected pages and details of them in colour, by the Courtauld Institute. The binder photographed many other details to illustrate technical points.

It cannot be over-emphasized that the best chance of investigating the intricacies of early manuscript books is while they are unbound, though the desire 'to find out' is not by itself justification for pulling a book! But even with the book in pieces, much is likely to be missed in unsuitable lighting conditions. All-over strip lighting is virtually useless – the Students' Room in the Department of Western Manuscripts at the British Museum is no place for this kind of research. Good directional lighting from a rather narrow source is a *sine qua non* (Plate 98, left). And, because there is often so much to be seen, look for and record only one feature at a time! With these things in mind the first problem with this book was to establish the original quiring before it was cut into single leaves. The make-up of an early manuscript, and other idiosyncrasies of the scribe, are important pointers towards identifying its provenance. And re-establishing the original quiring is not so difficult a process as might be supposed even when dealing with an early, irregularly arranged, Irish inspired manuscript. But to do so with a bound book would be quite impracticable. What is needed is the recognition and recording of the character and arrangement of the vellum, and of the scribe's, and sometimes of the binder's techniques; the answers will follow almost of their own accord.

A ruled book is prepared. At each opening the right-hand page carries a line for each leaf, and vertical columns in which to record classified features. The left-hand page is left blank for other notes. It is usually space-saving to adopt a series of conventional signs to represent recurring features. The comparison of what is found on each leaf in relation to its neighbours quickly establishes which were originally conjoint.

The all-important points in most cases are the recognition of hair- and flesh-sides of the vellum, and the direction of the animal's spine in relation to the manuscript. Other things being equal, neither is likely to present any major difficulty in a large-page manuscript: obviously, a leaf with hair-side on the recto could never have formed a conjoint bifolium with another leaf also with hair-side on the recto. Similarly, a leaf with the animal's spine running vertically could not be a pair with one where the spine runs horizontally. If the animal's spines run vertically it is probable that two bifolia were cut from each skin, and because of the behaviour of the fibres at head and tail of the skin, there are likely to be ripples on the edges at head and tail of the book, which will however lie open comparatively easily. Where the animal's spines run horizontally only one bifolium can be cut from the skin and any rippling will appear at the foredge, and the book will lie open comparatively uneasily. The recognition of hair- and flesh-sides comes with practice; the differences depend on the type of skin and how it was prepared. In the book in question it was remarkably easy; in the Lindisfarne Gospels it is often extremely difficult.

Another aid in establishing the original quiring is the pricking for ruling the lines for the manuscript. In this instance it could be seen to have been done with awls while the quire was assembled and folded, the awl passing through all the leaves at one operation, the top leaf showing a larger hole than the bottom one because the awl was tapered. The shapes of the awls, two of them, were characteristic and these shapes still showed clearly in most places, even after all the vicissitudes of twelve hundred years. Occasionally the scribe had to re-prick where the first attempt had failed to pierce the lower leaves of the quire.

Other aids were the veining of the skins; marks left by the vellum-manufacturer's scraper, and signs that two quires had rubbed together leaving a smudged appearance on the outer leaves. Paper guards added by the eighteenth-century binder, either to join two leaves or to allow a single leaf to be sewn-in normally with the rest, helped in places; their remains showed as narrow strips on the inner edges, where they had been cut by the eighteenth-century binder's plough knife in removing the folds.

Chart 3 showing the information from a portion of the notebook was prepared by Sheila Waters. It is in fact self-explanatory but perhaps not too easy to follow at a first encounter. It will be more easily understood when it is realized that it was usual for these early manuscript books to be prepared for writing, and actually written and illuminated while assembled and stitched in quires; in some areas the practice continued up to the fifteenth century. The more elaborately decorated leaves were sometimes treated separately, but one of the most intricate in this book was illuminated while part of a quire. In this instance the impressions made by compasses in setting-out the decoration were clearly indented on a blank area of the leaf below. Among comparable manuscripts prepared in the same way, the Lindisfarne Gospels is certainly one.

The numbering to right and left of the chart is that of the folios and pages. The folio numbering is in pencil and indistinct, the page numbering is in ink and clear; both are referred to in the notes. The second column shows the original arrangement of the quires so far as it can be deduced from the information recorded in the next five columns; in a few places there is doubt whether a leaf belongs at the end of one quire or at the beginning of the next. In the two right-hand columns the series of three horizontal lines between each group of six leaves indicates the limits of the quires in which the book is now sewn.

In addition to the information available from the chart's diagrammatic cross-section with its classified notes, a leaf attached within the back board of the new binding carries information describing the structure and condition of the book as received, and

Chart 3 Lichfield Gospels of St. Chad. *Cross-section of part of make-up*

| ff | pp | Original quire arrangement | Hair side recto or verso | Direction of animal's spine horiz. or vert. | Character of vellum HxF: hair and flesh markedly dissimilar H=F: hair and flesh similar | Pricking for ruling etc. FP: top leaf of fresh pricking K: with knife-point making a wedge-shaped hole A: with awl making less elongated hole and with rounded ends | Features and notes | pp | ff |
|---|---|---|---|---|---|---|---|---|---|
| 57 | 113 / 114 | | V | — | ← rubbed / H x F | FP A | Hair visible | 113 / 114 | 57 |
| 58 | 115 / 116 | | R | — | H x F heavy | FP K | The vellum in lower margin is an earlier addition | 115 / 116 | 58 |
| 59 | 117 / 118 | | R | — | H = F heavy | | Paper on inner edge / heavy ruled lines and thinning | 117 / 118 | 59 |
| 60 | 119 / 120 | | V | — | average | | Ruled on recto / Ruling on verso disregarded by the scribe / at inner edges as at ff 49-55 | 119 / 120 | 60 |
| 61 | 121 / 122 | | R | — | H = F average | | | 121 / 122 | 61 |
| 62 | 123 / 124 | | V | — | thinnish | | | 123 / 124 | 62 |
| 63 | 125 / 126 | | V | — | H x F heavy | | Hair visible | 125 / 126 | 63 |
| 64 | 127 / 128 | | R | — | ← rubbed / H x F heavy | | Hair visible | 127 / 128 | 64 |
| 65 | 129 / 130 | | R | — | H = F average | | | 129 / 130 | 65 |
| 66 | 131 / 132 | | V | — | H x F heavy wetted? | | Horizontal ruling clear | 131 / 132 | 66 |
| 67 | 133 / 134 | | R | — | H = F thinnish | three sets of pricking | Ruling to wrong points / see also ff 57 and 58 | 133 / 134 | 67 |
| 68 | 135 / 136 | | V | — | H x F heavy | | | 135 / 136 | 68 |
| 69 | 137 / 138 | ? | R | — | H x F thinnish | four sets of pricking 2K 2A | Mark of sewing thread at inner edge suggesting the 5 stabbed holes were opp. sewing throngs but this is not middle of quire. Hair visible. Line 2 p. 138 in different hand. | 137 / 138 | 69 |
| 70 | 139 / 140 | ? ? | V | — | H x F heavy wetted? | FP A see f 69 | Stylus drawing in margins / cf. drapery in Mark and Luke portraits | 139 / 140 | 70 |
| 71 | 141 / 142 | | V | — | H x F heavy uneven | No pricking in margins but inside frame | End of Matthew 'equum optimum' / Mark portrait | 141 / 142 | 71 |
| 72 | 143 / 144 | ? | V | — | H x F average | FP A | This leaf reversed when cut so leaving widest outter margin: 1 5/8" | 143 / 144 | 72 |
| 73 | 145 / 146 | | R | \| | H = F very heavy wetted? | | The thickest leaf ·034 had been cut from head to tail near inner edge on R. cf. heavy ruled lines ff 49-55. Compass marks indented from setting out at top of p. 143. | 145 / 146 | 73 |
| 74 | 147 / 148 | | V | — | H x F average | | Red edge-colouring by earlier binder retained on verso. | 147 / 148 | 74 |
| 75 | 149 / 150 | | R | \| | H = F very heavy | | | 149 / 150 | 75 |
| 76 | 151 / 152 | | V | \| | H x F very heavy | | | 151 / 152 | 76 |
| 77 | 153 / 154 | | R | — | H x F heavy | | | 153 / 154 | 77 |
| 78 | 155 / 156 | | V | \| | H = F very heavy wetted? / → rubbed | | Double vertical ruling on verso (i.e. as horizontal ruling) | 155 / 156 | 78 |
| 79 | 157 / 158 | ? | R | — | H x F average | FP A | ← Set-off while wet and under pressure | 157 / 158 | 79 |
| 80 | 159 / 160 | ? | V | — | H x F heavy | | ← Set-off while wet and under pressure | 159 / 160 | 80 |

Annotations in pricking column (vertical): two types (K and A) and two scales of pricking in inner margin, 20 lines and 21 lines; (opp. sewing throngs?); 5 heavy stabbed holes at inner edges; 5 holes at inner edges; paper on inner edges cf. ff. 45 and 59; damage to colour ?) damage by water ?) comparatively much less water what was done in the processes of repair and rebinding, including specifications of the materials and adhesives employed. The wording below is modified from the information attached in the book. In describing the state before repair, the repair itself and the rebinding, the observations and the actual work on the book are given in chronological order so far as is practicable. With exceptions, features easily visible in the bound book are not described.

When received the book was in a red plush jacket with gilt brass mounts which had covered it for many years. The dark-brown morocco, decorated in blind tooling with a diaper pattern and bearing a large cross in blind on the front board was almost unmarked after one hundred years, but the leather was broken down the joint of the front board as were all but one of its slips. It was titled in gold on the spine. The leaves had become so cockled that the boards could not close properly. All the slips had been laced into heavy millboards. After cutting the whole book into single leaves, and sawing-in for six cords they had been overcast very carefully into sections of two or three leaves with stitches about 12mm ($\frac{1}{2}$in) apart; the spine was glued, rounded and backed.

Many of the leaves had been very wet at some time, and pressed while wet – the ink on some leaves had set-off onto their neighbours (this was probably one of many misguided eighteenth-century attempts to flatten vellum). There was very obvious damage to the colours by water, abrasion and flaking, and damage to the vellum by moulds. The writing looked remarkably fresh. In most of the leaves the animal's spine runs vertically, so, assuming two conjoint bifolia from each skin, and that originally the manuscript ran to 240 leaves, it needed the skins of 100 or 120 animals to provide the vellum. There is a marked tendency for hair-sides to face hair-sides, and for flesh to face flesh, but only within the quires. Because there were some single leaves this agreement could not be regular.

With very few exceptions the pricking and ruling is constant throughout. Four holes pricked at the corners of a rectangle set the limits to the writing area, the decorated area of the portrait-pages and to the frame areas of other special pages; the areas are the same in all three categories. On the written pages these four prick-marks were used for the vertical ruling, and for the top and bottom lines for writing, the lower of the double lines passing through the marks. The intervening eighteen double rules were made to pricked marks in the margins, where they are 6–12mm ($\frac{1}{4}$–$\frac{1}{2}$in) outside the vertical rules in the outer margins and about 25–30mm (1–1$\frac{1}{4}$in) outside the vertical rules in the inner margins.

Two different tools were used for pricking. One (a knife point?) made a wedge-shaped hole, the wedge lying always horizontal, with the thick end to the left, the other was much more awl-like leaving a rounder hole. At pp. 113 and 115 there are two scales of pricking: one for twenty lines made with the knifepoint, the other for twenty-one lines made with the awl. There are several re-prickings and unusual features in this quire. The horizontal ruling was done with a double stylus, and often extends well into the margins; all the rectos were ruled and many versos also. The original quiring was irregular, the number of leaves in each quire ranging from eight to thirteen. In places a series of larger pierced holes spaced at regular intervals appears on or close to the inner edges; at f. 81 (not shown on the chart) a few more holes are to be seen near the tail which can hardly be anything but earlier, perhaps the original sewing holes. If so they fix the width of the inner margins at approximately 40mm ($1\frac{5}{8}$in).

Clearly to be seen on p. 145 are the indented marks of compasses used to set out the decoration on p. 143. The decoration is no longer directly superimposed on the blind indentations because p. 143/144 (f. 72) was reversed at the time when the edges were so severely cut in the eighteenth century, so whereas all the other leaves now have inner margins that are wider than their outer margins f. 72 has a narrow inner margin and a wider outer margin.

All the leaves were relaxed[1] in a sandwich of damp 'Photoprinto' (Fords). While relaxed, lined bulldog clips were attached to the edges and pinned out on insulating wallboard (visible in Plate 98). The final drying was completed between changes of 'Photoprinto' under pressure. While still damp from relaxing most of the patches added at an earlier repair were removed; after flattening some slits were stitched with linen thread, and many vellum patches were stuck with Scott Bader's VJC555 or V.1000 plus polyvinyl alcohol. Some areas in the margins of the St Luke portrait page were reinforced with transparent vellum over marginal manuscript; other margins have been reinforced with Green's lens tissue stuck with V.1000 used dry with local heat and pressure.

Because of the insecure condition of the coloured pigments many of them have been treated with Maranyl Soluble Nylon C.109/P DV.55 (ICI) using a 3 per cent solution in industrial methylated spirit. Soluble nylon was used also on areas of vellum much damaged by moulds, particularly in the margins and at beginning and end, where they were very porous and weak.

The leaves were joined in pairs after arranging them in quires of six leaves (one of four leaves). The strips of new vellum between them were cut, so far as possible with the direction of the animal's spine running in the same direction as in the leaves they were to join. In the 118 joins the spine direction agrees in all but twelve. With one or two exceptions (to allow existing features to remain) the inner edges of all the leaves were scarfed on the versos. The strips of new vellum were toned to match, using Winsor & Newton's Artists' Water Colours and scarfed to fit the inner edges of the leaves (as in Fig. 62). The edges were stuck with V.1000 used wet and pressed between waxed paper and hard rubber, drying being completed between changes of 'Photoprinto' under pressure.

The original leaves were given new fly-leaves – a fold of vellum with alum-tawed pigskin joints reinforced with linen. Fly-leaves and text were sewn all-along with Barbour's No. 1 3-cord flax seaming beeswaxed, on six double cords of Barbour's $2\frac{1}{2}$/10-cord Special

1 Relaxing vellum manuscripts in a damp sandwich calls for experience and very great care. Hanging the leaves in lines in a humidifying cabinet allows the relaxation even of illuminated manuscripts. Depending on the relative humidity in the cabinet and the character of the vellum, leaves may need to remain in the cabinet for as much as twelve hours.

Hilden Netting Twine, the sewing of each quire picking-up
the sewing of the preceding quire at the cords. Headbands of
Barbour's Best Quality 16/4-cord linen thread over cores of
$2\frac{1}{2}/10$-cord were tied-down in the middle of each quire, and
unusually, with the cross-over bead behind the band instead of in
front. All the slips were laced and pegged into quarter-cut English
Oak boards rebated inside and out two or three inches wide
(50–75mm) to accommodate the cover and joints; the slips were
neither thinned nor untwisted. The spine was covered with
alum-tawed pigskin stuck only to the boards, not the spine. A
secondary headband was sewn linking the primary headband and
thus the leaves to the cover: the thread passes under the primary
headband and through the cover, and also through an additional
thickness of pigskin. The thread then passes round lengths of gut
('cello string) in front where the bead normally appears and behind
the extra piece of pigskin. When completed the extra pigskin is
folded down making a pad, easily replaceable, at the most vulnerable
spots at head and tail; wings of the pad were laced to the boards
over the leather cover with vellum thonging (Fig. 102). (Plate 60
shows the *Book of Kells* with a similar pad screwed in *48*.)
Vellum when left entirely to its own devices in uncontrolled
atmospheric conditions tends to cockle. Cockled leaves prevent the
boards closing properly, and the leaves will not lie open comfortably.
In days when vellum was the normal material for the leaves, clasps
were fitted and used. Today very few people handling books
regularly can be persuaded to use clasps, and they make very bad
neighbours by scratching other books in the shelves. But special
books need special treatment, and vellum-leaved books, among other
things need to be kept under slight pressure. Custodians will put
books in some form of restraint if it is easily done. In this instance
the restraint provided is a wedge-shaped slip-case of wood (see also
Plate 62). The boards of the book are markedly cambered on the
outside so that the action of pressing it into the slip-case presses the
boards against the leaves. A simple lever working against the
foredges of the board ejects the book as needed.

R. P. 1972

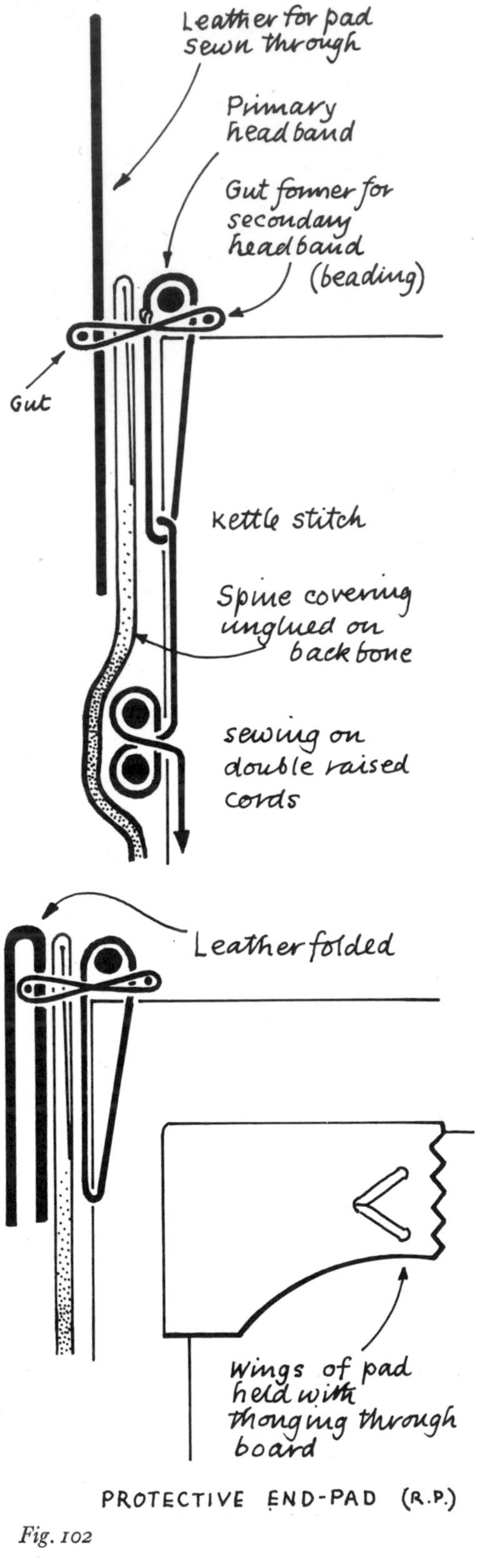

PROTECTIVE END-PAD (R.P.)

*Fig. 102*

182

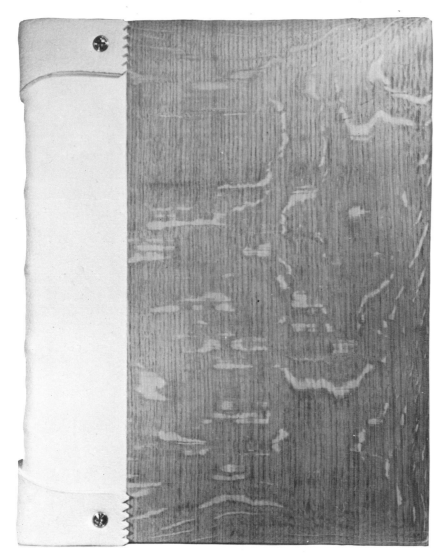

102    Roger Powell
*The Book of Kells* (one of the volumes)
Re-bound in oakboards and alum-tawed
pigskin.Note the protective pads, sewn
through with the end-bands, turned down and
fixed to the boards with stainless steel screws
(gold washers) 1951
Trinity College, Dublin

103    Roger Powell
*Book of Durrow*
Re-bound in oak boards and alum-tawed
pigskin 1952
Trinity College, Dublin (Section 22)

103

104   Marcel Duchamp/Mary Reynolds
Alfred Jarry *Ubu Roi* 1935
Tan morocco, shaped book-block, cut-away boards. Black silk doublures and
flyleaves. Gold crown stamped on front flyleaf. One of two identical bindings in
The Philadelphia Museum of Art and Art Institute of Chicago
168 × 130mm (6¾ × 5¼in)

105   Jeff Clements
Sophocles *Antigone* 1972
Orange-rust morocco inlaid black and natural moroccos, blind tooling
292 × 208mm (11½ × 8¼in)

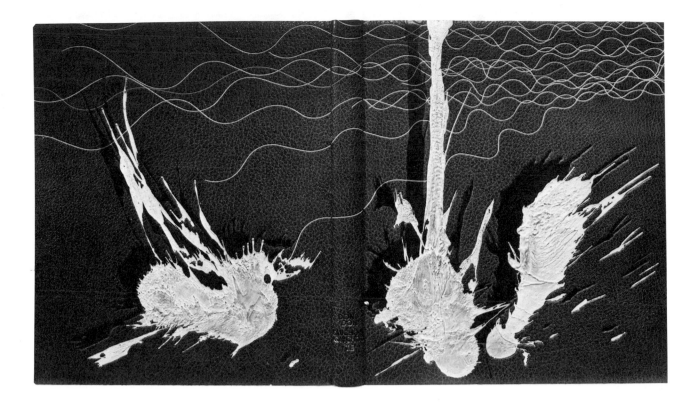

106 Henri Mercher
Cervantes *Don Quichotte* illustrated by Dali
Molten tin encrustations. Black calf shadows. Orange and yellow tooling
410 × 325mm (16 × 12¾in) 1959

107 Henri Mercher
*Promethée* illustrated by Henry Moore
Bright-green morocco. Red tooling. Painted and sculpted plexiglas (perspex)
reliefs 270 × 370mm (10⅝ × 14½in) 1958

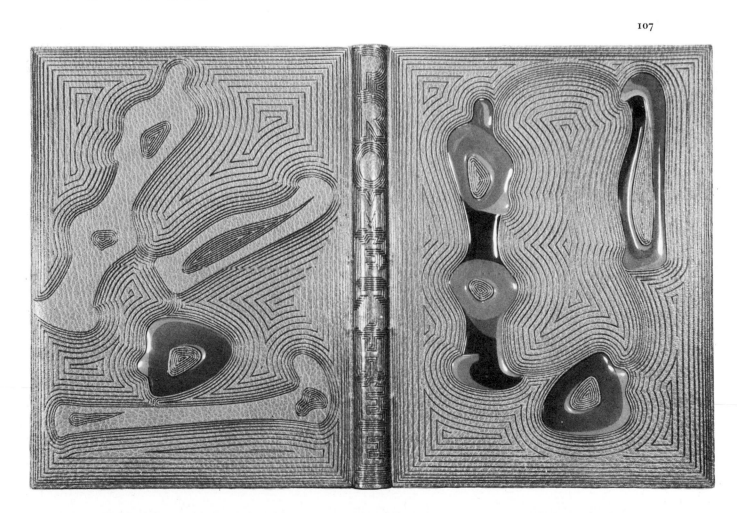

## 23 Technical and directional notes from the international bookbinding scene

This section is devoted to extracts from contributions to this book sent in by representative bookbinders of the various modern schools. In France, where the tradition of working in collaboration with the craft atelier in the production of the hand-bound book reached its zenith under the designer Paul Bonet, most of the work sub-contracted from the design studios has a uniformity of technical accomplishment and style, so that throughout the Paris school the work varies only in the designer's style. The French designer feels free to produce the almost impossible design specification in the secure knowledge that the skilled atelier craftsman will somehow be able to conjure it up. Many designers have remarked that they just would not be able to operate if it were not from this mutual collaboration.

There are still those like Henri Mercher who prefer to carry their own designs into the materials.

The painter and sculptor create as they carry out their work, and one cannot imagine these artists entrusting the execution of their projects to others, even with the aid of an elaborate model. The same is true of the binder, provided he has sufficiently mastered his technique to make them serve his needs instead of being restricted by them . . .

For me, technique plays so important a role that I wonder whether an artist who decorates objects but remains ignorant of how they are made is not putting the cart before the horse . . .

I sculpt bindings without increasing the thickness of the covers by using duralumin supports instead of board. This means that the supports can be thinner and still have the same weight and strength. I have observed that 1mm duralumin corresponds to a 3mm board. This thin metal plate, angled next to the spine, can fill the joint and still leave a well of 2mm, allowing for encrustations and sculpture without making the covers heavier, so that the elegant proportions of the binding are preserved.

For more than twenty years I have been working with plexiglas (perspex), to paint transparently on it, to sensitize it with photographic emulsions, to gild it, and to obtain effects on it by using static electricity with which it is charged. Projections of cast metal mouldings transformed by electro-chemical deposits (Plate 106), the use of anodized aluminium, and the use of natural objects, are all means of expression available to the modern bookbinder.

A few years ago, I created my first mobile decorations using different coloured strips of plexiglas, attached beneath the morocco of the binding, which shone with an undulating light. Later, solid sections were set in motion by manual contact. Today, I achieve movement by the interplay of air and coloured liquids of different densities, a technique similar to that of kinetic art (Plate 61). I have in mind the possibility of mobile decoration created by using the motive force provided by the opening of the binding with the automatic restoration of the shapes when it is closed (Plate 60).

If bookbinding is seen in the light of these possibilities, it seems to me that it has now been set free from the traditional techniques and tools which restricted it, has emerged from the level of handicraft, and is no longer an artisan's skill.

There are of course many artists who employ expert craftsmen (sign-writers) to execute their designs, e.g. Bridget Riley, Vasarely. Monique Mathieu is another French bookbinder with considerable creative sensibility, but who has now adopted a different standpoint to that of Henri Mercher. Whereas his main interest seems to be technique and novel application, for her the typographic character and especially the illustration style are the main sources for bookbinding decoration. Below she has written some notes on her works reproduced in the Plates, and some remarks which explain her particular approach.

Plate 72. It was necessary to select a strong material to re-bind this book designed by Vollard in 1939, for the type is very bold and Roualt's etchings are in strong blacks or unusual colours. It was not a matter of 'doing a Roualt'. It never is a question of paraphrasing the illustrator as this is not what is expected of the designer bookbinder. It is necessary to be wholly oneself in discovering an intimate relationship with the text and illustrations, suggesting them in the covers before they are seen. All this is to be achieved using one of the most constraining of media. Our work is not straightforward, but is of such complexity that one needs to be a conjuror, possessing more than one trick up one's sleeve.

Gold need have no part in it now. Any functional material which may be formed into thin sheets and fixed to a flat surface is good for the job. All kinds of tools can be brought into play, for drilling, planing, routing, incising, stamping and modelling. Any relief effect need rarely exceed a thickness of 3mm. So in this particular binding, where the same cleanly cut calf leather is used throughout, I have made a representation of Jerusalem's hills by contouring four levels. The title letters are treated in the same way.

In Plate 71 I have been induced to draw with a hot tool on black calf in order to relate to the Ubac woodcuts. The title is also black on black so as not to break the monochromatic unity.

Plate 73. The typography of L'Air and the wood engravings are extremely light and the binding demanded a delicate treatment. The use of mother of pearl fragments inlaid in an ivory coloured box calf, together with fine lines incised in the leather, make for an effect with greater subtlety than could be obtained with traditional tooling.

Perhaps these few explanations will show why it is that it seems to me impossible to be both the conceptual designer and the executive craftsmen of such bindings. The slow maturation of the myriad processes required to integrate design concepts of this complexity cannot develop parallel with the work of extremely fine craftsmanship, which must be clever, careful and also inventive, and which demands a degree of skill developed only by dedicated practice day after day. This is why, having executed my own bindings for several years, I now prefer, in order to develop more sophisticated and ambitious projects, to consign the realization of my designs to highly trained artisans who have a remarkable understanding of them. I take along maquettes and materials to these craftsmen and together we discuss them in minutest detail. Their long experience of this mutual way of working does the rest.

Some fine binders in Germany, like Gerhard Hampe, one of the leading bookbinders, and especially the hand-bookbinders in Denmark such as Jens Hansen and Knud Erik Larsen, favour the use of paper (sometimes with narrow leather edge strips) as a medium of creative expression. Gotthilf Kurz, a bookbinder, letterer and teacher with a wide influence in Germany, gives below his view on the value of materials in hand-bookbinding.

> Durability has always been an important criterion, but the life of the book and the binding should correspond. This may be difficult to estimate, yet there are valuable books, not yet fifty years old, in which the paper shows clear signs of decay. Is it right to force such copies into a binding made of the most durable materials known? There are more appropriate ways of binding such books which take into account their true value . . .

> There are books which cannot be bound with classical techniques used for centuries. 'Perfect binding' (with adhesives) is just as valid in its place as sewn binding. Some books, for example, art books, often printed on heavy paper or card, need not be forced into a rigid binding, or one with a deep shoulder, because this would make impossible the proper display of the pictures. We must always be conscious of the ancillary function of bookbinding and use our creative urge appropriately.

> The way a material is worked and presented anew changes its real value, and the value of the finished binding can be in inverse proportion to the cost of the material. Artistic quality is never judged primarily by the value of the materials, for any kind may be used to achieve it . . .

> The total artistic impression, and therefore the true value, of a book bound in paper can be much greater than that of a leather-bound book.

For many of his leather-bound books Kurz draws out and hand-cuts his own over-all stamps, which are put in cold on wet leather. Plate 76 shows one such freely cut stamp (made from acrylic sheet) on a completely flat board. The lettering on the spine is carefully built up from small tools. Kurz seems to be particularly interested in the play of light and shadow on blind tooling and stamping. Changing the directional lighting on the bindings shown in Plates 74 and 75 considerably alters the surface effects. These designs are built up from small pallets.

Ivor Robinson is another designer who makes use of a small number of pallets by which he interprets small pencil doodles collected in a quasi-developing series in his sketch book. His current method is to select a drawing which he feels will not be inappropriate to a book he is asked to bind. By limiting himself to a simple formula of black and earth colours punctuated here and there by a blacker (smooth calf) or white shape he maintains a series of variations from binding to binding (Plates 84–87), using string-like gold lines which jerk this way and that keeping to the spontaneity of the original pencil lines. Robinson has adapted his work admirably to the often conflicting demands of the craft; demands of the medium of tooling (usually hard-edged and tight); limited time (he is a full-time teacher of bookbinding) and resources (his bindery measures about 9ft × 7ft). He writes:

> The making of a book is a unique act, the realization of which will have been directed by one of a small number of clearly discernible initiatory intentions. A specifically craft-orientated bias tends to engender a predilection to technique and surface finish as ends in themselves. Prodigious efforts can be expended towards a pointless perfection in the inlaying and tooling of images which are utterly banal. At another extreme, bookbinding design produced apart, from and subsequently imposed on the craft, relying for its interpretation on another's or several others' individual skills, degrades craftsmanship by transforming it into a mere reproductive process, however brilliant and highly acclaimed the levels of specialized attainment might be.

> In the arts of painting, sculpture and music, the works of major exponents normally progress along a rational line of development. Although influenced by a wide range of conditioning factors – powered by the inner compulsion of the artist, the line of development most frequently exhibits a palpable commitment to a dominating and all-pervading idea or 'motif'. Its recognition and periodic isolation must be capable of providing total or provisional solutions to the artist's immediate creative needs . . .

> The problems likely to be conferred by a specific book title, with its subject emphasis, and style of illustration and/or typography, may or may not be consistent with the expressive outlet required by an artist bookbinder at any one particular moment.

> Presuming an advanced technical maturity and dexterity capable of acting as a complementary and positive means to creative and artistic ends, then various alternatives suggest themselves. The selection of one single title, for example, perhaps varied by edition, would allow a binder to work out developing designs 'in series', on different volumes of the same literary work.[1]

> Alternately, a range of carefully selected titles might, by a similarity of literary composition, theme, structure, or authorship, be capable of supporting a development from book to book without undue divergence from the evolutionary direction.

[1] cf:E. Mansfield's *Through the Woods* series (CPS).

In Britain no collaboration seems possible between the independent designer and the trade craftsmen. Although this might raise the all-round standards of design and finish some designer-bookbinders would still prefer to carry all aspects of the work themselves. Some of them are aware that only continual dedication to each aspect all the time will enable them to overcome technical and even design limitations. Several operators have found ways to adapt limited skills to good effect in one or more ways. The craftsman who does not continually practise tooling straight parallel lines (because for economic reasons he is occupied at another job) may purposely use a 'wandering line' where deficiencies show up less; or the unsymmetrical shape; the not-too-precise positioning of detail; the broken line; or by keeping to a simple, not-too-ambitious effect. The apparently unkempt appearance, skewed shapes and compositions made acceptable by abstract and expressionistic art has lured the unwary, uninformed or insensitive into the trap of believing that any arrangement of shapes and lines will do on bookbinding. On the whole, however, bookbinders are more deficient in design ability and sophistication than in technical prowess. It is easier to hide deficiencies of technique than deficiencies of design (but either of them only from the un-trained eye). This is where the patron or collector has a duty to the art. The undiscerning collector keeps standards low by being uncritical of both finish and design, and will often select the derivative or immature work (usually cut-priced!) instead of the original.

The serious collector (of whom there are still too few to support the further development of this art form) can do a great deal to improve matters in ensuring the survival of the more dedicated and original bookbinders. A good deal of the carelessness in design (in organizational unity as well as drawing) apparent even at national exhibition level is responsible, along with indecisiveness of aim, for the low general standard of performance in the craft, which remains on the whole a part-time and amateur occupation. I hope that many of the principles and factors elucidated in this essay will help towards the realization of greater integration in their work amongst bookbinders, leading to a new and special role amongst the arts.

108 John Latham
*The Bible and Voltaire* (Detail) Book Relief
Canvas on hardboard with wooden framework.
Damaged books, cellulose filler, wire mesh and
other materials
1600 × 1830mm (63 × 72in) 1960
The origin of the concept could be as presently
stated in the form of a theorem which defines a
principle of structure. It is pre-linguistic in so
far as the important question given an answer
is: "What could be said to have been going on
that this situation occurred?" In other words,
"How do you account for an event which
appears stable?" (Time-base theorem required
to go further.)

109 John Latham
*Book Relief.* Damaged books, cellulose filler,
spring wire, etc. mounted on canvas-covered
board 915 × 610mm (36 × 24in) 1960

108

109

# Appendix I

**Planning**: Factors determining decisions on the structure of binding mechanism

| *Element* | *Check list of variables* | | |
|---|---|---|---|
| Paper (Kind and substance) | Thick, medium or thin (substance in gsm) Soft or hard sized Filled, coated Hand-made, mould-made or machine made, other | | |
| Leaf area (Nearest A size) | Large (A2, A3) A2 23·4 × 16·5in; 594 × 420mm. A3 16·5 × 11·7in; 420 × 297mm. Medium (A4) A4 11·7 × 8·3in; 297 × 210mm. Small (A5) A5 8·3 × 5·8in; 210 × 148mm. | | |
| Sections (Number of folds) | Thick (4+) | Medium (3–4) | Thin (1–2) |
| Bulk of Book | Number of sections in book | | |
| Back (or hingeing) margins | Wide (1½in+) 40mm+ | Average (¾–1½in) 20–40mm | Narrow (0–½in) 0–12mm |
| Plates and fold-outs | Many, few, none | | |
| Type of book | Creative writing e.g. fiction, poetry, drama, biography | Reference e.g. atlas, technical, art | Commemorative e.g. Roll of Honour, Presentation, Liturgical |
| Possible usage and environment | Cannot be known (long term) | | |

| *Structural mechanisms* | *Check list of variables* |
|---|---|
| Pressing | Amount and weight and kind, e.g. India paper sections should not receive much pressure on the folds (swelling, aeration) when backing |
| Sewing thread | Size, type and material |
| Sewing supports | Type, size, material and number |
| Sewing method and style | Raised cords (double or single); webbing or tapes; recessed cords; number of sewing stations; kind of stitch (plain or link); sewing all-along, two-on, three-on; stab sewing; Coptic, oriental, french sewing |
| Back-fold treatment and make-up | Direct, loose guards, zig-zag guards, kind of reinforcement (linen, etc.) conjoining guards (scarfed, staggered, cut or torn strips), stubs, meeting-guards, overcast leaf grouping, adhesive binding |
| End (paper) sections | Waste sheet (good quality), number and type of flyleaves (coloured, plain), free or made (stiff-leaf); hand-made or machine made papers, fibre direction (grain); gusset and make-up |
| Joints and reinforcements | Textile (type of cloth), leather or cloth/leather laminate, paper, vellum (too hygroscopic and tending to stiffness), plastics; sewn-in or unsewn with endpapers |

| Structural mechanisms | Check list of variables |
| --- | --- |
| Type of boards | Wood, metal, plastics; millboard, strawboard, chipboard, fibreboard, pasteboard; reinforcements at corners, etc. Cut-outs, insets, built-up; laminates, linings. Thick, thin. Flat, cushioned, bevelled inside or outside face, wide or narrow |
| Board attachment | Laced-in, pegged, split-board, pre-tongue-and-slot variations, tongue-and-slot; cased, etc. Tight joint, groove, supported groove |
| Back-linings | Paper, mull, linen; direct, hollowback (number of folds or layers, e.g. one-on two-off) folds reinforced (linen); down-the-spine (back-bone), between the sewing supports; overlap tongue flap; extra leather, built-up, modelled over hollow |
| Type of back | Flat, rounded, rounded and backed; heavy or low shoulder, natural or built-up. Tight or hollow-back |
| Endbands | Type of former or core; sewn or stuck-on; single, two- or three-tier; primary or secondary, laced-in; linen, silk; one, two or more colours; with or without beading at front; braided, etc. |
| Caps (type and shape) | Vertical (un-moulded); set narrow or wide; overcast, plaited; modelled over string former, sloping or square; extra endpads, end of spine flaps and other structures |
| Edge-squares | Flush, narrow, wide |
| Book-edge treatment | Gilt, palladium, plain, coloured; one metal or more together; deckle, trimmed; under-gold painting (foredge); engraved, painted, marbled, sprinkled; combined media; tooled or gauffered. Rough or solid |
| Covering | Types of material; paper, cloth, leather, plastics and their varieties |
| Board linings | Type of material and method of fitting |

## Other factors for consideration in the binding programme

| | |
| --- | --- |
| Finishing | Kind of surface treatment; identification, decoration and expression (titling, tooling, onlays, insets, etc.) |
| The binder (operator) | Type of binder, his temperament, inclinations and procedural habits. His knowledge, experience, abilities and talent. On balance does he operate as a craftsman, designer or artist? Is he inventive, innovative, original. (See *Chart 1*.) |
| The client | His specification or special requirements; economics |
| Working conditions | The bindery and its equipment; availability of tools, materials and processes |
| Storage | The book container, e.g. book-box, slipcase; book-stack; location |

## Books for re-binding: check present condition and decide relevant treatment

# Appendix II

## Manufacture of Leather

| Process | Method | Function |
|---|---|---|
| **PRE-TANNING** | | |
| Flaying | Butcher cuts or peels | Produces raw hide – large animals (cattle, horses, etc.) raw skin – small animals (goat, sheep, seal, etc.) |
| Curing | Drying, wet or dry salting, brining | Prevents decay and putrefaction |
| Soaking | In water with bactericides, in pits, paddles, rockers or drums | Replaces lost moisture, cleans and softens |
| Liming and un-hairing | Lime-wash paint, immersion in lime solutions | Loosens and removes hair and epidermal layer |
| Fleshing | Fleshing machine or knife and beam | To remove adipose tissue and flesh |
| Splitting | Plumped larger hides, layer split in band-knife machine | To obtain greater area of hide of right thickness for use |
| Lime-scudding | With blunt 'knife' over beam pushing the grain | Further removal of epidermis, hair roots, etc. with surplus lime |
| De-liming | With water flow or weak acid bathing in paddle or drum | To neutralize alkalinity of hide |
| Bating | Paddled or drummed in powdered enzyme mixture (formerly dog or chicken dung) | Removes more lime and renders skins more flexible and stretchy |
| Scudding | In scudding machine | Removal of any unwanted material in skin |
| Pickling, drenching and scouring | Immersion in acid and salt | Corrects acidity level in skin prior to tanning, and also acts as a preservative and de-greasing agent |
| **TANNING PROCESSES** | Depends on qualities desired in finished article | To stabilize the raw material by conversion of collagen proteins |
| Vegetable tanning | By infusion of leaves, berries bark or roots of certain plants | Gives a firm leather which moulds well, gives a clean cut edge and takes tooling and stamping. Good grain pattern and flexibility. 'Oasis' goatskin is a favoured leather for bookbinding and is made from the red 'Sokoto' goat from NW Nigeria. It is imported as a rough-tanned crust (undyed), washed out and re-tanned with Cyprus powdered sumac for one week. |
| Chrome tanning | Usually chromium sulphates or chlorides | Gives a soft or resilient leather indentified by a bluish green cast (undyed). Not very flexible. The tan does not wash out. Difficult to tool. |

| Process | Method | Function |
|---|---|---|
| Zirconium tanning | Zirconium sulphates or chlorides (acid) | Gives a white washable leather, tight and firm, fast to light |
| Alum tanning or tawing | Aluminium salts (Alum and salt) | Gives a soft, usually white leather. The tannage will wash out to leave raw-hide. Alum-tawed pigskin is a very strong, beautiful bookbinding leather, but rather resilient to tooling. It is usually stuffed with egg-yoke, etc. Alum tannage is used as a pre-tan for chrome and vegetable tanned leathers |
| Oil tanning (Chamoising) | Fish and marine animal oils, (e.g. cod liver oil) partly oxidized, hammered (fulled) and drummed in. (Emulsified oils) | Very soft and stretchy. Commonly used for dressing the flesh splits of sheep-skin for wash leathers |
| Aldehyde tanning | Formaldehyde (to formalin) | Used in the production of 'doeskin' products and sometimes used before other tannages to 'set' the grain. |
| Semi-chrome | Vegetable tan followed by chrome tan | Gives a softer more flexible leather with good dye-uptake |
| Chrome re-tan | Chrome tan followed by vegetable tan | Produces a fuller and firmer leather with good rot-resistance |
| Combination-oil | Formaldehyde tan followed by oil tan | Gives leather with similar qualities to vegetable tanned leather. It often replaces the latter as the tannage does not wash out. Speciality leathers. |
| Syntans or synthetic tanning | Cresols, phenols, napthalenes plus formaldehyde and sulphuric acid | As an auxiliary this method can improve the penetration of vegetable tannages. It produces a paler coloration in dyeing, retards mould growth but by itself gives a rather thin-bodied leather |
| POST TANNING OR FINISHING PROCESSES | Methods apply here (mainly) to light or bookbinding leathers | Re-inforces the natural qualities of leather and can impart special surface characteristics |
| Drying out | | The vegetable tans in crust leather are further fixed by standing |
| Draining | Horse-up, etc | Drains away excess tan liquors |
| Washing | In drum or paddle | Washes out excess tan |
| Neutralizing | Chrome leather is neutralized in mild alkali and re-washed | Chrome leather develops further acidity by standing |
| Splitting or shaving | Splitting or shaving machines | Thickness is rendered uniform and levelled up |

| Process | Method | Function |
|---------|--------|----------|
| Dyeing | Various types are used. Acid dyestuffs, direct dyestuffs or basic dyestuffs | Leather in drum or paddle has ready dissolved and diluted dyestuff added to it. Almost any colour may be given to bookbinding leathers |
| Fatliquoring | Emulsified oils, coconut oil, neatsfoot oil, etc | Gives greater body, flexibility and softness |
| Setting out and Sammying | Striking out with a slicker or machine | Samm to remove surplus water by pushing it out by 'mangle' or hand. Setting out removes creases which would dry in |
| Softening | On a stake by hand | Stiff leathers are staked to loosen the fibres, some chrome leathers are damped to prevent breaking of the fibrous structure during staking |
| Boarding | Folding of skin grain to grain and working a crease about under pressure. By hand with a graining board or on a machine | Brings out the grain qualities of the skin. 'Oasis' for example has a natural irregular grain configuration. Boarding in one direction produces straight or willow grain. A second pass at right angles to this creates box grain. The grain appearance may be further detailed by boarding in all directions |
| Brushing | By rotary stiff brush or by hand | This polishes the grain |
| Plating and embossing | Hot plates and stamps | Hardens the surface and imparts many kinds of 'grain' patterns |

Not all of these processes are used on all leathers or in this exact order of operations. (*32*, *55*, *67*)

# Appendix III

**Check-list of binding operations** extracted from the processes typified in the case history, Section 19. Main and conventional processes are italicized.

Read book, make notes
Check pagination, pencil in un-numbered leaves
*Remove endpapers, joints, boards*
Soak off board-papers
Cut thread loops in centre of sections
*Remove sections from back linings,* one at a time. Retain all endbands, etc
Remove all thread and glue from sections
Clean surface grime from paper with soft eraser
Make mild bleach solution and immerse folio by folio
Wash in running water (bath)
Test for acidity and de-acidify; leave buffer against acidity
Immerse in fungicide; leave buffer against mould formation
Re-size with toner (to colour); use a polyvinyl-alcohol for surface wear resistance
Fragile papers are interleaved with wet-strength papers in wet processes
Squeeze out size; peel up to dry or use drying cabinet, etc
Pare leather joints and *make up endpaper sections,* thin leather joints to be laminated to fine linen, organdie, etc; make special papers
Insert soft barrier sheet between joint and fly-leaf
Gather book off lines or drier
*Collate book*
Mend tears, backs of folios, guard plates, maps, etc.
Re-collate book. Read and make verbal and graphic notes
*Stack* in 3-4 signatures between boards *in press,* alternating groups spine to foredge
Make colour sketch and maquettes
Remove from press, knock up head and spine to square, press as block
Tidy deckle edges, light trim or scrape head (old gilding)
Alternately, trim edges for gilding
Gild, or gild on deckle
Other edge treatment may be done before or after sewing depending on effect required
Remove end sections
Knock up square, insert in lying press, *mark in sewing stations;* check collation and make collation mark
*Saw in kettel kerf, stations for semi-recessed cords, etc.*
Replace end-sections and pencil in sewing stations
Prick sewing holes at angle to avoid joint 'show'
Set up single-post sewing-frame with selected cord or tapes
Wax thread
*Sew book*
Use heavy band-stick between supports to compact every 3-4 sections
Cut off cords, dismantle tapes and pull through to cut off economically
Knock book square, tip up end sections along back edge to glue to book
Place waste millboard each side and knock up square, lower into press
*Beat out surplus swelling* in lying press, slips out; close sewing holes, knock up perfectly square to head and spine, *glue spine*
*Round the spine*
Set backing boards; lower in lying press; *back the spine* after gluing again
Glue spine (backbone) again and line between slips with fine lawn or handkerchief linen
Leave overlap for split board tongue
Unravel cords and feather out (obligatory for laced-in styles)
*Prepare boards* and make up allowing for modelling, recesses, slot, etc.
Shape and bevel boards, back-corners holes for slips, etc.
Glue fanned-out cords, slips and linen on to waste sheet (groove style)
*Attach boards* by lacing cords in holes (tight joint style). Split boards are attached at this stage also
Press book in boards with tins
Correct squares of boards
Prepare and *sew endbands* through lawn lining

Cap-up text (book-block), use damp-proof or one-sided release (siliconed) paper for this wrapper
Insert any compensating card to bulk of doublures, suede fly-leaves, etc.
Waste sheet with lawn, slips, etc. is tongued-off with pinking shears
Split boards are attached as above
Heavy books may be stab-sewn through first few sections from centre fold of ends
*Make up* linen re-inforced *hollow back*
*Attach hollow* before or after lining the backbone with leather depending on circumstances
While pressing hollow off book insert strip of release paper down length
Glue spine, glue hollow, press on with folder (or hold in press with tight 'dust wrapper')
Pare waste leather for lining over hollow
Glue and apply leather liner, allow to dry, sandpaper smooth all irregularities
Place brass rods in joints and press to crush flat any slips in groove
Pare leather for onlays to spine for tongue and slot (t+s) style
Assemble onlays and glue in position on spine leather strip (t+s)
*Pare spine strip* to level onlays and thin for turn-ins head and tail (or *pare whole cover*)
Prepare any built-up relief work on hollow back; or recess work (t+s)
Paste up spine strip at least twice
Apply paste or glue to spine liner
*Cover spine* and form headcaps, etc. (or *cover whole book*)
Nip in press with formica-covered boards up to the shoulder with release paper
Glue/paste leather joint to inside of waste sheet tongue, after local paring
Nip with barrier sheet to book-block
When dry trim tongue to shape with template (t+s)
Cut out leather for board covering (t+s) or for full covering; board grain
Prepare cut-out card frame in which to compose loose leather onlays for cover
Pare and roughly shape leather for onlays
PVA/paste mix on plastic sheet on which to apply adhesive to onlays
Damp loose leather cover and assemble onlays referring to sketch, etc
Rub down with smoother through release materials (paper, plastic)
Nip in press with siliconed paper every twenty minutes
Pare flesh side of cover leather to compensate and sink onlays
Pare edges for turn-ins, etc.
*Cover preparation*,[1] board preparation
Damp grain side; paste flesh side; leave to soak for ten minutes
Second pasting; leave five minutes; scrape off surplus paste
Paste spine (not t+s); paste cover
Cover board into slot (remove slot template but put back after covering)
(t+s) Trim out and fill-in board to level with turn-ins; nip in press
With damp covering leather press with foam-plastic or rubber sheet (t+s)
Allow to dry in air; then under weight
Open book gently (full covering: fc); support board open flat
Glue thin manilla strip (up to 2cms wide) down inside edge of board, to back up joint
Pare leather joint at ends to feather; damp grain side and paste flesh side
*Put down leather joints*
Tight hinge (joint) close board by 30° every twenty minutes until set
*Fill in boards* to level. Trim through in-fill card and turn-ins together
Allow to dry; line boards to pull flat
Sand-paper inside of boards level
Damp outside of covers and press to level onlays; allow for recesses, etc
Make any inlays and apply
*Tooling;* blocking; conventional onlays applied
Polish with heated iron
Press with tins inside and out, having removed doublure or special fly-leaf compensator sheet
Prepare doublures; line suede with thin h/m paper; pare edges; seal edges
*Put down doublures*; leather lining, etc. (or paste-down of endpapers)
*Treat leather* with micro-crystalline wax or a stable colourless varnish
Make book-box; this may be made as soon as the book is covered, for protection

Make out brief 'case-history' and tip on guard provided for it in end section

The above is a general check list to the author's methods (used mainly in Section 19); it is not comprehensive or elaborately detailed, but would be more so used with reference to the diagrams. Many of the elementary processes are fully described in several excellent books on the techniques of bookbinding. See Bibliography (*14, 18, 35, 39, 52, 58, et al.*).

[1] This precedes conventional covering (above); where a particular method is not used (e.g. feathered onlays or t +s), the operator should proceed with the relevant operation.

# Appendix IV

## Adhesives

| Product constituents | Process | Remarks |
|---|---|---|
| Synthetic resin adhesives | Aqueous dispersion of polyvinyl acetate (co-polymerized with plasticizing agent) Dilute with (distilled or purified) water Various formulations according to requirements of use. Some contain PVOH.[1] Used in the cold state Very poor medium for mould growth Relatively non-soluble when set | The best kind are internally plasticized Scott Bader's VJC 555 National Adhesives 232 1720 (WS 3836) They do not dry too rapidly. Can be used for most hand-binding operations except (soak) covering with leather. Remains flexible |
| Animal glues | Made from the collagen proteins in bone and hide, and usually include preservatives and plasticizers<br><br>Generally used hot but cold state formulations may be had<br><br>Susceptible to mould growth and pests | Presented in cake form (ready for the pot) Bead form (is soaked to prevent stringing, before heating) and powder. Glue should not exceed 40°C (104°F). Quick tack but tends to brittalize. Used on spines, cloth, board |
| Vegetable paste | Starch from wheat, corn (maize) rice cooked with purified water, with additions of anti-acid, preservatives | Good penetration of adherands, very good for covering in leather. Slow drying. Brittle. Used for setting spines, board linings, paper. Susceptible to mould growth and pests (Plasticize with a little PVA) |
| Glaire | Traditionally the beaten and distilled albumen of egg, with a preservative (formalin or acetic acid) Shellac mordants now widely used Dilutes with purified water | Used in gold finishing Edge gilding Retains adhesive properties with age |
| Epoxy resins | Usually two-shot type, resin plus catalyst Drying time speeded by gentle heating<br><br>Acrylic based adhesives are best for gluing plexiglas, perspex or use solvents of these | A useful and versatile adhesive for gluing decorative insets, rigid materials such as ceramics, stone, metal to boards, etc. Araldite, Twin-bond, etc.<br><br>1 Mr. J. Halifax (Williams Adhesives, Slough, England) tells me that modern PVAs contain lower hydrolysis PVOH. Their PVA WS3836 (which I use) contains a percentage and so is re-dispersible. PVA is usually pH5. |

## Chemicals (mainly used by the conservator)

These are constantly under review (see A. Cains article)

| Process | Product | Remarks |
|---|---|---|
| Dry cleaning | Kneaded rubber Putty rubber 'Draftclean' powdered rubber Powered eraser Mini vacuum | General dust stains Unwanted pencil marks<br><br>Dry mould |

| Process | Product | Remarks |
|---|---|---|
| Image fixing | Gelatine plus formaldehyde | Tempera |
| | Nylon soluble in methanol or industrial white spirit (alcohol) | Autographs, etc. (before washing) |
| | Vynalak | |
| | Paraloid B72 and Xylene | (See A. Cains) |
| | Isinglass | Fixing pencil |
| Dilutant | Distilled or purified water | Chemically and biologically inert |
| Wetting agents | Mild detergents | Washing additive |
| | Cellulose derivatives | |
| | Methanol and industrial alcohol | Help penetration of size, carries thymol (anti-mildew) into fibres |
| Bleaching (Use only if informed) | Sodium hypochlorite | Use anti-chlor after |
| | Ethereal-hydrogen peroxide | |
| | Permanganate | |
| | Chloramine T | Mild stains |
| | Chloramine dioxide | In bleaching chamber |
| | Wash after all treatments | Use wet-strength paper or mesh supports for weak and fragmented subjects |
| Sizing | Polyvinyl alcohol (PVOH) | Clean the subject first and use a bio-static size where possible. A buffering agent against acid formation and bacterial action may be used simultaneously |
| | Gelatine | |
| | Vellum parchment size | Sizing strengthens, hardens and renders papers more resistant to handling and decay |
| De-acidifying and buffering | Magnesium bicarbonate in solution | Can be prepared in a domestic sodawater syphon (small quantity) |
| | Orthophenylphenol (Topane) | Fungicide |
| | Thymol (crystals) | Paste preservative |
| | Barium hydroxide in methanol (methyl alcohol) | |
| | Potassium lactate solution | For treating leather, but is hygroscopic (can encourage mildew in humid conditions) |
| | Disodium dihydrogen pyrophosphate solution (white powder in water) | Inhibits acid formation in leather, but a slight white bloom is left |
| | Magnesium acetate (white powder) | Neutralizes acidity in paste, leaves a buffer. Soluble in water or spirit |
| | Crystalline phenol | Paste preservative (turns slightly pink) |
| | Calcium carbonate (precipitated chalk) | Anti-acid and whitener in paste |

## Appendix V

### Tools and equipment

*Binding studio*

- —Good over-all lighting
  Several local (shadow casting) angle
    lamps, clamping type
- +Light-box let into bench top (for
    mending and tracing)
- —Water source nearby
  Power points
- +Sanding and spraying bay (with
    extractor fan)
  Working surfaces (Formica plastic)
    or lino tops, 915mm (36in) high,
    763mm (30in) deep and as long as
    possible. Storage under.
  Drawing board and stand with
    T-square.

*Storage*

Plan chest with 152mm (4in) drawers
  1,220mm (48in) wide (useful as
  working surface) for flat papers
Tower rack with removable slatted
  shelves 1,220 × 915mm (48 × 36in)
  for storage of leather and cloth
  rolls.
Vertical compartmented storage rack
  for millboard (off-the-floor
  ventilation)
Wall-board tool-racks with hooks
  and painted silhouette location and
  shelf
Finishing tool storage unit with racks
Chemical cupboard

*Cutting tools*

Board cutter (610mm (24in)
    minimum cut)
- +Grindstone (powered)
- +Guillotine (for book edges)
- —Leather strop
- —Oil stones
- —Paring knives ('German') large and
    small
  Paring machine (Fortuna, etc.)
- —Penknife
  Plane (Smoothing or jack)
  Plough (with lying press)
- —Saws (tenon, coping or fret)
  Scalpels
  Stencil cutter rods

- —Spokeshave (blades for leather and
    board)
  Shears, scissors
- —Trimming knives (changeable
    blades)

*Holding tools*

- —G-cramps
  Clamps (small)
  Forceps
- —Grip stick
  Band nippers
  Pliers
  Tweezers (philatelists)

*Drawing and measuring tools*

Dividers (spring)
Typographer's steel rule
Steel tape measure
- —Steel straight edge (calibrated)
- +Drawing office instruments
  Colours, brushes
  Carpenters square
  Set squares

*Sewing equipment*

- —Sewing frame (preferably alloy
    single post)
  Mounted needle piercers
- —Bodkin or awl
  Rosewood band-stick
- —Beeswax
- —Cord
- —Tape
- —Thread
- —Endband silks
- —Needles (various)

*Presses*

Lying press (610mm (24in) between
    screws) (with plough runners)
- +Standing press
  Nipping press (large platen and
    daylight)
- —Small nipping presses
  Finishing presses (bench)
- —Pressing boards (Formica surface)
    various in pairs
  Pressing tins

+Blocking press
+Small printing press (adapted for
    heating type)

*Finishing tools*

Finishing stove and ring (Cockerell
    electric)
+Handle tool die holder (electric)
Various dies and blanks
Fillets
Pallets
Gouges, dots, rings, etc.
Handle letters
Type
Type holder
Gold cushion
Gold knife
Latex (separate for collecting
    palladium)
Glaire (egg or shellac, various)
Cotton wool
Benzine
Acetic acid
Pencil brushes

*Miscellaneous tools and equipment*

—Paring stone (litho, marble slab,
    thick plate glass) 763 × 508mm
    (30 × 20in)
Knocking down iron
Various weights (covered in leather)
—Backing hammers (2lb)
+Power drill (on stand) with bits
—Bone folders (various shapes)
Backing boards
Gilding boards

Miscellaneous carpenter's and metal
    worker's tools
Hypodermic syringe and needles
    (for inserting adhesive)
Glue pot (electric water-jacketed)
—Paste container
—PVA container
—Brushes for adhesives
Sponges
Vice
Tying-up boards (for banded books)
Newsprint (white – printer's reel-
    ends)
+Erasers (powered for conservator)
Hygrometer (dial, hair; with
    whirling hygrometer for
    calibrating) or wet and dry bulb
    psychrometer, with tables
Thermometers
+pH Meter
+Humidity control
Photographer's dishes (large)
+Type cabinet and cases
+Hand compositor's equipment

*Barriers and release papers*

Silicone papers, one sided brown
    kraft, for pressing and capping-up
White siliconed release paper
—Waxed papers
Oil-board (fixed)
Cellulose acetate film
Various calipers for capping
    (banding) and pasting upon
—Un-watermarked blotting paper
Wet-strength (carrier) paper

*Note:* Tools and equipment are best bought when needed. See Designer Bookbinders' Directory (Acknowledgements
    and Notes)
—Minimums for the amateur
+Specialist equipment

# Bibliography

*1*  Banks, P. Paper Cleaning, *Restaurator* 1, 1969, 52–66.

*2*  Barrow, M. The Barrow method of restoring deteriorating documents, W. J. Barrow Restoration Shop Inc., State Library Building, Richmond, Virginia, 1959.
Deterioration of bookstock: causes and remedies. Richmond, Virginia, 1959.

*3*  Bayerische Staats Bibliothek, Munich, '*Buchrestaurierung Methoden und Ergebnisse*'. A catalogue of an exhibition of restoration methods with contributions by Dr Karl Dachs, Friedrich Butz, Barbara Fischer, Karl Jackel, Wilhelm Ziegler and Dr Helmut Barrsa. 11 November 1971–15 January 1972.

*4*  Baynes-Cope, A. D. 'The non-aqueous de-acidification of documents', *Restaurator* 1, 1969, 2–9.

*5*  Biblioteca Nazionale Centrale di Firenze, *A guide to the BNCF restoration system*. Compiled by A. G. Cains with an introduction by Dr L. Crocetti. 2nd edition, 1970.

*6*  Birren, Faber *Principles of Colour* Van Nostrand Reinhold, 1969.

*7*  Bono, Edward de *Lateral Thinking: A Textbook of Creativity* Ward Lock Educational London, 1970.

*8*  Bono, Edward de *Practical Thinking* Jonathan Cape, 1971.

*9*  Bono, Edward de *The Mechanism of Mind* Jonathan Cape, London, 1969.

*10*  Bono, Edward de *The Uses of Lateral Thinking* Jonathan Cape, London, 1969.

*10a*  Burdett, Eric *The Craft of Bookbinding* David & Charles, London, 1974.

*11*  Cains, A. G., Guiffrida-Ruggeri, Barbara *Council on Library Resources Grant* – 545, September 1972. A report or manual of methods provisionally recommended for use in the BNC Florence. Revised version to be published. Produced in collaboration with Margaret Hey, CLR researcher.

*12*  Chevreul, Michael E. *The Principles of Harmony and Contrast of Colours* (Introduced by Faber Birren) Reinhold, 1967.

*13*  Clarke, Peter J. *Plastics for Schools* (Applied Polymer Guide) Allman and Son, London, 1970.

*14*  Clements, Jeff *Bookbinding* Arco Publications, London, 1963.

*15*  Cockerell, D. *Bookbinding and the Care of Books*. Pitman, London and New York, 1963.

*16*  Cockerell, S. M. *The Repairing of Books*. Sheppard Press, London, 1960.

*17*  Coomaraswamy, Ananda K. *Christian and Oriental Philosophy of Art* Dover Publications, New York, 1956.

*18*  Corderoy, John *Bookbinding for Beginners* Studio Vista, London, 1967; Watson-Guptill, New York, 1967.

*19*  Couzens, E. G. and Yarsley, V. E. *Plastics in the Modern World* Penguin Books, London and Baltimore, USA, 1968.

*20*  Dreyfus, Henry *Symbol Source Book* McGraw-Hill Book Co., New York, London, 1972.

*21*  Flyate, D. M. (ed.) '*Preservation of Documents and Papers*' Translated from the Russian, Israel Programme for Scientific Translation, Jerusalem, 1968.

*22*  Gansser, A. *The Early History of Tanning* CIBA Review 81, Basle, August, 1950.

*23*  Gettens, R. J. 'The bleaching of stained and discoloured pictures on paper' *Museum* (UNESCO Paris) 5 (1952) 124.

*24*  Goethe, J. W. von *Goethe's Colour Theory* (ed. Rupprech Matthaei) Studio Vista, London, 1971; Van Nostrand Reinhold, New York, 1971.

*24a*  Gregory, Richard L. *Eye and Brain* Weidenfeld & Nicolson, London, 1966.

*24b*  Gregory, Richard L. *The Intelligent Eye* Weidenfeld & Nicolson, London, 1971.

*25*  Hey, Margaret 'The bleaching of paper-based library materials – a preliminary study'. Paper presented to the Oberlin, June 1971, meeting of the American Group, IIC.

*25a*  Hey, Margaret and Cains, A. G. 'The use of heatset paper tissue in the repair of library and archive material' (in preparation 1972).

*25b*  Hofenk-de Graaff, J. H. 'The constitution of detergents in connection with the cleaning of ancient textiles, *Studies in Conservation* 13 (1968), 122–41.

*26*  Jung, Carl G. *Man and his Symbols* Aldus Books, London, 1964.

*27*  Kandinsky, Wassily *Concerning the Spiritual in Art* George Wittenborn, Schultz, New York, 1947.

*28*  Kathpalia, Y. P. 'Hand lamination with cellulose acetate', *American Archivist 31* 3 (1958), 271–5.

*29*  Koestler, Arthur *The Act of Creation* Pan Books, London, 1966.

30  Kyriss, Ernst 'Bookbindings in the Libraries of Prague', in *Studies in Bibliography* The University of Virginia, III. I (1955), 14.

31a Langwell, W. H. 'Permanence of paper', *Technical Bulletin* British Paper and Board Makers' Association, *29* (1962), 21; *ibid.*, p. *52*, *ibid. 30* (1953), 2; *ibid. 36* (1955), 199.

31b Langwell, W. H. 'Vapour-phase de-acidification of books and documents'. *Journal of the Society of Archivists, III*, no. 3, (1966), 137.

32  Leather Institute *International Glossary of Leather Terms.*

33  London Conference on Museum Climatology 1967. National Gallery London. Revised edition 1968.

34  Lüscher, Max *The Lüscher Colour Test* Jonathan Cape, London, 1970.

35  Mansfield, Edgar *Modern Design in Bookbinding* Peter Owen, London, 1966; Boston Books, Boston, USA, 1966.

36  Martin, A. G. *Finishing Processes in Printing* Focal Press, London, 1972.

37  Maslow, Abraham H. *Towards a Psychology of Being* (2nd edition) Van Nostrand Reinhold, New York, 1968.

38  Middleton, Bernard C, *A History of English Craft Bookbinding Technique* Haffner, New York and London, 1963.

39  Middleton, Bernard C. *The Restoration of Leather Bookbindings* American Library Association, Chicago, 1972.

40  Norstrand, Ove K. 'Chinese double-leaved books and their restoration', in *Libri 17*, 2, (1967), 104–30.

41  O'Flaherty, F., Roddy, W. T. and Lollar, R. M., *The Chemistry and Technology of Leather* Reinhold, New York, 1965.

42  Ostwald, Wilhelm, *The Colour Primer* (ed. F. Birren) Van Nostrand Reinhold, 1969.

43  Petersen, T. C. 'Early Islamic Bookbindings and their Coptic Relations' in *Ars Orientalis*, 1954.

44  Petrova, G. I. *et al. 'Restoration and Preservation of Library Resources, Documents and Books* Translated from the Russian, Israel Programme for Scientific Translation, Jerusalem, 1965.

45  Plenderleith, H. J. *The Conservation of Antiquities and Works of Art* Oxford University Press, 1956

46  Pollard, G. 'The Construction of English Twelfth Century Bindings' in *The Library 17*. 1, (1962), 1–22.

47  Potter, Norman *What is a Designer?* Studio Vista, London, 1969; Van Nostrand Reinhold, New York, 1969.

48  Powell, R. The Book of Kells. The Book of Durrow. Comments on the vellum, the make-up and other aspects. *Scriptorum* X.1 (1956),3–21.

48a Powell, R. and Waters, P. *The Stonyhurst Gospel of St John* (T. Julian Brown) Description of the binding. Roxburghe Club, Oxford, 1969.

49  Prideaux, Sarah T. *Bookbinders and their Craft* Charles Scribner's Sons, New York, 1903.

50  Pye, David *The Nature of Design* Studio Vista, London, 1964; Reinhold Book Corp., New York, 1964.

51  Rapson, W. H. The role of pH in the bleaching of pulp. *TAPPI 39* (1956), 284–95.

52  Robinson, Ivor *Introducing Bookbinding* B. T. Batsford, London, 1968; Watson-Guptill, New York, 1968.

53  Ryder, M. L. Parchment, its history, manufacture and composition. *Journal of the Society of Archivists*, vol 2 (9), (1964), 391–9.

54  Schunke, Ilse *Der Einbande der Palatina in des Vatikanischen Bibliothek* Biblioteca Apostolica Vaticana, Rome, 1962.

55  Sharphouse, J. H. *Leather Technician's Handbook* Leather Producers' Association, London, 1971.

56  Smith, C. Philip *The Lord of the Rings and Other Bookbindings* London, 1970 (published by the author).

57  Smith, R. D. 'Paper de-acidification: a preliminary report' *Library Quarterly 38* (1966), 273–92.

58  Town, Laurence *Bookbinding by Hand* Faber & Faber, London, 1951.

59  Trobas, C. 'Ein neue papierestaureiergerät' (liquid fibre infilling) *Allgemeine Anzeiger für Buchbindereien 81* (1968), 662–6.

60  Van Regermorter, B. 'Ethiopian Bookbindings' in *The Library*, 17, 1 (1962), 85–8.
61  Wächter, O., Lesky, E. and Kortan, H. *Anatomiae Universae Pauli Mascagni Icones* Vienna 1968. The documentation of the restoration for the BNC Florence.
62  Wächter, O. 'Das Reinigen und Bleichen von Drucken, Graphiken und Aquarellen', *Algemeine Anzeiger für Buchbindereien 76* (1963), 156–63.
63  Wallace, R. K. and Benson, H. 'The Physiology of Meditation', *Scientific American,* 226, No. 2, 1972.
64  Wallace, R. K., Benson, H. and Wilson, A. E. 1971. 'A Wakeful Hypometabolic Physiological State', *American Journal of Physiology*, 221, no. 3, 1971.
65  Walters Art Gallery *The History of Bookbinding 525 – 1950* Walters Art Gallery, Baltimore, 1957.
66  Wardle, D. B. *Document Repair* Society of Archivists, London, 1971.
67  Waterer, J. W. *Leather Craftsmanship* G. Bell & Sons, London, 1968.
68  Willcox, Donald *Modern Leather Design* Watson-Guptill, New York.
69  Zechlin, Katharina *Setting in Clear Plastic* Mills & Boon, London, 1971; Taplinger, New York. 1971.

# Index I General

Key: Figure numbers in *italics*; Plate numbers in **bold** type; Page numbers in roman

## Index II Names